Could Have Been
Should Have Been
HERE I AM

An Autobiography

ERIC KOSLOWSKI

Copyright © 2024 Eric Koslowski
All rights reserved
First Edition

PAGE PUBLISHING
Conneaut Lake, PA

First originally published by Page Publishing 2024

ISBN 979-8-89315-797-0 (pbk)
ISBN 979-8-89315-818-2 (hc)
ISBN 979-8-89315-812-0 (digital)

Printed in the United States of America

CONTENTS

Preface ix
Chapter 1: Before Me 1
                My Grandparents (1890–1951) 1
                My Parents (1926–1954) 12
Chapter 2: Starting with My First Breath 28
                March 9, 1954 28
                Major Events of 1954 29
                My School Years (1961–1972) 34
                Becoming an Adult 37
                It's Now Time to Work 42
                Moving on to Higher Learning 44
Chapter 3: Family Hood 52
                Family Ties 52
                Marriage Years 55
Chapter 4: Could Have Been, Should Have Been 60
                Medical Doctor 60
                A "Fix It" Man 61
                Mechanics and Science 64
                Tradesman 68
                Stand-up Comedian 70
                Rock Star 73
                A Pilot 81
                An Electronics Engineer 97
                A PVC Research and Development Chemist ... 114
                Retired at Sixty-Seven 135
Chapter 5: Taking Care of Business 139
                Self-Employed Entrepreneurial Journey 139
                Building a Drinking Water Testing Business ... 145

Chapter 6:	Going Forward: What to Expect for Completing My Career Journey 180
	A Profession Is Like Trying on Pants for Fit 181
	Lessons I've Learned 184
	Pathways and Doors 184
	There Is a God 186
	The Black Box in Your Life 190
	Charting My Own Path: The Journey of Self-Growth 194
	Hey, Buffalo Bill, What Did You Kill? 196
	Relationships 197
	Hobbies 206
	Our Inner Self 208
	Controlling and Eliminating Unwanted Habits through Distraction Techniques 211
	Don't Always Look for Absolutes or Certainty, Instead Look for All the Possibilities 216
	Only You Know You Best 218
	Who Are These Inner Voices and What Are They Telling Us? 221
	Distractions 223
	Storytelling to Yourself 226
	There Are No Excuses in Life, Only Your Choices 228
	Don't Make a Permanent Decision over a Temporary Situation 231
	Where Is Your Life, Ahead or Behind You? 232
	Practice Your Calling 235
	When the Time Is Right, You'll Know 239
	The Power of Walking Away 240
	Inch by Inch, It's a Cinch 241
	A Winning Strategy: The Best Solution Wins 245
	Don't View Yourself through the Eyes of Your Enemies 246
	Transforming Ideas into Reality in Three Steps 248
	Diet, Alcohol, Drugs, and Gambling 250
	The Dirty Truth about the COVID-19 Pandemic 253

	The Events That Could Have Taken My Life 258
	Suicide 266
	Skydiving 272
	Stories I Keep to Myself....................................275
	A Time to Surrender...278
	Understanding One's Death 281
	Reflections on My Fiftieth Class Reunion: A 2022 Retrospective...288
	Unlocking the Secrets to a Fulfilling Life.................290
Chapter 7:	Time to End..293
	Everything Must Come to an End Someday............293
	Final Wishes: Crafting Your Will and Planning Your Legacy......................................296
	On Top of the Hill, What's Next?.........................298
	A Message to My Unborn Son...............................301
	You Will Soon Become a Memory.........................302
	My Final Thoughts..304

This book serves as a cherished chronicle of my family's history, to which I am profoundly connected. The enduring legacy of their hard work and sacrifices will illuminate the path for future generations, offering wisdom to weave into the tapestries of their lives. To my children, my beloved wife Lori, my new granddaughters Alayah and Kali, and all those who came before me. I dedicate this work.

PREFACE

*I know I can't change the past, the question
is, did I choose my own destinies.*

So what prompted me to pen down my thoughts and compile them into this book? The answer stems from a journey I have embarked upon over numerous years, filled to the brim with adventures that can only be described as extraordinary. It is through these unique experiences that I have come to a profound realization, one that resonates with my core, revealing my true purpose. It is this sense of discovery, this newfound enlightenment, that I am eager to share with you, the reader. My belief is steadfast in the idea that every single day we experience, as long as we continue to breathe and move on this vast planet, carries with it a significant lesson. These daily experiences, no matter how minor they may seem, all contribute equally to the grand design of the cosmos. Furthermore, I embrace the notion that you, the individual, are the central figure in your own cosmic narrative, with everything in your life revolving around this central axis. It's akin to being the sun in your own solar system, influencing and affected by the celestial bodies that orbit around you. This leads to an intriguing principle, one that suggests the universe operates somewhat like a cosmic vending machine. If you express a clear desire to the universe, it is likely to fulfill it, albeit in its own time and manner. This is why it is imperative to be mindful and deliberate about what you wish for.

As we move forward in this book, I will explore this concept in greater depth, examining the implications of our desires and intentions and how they shape the fabric of our reality. I have often found myself deep in contemplation about the fundamental essence of human existence and the intricate concept of individuality. There's an undeniable truth that we all share a common beginning: birth, emerging into this world from our mothers, devoid of any physical belongings. Similarly, we all share a common finality; we depart this life alone, relinquishing all that we have amassed.

Despite sharing the earth at the same time, each individual embarks on a distinct journey, our life paths diverging in duration and trajectory. It is a fascinating aspect of life that while some paths are transient, merely brief flashes in the grand scheme of time, others span the entirety of a lifetime, rich in experiences and lessons. In my philosophical musings on destiny, I often picture myself as a solitary rower in a small boat, adrift in the vast expanse of life's ocean, seemingly without direction, endlessly rowing in pursuit of a place of safety and peace. It's a metaphor that speaks to the varied nature of our destinies: some appear deceptively simple to attain, invitingly close, while others are laden with hurdles, resembling a beleaguered vessel that is overwhelmed with incoming water on the verge of succumbing to the depths. Regardless of the length or complexity of our paths, they all inevitably lead to the same conclusion. This brings me to ponder whether we possess the ability to foresee our own destinies and alter our paths through sheer will or actions or if they are irrevocably etched by fate, compelling us merely to discover our predetermined positions in the grand narrative of life. These are the persistent inquiries that occupy my thoughts, leading me to explore the depths of our existence and the mysteries that it holds.

I vividly remember a particular day when I found myself meandering through the solemn grounds of the cemetery that has become the final resting place for both my mother and father. As I walked, I couldn't help but take note of the multitude of headstones scattered across the terrain, each marking the memory of a distinct individual. These markers varied immensely in their physical characteristics—some were tall and imposing while others were modest and unassuming; their designs ranged from elaborate sculptures to simple plaques. Despite the diversity in their appearance, there was a singular, unifying element present on each one: the modest dash (–) etched between the dates, marking the birth and conclusion of each life.

COULD HAVE BEEN; SHOULD HAVE BEEN; HERE I AM

This seemingly insignificant line, a mere punctuation mark on the stone, holds a profound significance. It represents the entirety of a person's existence—the myriad experiences they had, the choices they made, and the paths they traversed throughout their time on earth. This small dash stands as a symbol for all the laughter, tears, triumphs, and trials that filled the days from their first cry to their final breath. It serves as a reminder that, while we may be remembered by a name and bookended by dates, it is what lies between—the life lived—that truly defines us. One profound lesson that has emerged from my reflections is the realization that the specific dates marking our entrance and exit from this world anchor us within a distinctive and momentous era. The dash (–) positioned between the date of our birth and the date of our death is not merely a separator; it symbolizes the entire span of our existence. This small line is a container for the duration of our lives, embodying our individual purpose and the broader meaning we bring to the world. It serves as a silent prompt, urging me to contemplate the reasons for my existence within this precise historical context and the responsibilities or roles that are expected of me during this time.

The randomness—or perhaps the destiny—of being born at a certain moment in time fascinates me. I often muse on the alternate realities of my existence. What if I had been born five hundred years earlier, in a time devoid of modern conveniences and facing entirely different global challenges? Or imagine if I were to arrive a thousand years into the future, navigating a world reshaped by centuries of technological advancement and cultural evolution? Yet here I stand, brought into existence on March 9, 1954, a date that has placed me at this particular crossroads of history. It's a period marked by its own unique challenges, advancements, and cultural shifts—a time that requires me to navigate with understanding, purpose, and contribution.

Reflect on the multitude of individuals with whom you share the planet during your time here. They are your companions, your fellow passengers, as we all navigate the river of time. It's an inevitable part of life that some of these individuals will exit the journey before you while others will remain long after you've reached your final destination. Among these interactions and shared timelines, there are fleeting, significant instances when all those who play crucial roles in your life are present simultaneously. These instances, which I like to think of as the zenith of life, represent a rare and invaluable alignment within the vast expanse of our shared human experience.

This brings us to ponder the nature of our life paths. Are our lives akin to parallel lines, running alongside each other, occasionally intersecting at crucial junctures, sharing fragments of a larger narrative? Or do they exist in isolation, each narrative unfolding in its own bubble, occasionally observed but never truly intersecting? As we navigate through the complexities of life, gathering stories and experiences, a clear pattern begins to emerge, crystallizing into the essence of our being, sculpting our identities and destinies.

My own narrative is a mosaic of encounters, decisions, and moments, each piece influenced not just by my actions but also by the legacy of those who came before me. It's a story that doesn't start with my first breath but stretches back to the lives of my grandparents and beyond. Their experiences, their decisions, and the paths they chose have, in various ways, paved the way for my own journey. Let me take you through the saga that led to my existence, a tale woven through time, connecting past generations to my own steps through life.

CHAPTER 1

Before Me

My Grandparents (1890–1951)

US presidents: Benjamin Harrison, Grover Cleveland, William McKinley, Theodore Roosevelt, William Taft, Woodrow Wilson, Warren Harding, Calvin Coolidge, Herbert Hoover, Franklin D. Roosevelt, and Harry Truman

Major world events: Discovery of X-rays, radio, television, jet airplanes, theory of relativity, World War I, World War II, atomic bomb

Music styles: Classical, ragtime, vaudeville, jazz, blues, electric guitars, country, and R & B

In my family history, there are two distinct yet parallel stories of migration and hope, embodied by the lives of my four grandparents: the parents of my mother and the parents of my father. Each set undertook the formidable journey from Europe to the United States, spurred by the tumultuous backdrop of wartime. Despite the unique circumstances of each couple, their underlying motivations were remarkably similar—they were all in search of a brighter future, not just for themselves but also for the generations that would follow.

My mother's parents and my father's parents, though originating from different European countries, shared the universal immigrant dream of escaping the hardships and uncertainties brought on by war. They sought a land that promised freedom, opportunity, and the prospect of peace—a stark contrast to the battle-scarred landscapes they were leaving behind. This desire for a better life was the powerful driving force that led them to make the life-altering decision to leave everything familiar and embark on a journey to an unknown land.

Their migrations were not simple journeys but rather monumental endeavors fraught with challenges, risks, and the constant uncertainty of the unknown. Yet it was their resilience, hope, and the pursuit of a new beginning that propelled them forward. These stories of migration and settlement are a testament to their courage and determination to provide a stable and prosperous future for their children. In doing so, they laid the foundations for the life I came to know, influencing not only the immediate circumstances of their offspring but also the opportunities and challenges faced by the generations that followed.

My maternal grandparents, Irene and Paul Cherries, were true to their Italian roots, originating from the picturesque city of Florence. The turbulent aftermath of World War I, marked by economic instability and political unrest, prompted their decision to leave their homeland in search of a more stable and prosperous future. Around the year 1920, they embarked on a significant journey, leaving Italy behind to cross the Atlantic aboard a steamer, their sights set on Ellis Island, the gateway to new possibilities in New York, USA.

Upon their arrival in the bustling metropolis of New York, they underwent the customary immigration procedures and were soon able to begin their new life in America. They initially settled in Monson, Massachusetts, a decision influenced by the presence of other family members who had migrated earlier and had kindly sponsored their journey. This initial settlement provided them with the community support they desperately needed in this unfamiliar land.

My grandfather Paul brought with him not only dreams for a better future but also a valuable skill—he was a skilled stonecutter. This craft, honed over years, became their ticket to a more stable life. Seeking better employment opportunities, the family later moved to Fitchburg, Massachusetts, a town known for its thriving granite quarries. There, Paul found work that was well-suited to his skills, extracting granite stone, a trade that was in demand and offered him steady employment.

COULD HAVE BEEN; SHOULD HAVE BEEN; HERE I AM

Fitchburg eventually became the cornerstone of the Cherries family's new life in America. It was here that they put down roots, contributing to the community and building a new life from the ground up. They expanded their family, embracing the joys and challenges of raising nine children in this new world. Among these children was my mother, Rose, born in the year 1926. The Cherries family's journey from the cobblestone streets of Florence to the granite heart of Fitchburg encapsulates a tale of resilience, hope, and the relentless pursuit of a better future.

In the turbulent years following World War I, my father's family found themselves in a dire situation that led them to make life-altering decisions. My grandmother, a resilient and determined woman, made the monumental choice to leave Germany and start anew across the Atlantic. In 1920, amid the chaos and uncertainties of post-war Europe, she embarked on a journey to the United States with her three children, in search of a safer and more stable environment. This decision was made under the shadow of my grandfather's absence, making it even more daunting.

John Koslowski

John Koslowski, my father's father and a seasoned sea captain, found himself caught in the gears of geopolitical conflict far from home. Commanding a large German fishing vessel, he was engaged in what was supposed to be routine work, delivering their catch to a Russian port. However, fate took a dramatic turn when, during their voyage, Russia declared war on Germany. Unbeknownst to them, as they navigated toward their destination, they sailed straight into a new reality. Upon arriving at the Russian port, instead of conducting their usual trade, they were captured and designated as political war prisoners, a fate they hadn't foreseen when they set out to sea.

Detained in Siberia, a land infamous for its harsh conditions and brutal cold, my grandfather and his crew were thrust into an unexpected nightmare. They were initially forced into the grueling work in the salt mines, a punishing ordeal that tested the limits of human endurance. Despite being classified as political prisoners, which afforded them a marginally better treatment compared to military captives, the experience was harrowing and left indelible marks on all who endured it.

Meanwhile, across the ocean in the Bronx, New York, my grandmother faced the challenges of adapting to a new country, culture, and life without her husband while holding onto the hope that they would someday reunite. This period of separation and struggle would later become a chapter in our family's history, illustrating the resilience and sacrifices that shaped the generations to come.

In a daring escape that sounded more like a plot from a high-stakes adventure novel, my grandfather took a leap of faith to leave behind the harrowing confines of Russia. With a heart full of hope and desperation, he covertly boarded a ship setting sail for New York, driven by the unwavering desire to reunite with his family whom he had not seen for what felt like an eternity.

This act of boldness and sheer will was his declaration of resilience and his refusal to be a prisoner of circumstance any longer.

However, upon arriving in New York, his elation was quickly shadowed by the harsh realities of his undocumented status. Without a passport or any legal documents to prove his identity, he inadvertently became a fugitive in the eyes of US authorities. This predicament was a stark reminder of his vulnerable situation, as he was now in a country that promised new beginnings but also posed new challenges.

The situation reached a crescendo when, according to my father's vivid memories, US Customs officials, possibly tipped off about a stowaway, came knocking at their apartment door. In a scene filled with tension and urgency, my grandfather, with instincts sharpened by survival, made a split-second decision to escape. He dashed down the back stairwell, his heart pounding against his chest, as the customs agents ascended the front stairs, unknowingly just moments behind him. This cat-and-mouse chase was a dramatic twist in his journey, underscoring the precarious nature of his quest for freedom and reunion.

COULD HAVE BEEN; SHOULD HAVE BEEN; HERE I AM

After this hair-raising incident, the family decided that staying in the Bronx was too risky. They packed their lives into suitcases once more and moved to Connecticut, seeking a quieter existence away from the prying eyes of authorities. It was in this new setting that an unexpected turn of events awaited my grandfather, one that seemed like a twist of fate. This transition marked the beginning of a new chapter for the Koslowski family, offering them a chance at a fresh start and the hope of laying down roots in a new community, far from the shadows of the past. This move, prompted by necessity and fueled by the desire for safety, would lead to unforeseen opportunities and serendipitous fortunes, shaping the destiny of our family in ways they could never have imagined.

After their harrowing experiences and tumultuous escape from New York, my grandfather John, along with his family, sought a fresh start in Connecticut. In this new setting, away from the immediate threats of his past, John was able to secure a position as a crew member on the fishing vessel named *Gudrun*, a sturdy boat that called Gloucester, Massachusetts, its home port. The *Gudrun* was known for its extensive fishing ventures along the choppy northeast coast and into the colder, more unpredictable Canadian waters. These journeys were not brief; they could stretch out for weeks, the duration largely dependent on the success and quantity of the catch they were able to secure.

In the cold December of 1951, the *Gudrun* was preparing for a rigorous month-long journey targeting the rich fishing areas near Nova Scotia, Canada. This expedition, like many before, was expected to be challenging, testing the endurance and skills of all aboard. It was during this time that my uncle Rene, married to John's daughter, was scheduled to make his debut on the *Gudrun*, having been assigned the role of cook for the crew. This would have been Rene's inaugural venture into the demanding environment of a fishing vessel's galley.

However, fate intervened through the seasoned instincts of my grandfather. With a life steeped in maritime experience, John had a deep understanding of the sea and its whims. He noted the brewing storm systems and unfavorable weather patterns forecasted for the time of the expedition. Concerned for the safety and well-being of his son-in-law, especially given Rene's inexperience at sea, John advised against his participation in this particular journey. He promised Rene a spot on the following expedition, hoping for better weather conditions that would offer a more suitable introduction to the rigors of sea life.

Heeding his father-in-law's seasoned advice, Rene made the decision to stay ashore, a choice that unknowingly spared him from what was to become a fateful journey for the *Gudrun* and its crew. This moment, seemingly inconsequential at the time, would later be regarded as a significant twist of fate in our family's history, illustrating how a single decision, guided by experience and intuition, can alter the course of lives.

The *Gudrun*, a formidable two-hundred-foot, all-steel construct, was designed for the harsh and demanding conditions of the sea, especially the unpredictable nature of the northeast coast and Canadian waters. Central to its operation was the spacious hold, strategically placed at the vessel's core, where the fresh catch would be stored. As fish were brought aboard through the strenuous efforts of the crew, they were immediately transferred to this chilled sanctuary, layered with ice to preserve their freshness until the ship could make its return to the mainland processing facilities.

The operational efficiency of the *Gudrun*, particularly the storage capacity of its hold, was a balancing act that depended heavily on several factors. The quantity of fuel—a critical element for the long-haul voyages—directly impacted the available space for the catch, as more fuel meant less room for fish. Additionally, weather conditions played a crucial role; rough seas could lead to higher swells, challenging the vessel's stability and its ability to secure its valuable cargo.

On this particular occasion, as winter cloaked the docks in its icy grasp, the *Gudrun* was poised to embark on its scheduled journey to the fishing grounds near Nova Scotia. It was then that a last-minute hiccup arose; the crew found themselves shorthanded by two members, an issue that needed urgent resolution for the voyage to proceed. In a stroke of necessity, the captain turned to the docks, where he spotted two workers unaffiliated with the usual crew. Seizing the opportunity, he extended an impromptu invitation to these men to join the expedition. With little hesitation, they agreed, stepping into the roles vacated by absent crew members.

With these last-minute additions, the crew was deemed complete, and the vessel, now fully staffed and provisioned, set off from Gloucester, Massachusetts, into the biting December chill, its bow cutting through the cold waves toward the rich fishing areas near Nova Scotia. This decision to bring on untested crew members would not only fill the immediate need but also set the stage for unforeseen developments in the voyage ahead.

In what can only be described as a remarkable turn of events, the *Gudrun*, having experienced unexpectedly favorable fishing conditions, managed to fill its storage hold much faster than anticipated. This stroke of fortune allowed them to conclude their fishing expedition ahead of schedule. With their haul secure, the crew made the decision to head back to Gloucester, aiming to beat an approaching storm to the safety of the port. They were keen to unload their lucrative catch and avoid the impending bad weather, which threatened to turn the sea treacherous.

However, as they embarked on their return journey, the seas began to betray them. In the early hours, around 2:00 a.m., the *Gudrun* and its crew found themselves facing the very storm they had hoped to outrun. The vessel, already heavily burdened by its bountiful catch, struggled against the onslaught of the storm. It was a perilous situation, exacerbated by the ship's overcapacity. The furious wave swells relentlessly battered the ship, causing water to flood into the compartments. The crew, caught in an increasingly desperate situation, scrambled to bail out water and lighten the ship's load, but their efforts were in vain against the ferocity of the storm.

Gloucester Fisherman's Memorial

In a final bid for salvation, the captain issued an SOS signal, a desperate plea for rescue in the face of impending doom. This call for help was a beacon of hope in the storm-ravaged pitch-black December night. Yet despite their pleas, help would not come. The storm, indifferent to the plights of men, continued its wrathful assault. The tragic fate of the *Gudrun* was sealed as it succumbed to the sea, taking with it all seventeen souls on board, including the two replacement crew members, whose names and stories faded into the abyss alongside the vessel. This tragic event left a lasting scar on the community and my family, forever remembered as a stark reminder of the sea's merciless power and the unpredictable threads of fate that weave through our lives.

My introduction to the tragic story of the *Gudrun* and its ill-fated voyage came during my childhood, a time when the complexities and profound impacts of such events were beyond my young understanding. I knew only of the somber fact that my grandfather, a man I never had the chance to meet, had perished at sea, his life claimed by the ocean's depths a full three years before I was born. In our family narratives, his name seemed to hover in the background, mentioned infrequently, his story a quiet specter in our family's past. However, the presence of my German grandmother, John's widow, in my early years, was a silent testament to the loss and sorrow that lingered long after the tragedy. Curiously, throughout the years that we shared, she never once spoke directly to me, maintaining a kind of solemn distance that I couldn't understand as a child. Her sudden death, which occurred in such a mundane and familial setting as a card game at the dinner table, struck me as a shocking and reminder of how sudden and unpredictable life can be. The two events left a stark impression on my young mind, mingling with the lingering sadness of the losses of both my grandfather and grandmother.

It was not until years later, as an adult, that I delved deeper into the story of the *Gudrun*, guided by conversations with my uncle Rene. He, who had narrowly escaped the same fate because of my grandfather's wary advice, provided perspectives and details previously unknown to me. These discussions illuminated not just the tragic events that had unfolded at sea but also the profound and lasting impact they had on our family. The weight of the past and the resonance of my grandfather's untimely death began to solidify in my understanding, intertwining with my own sense of identity and family heritage. This exploration into our shared history brought to light the depths of loss, the bonds of family, and the silent currents of grief that had flowed beneath the surface of our family's outward appearance for so long.

During a particularly somber visit to the hospital where Rene, my uncle, was a patient facing the grim reality of cancer surgery, he recounted harrowing tales that sent shivers down my spine. Lying there, weakened yet resilient, he unveiled a part of his past that I had never known. He revealed to me that throughout his life, he had faced the grim specter of death not once but three times, each escape seemingly more miraculous than the last.

His first brush with mortality took place in his childhood, a time usually marked by carefree days and innocent adventures. He recounted a day from when he was just an eleven-year-old boy, filled with excitement and anticipation, at an air show in Orange, Massachusetts. This wasn't just any event; it was a special day where the thrill of flight was to become a reality for him and other attendees, as free airplane rides were being offered to the public.

After what seemed like an eternity of waiting, with anticipation building with each passing moment, Rene was on the cusp of his turn. He was next in line to climb aboard the small aircraft and soar into the sky, an adventure he had been dreaming of throughout the day. However, fate intervened in a most unexpected manner. Just as he was preparing to step forward, a father, eager to share the experience with his two children, bypassed the queue, taking the spots meant for Rene and the others waiting with him.

Disappointed but resigned, Rene stepped back, watching as the plane, now carrying the family that had just cut in front of him, began its takeoff run down the runway. He watched, perhaps with a mix of envy and relief at not having to confront any lingering fears, as the plane lifted into the air. His relief turned to horror as the aircraft, shortly after takeoff, experienced a catastrophic engine failure. Before the eyes of the shocked crowd, the plane spiraled uncontrollably nose down and crashed to the ground, a tragic end to what began as a day of joy and excitement, claiming the lives of all on board. This chilling story of missed fate and the fragility of life left me with a profound sense of the thin line between life and death and the mysterious forces that sometimes intervene in our destinies.

Years after his narrow escape from the air show disaster, another unsettling chapter unfolded in Rene's life, intertwined with the theme of aviation and the specter of death. His son Paul, at the cusp of adulthood and hungry for adventure, was drawn to the thrill of skydiving—a yearning that led them back to the very airfield shadowed by Rene's childhood trauma. The requirement for parental consent placed Rene in a harrowing position, torn between nurturing his son's aspirations and the haunting memories of past tragedies.

Despite reassurances from the skydiving instructor about the safety and regulations of the sport, Rene found himself paralyzed by an ominous feeling, an unshakable reluctance to sign off on his son's daring venture. His instincts, it seemed, were eerily prescient; in a cruel twist of fate, the same instructor who had attempted to alleviate his fears that week met with a tragic accident, perishing because of a parachute malfunction during a routine jump. This grim incident only deepened the eerie aura of destiny that seemed to loom over Rene's life.

It was within this context of narrow escapes and tragic fates that Rene recounted his second major brush with mortality—the forsaken journey of the *Gudrun*. His decision, influenced by his father-in-law John's wary counsel, spared him from joining the doomed expedition, marking yet another instance where fate seemed to veer him away from an untimely demise.

In the hospital, reflecting on these profound escapes from death, Rene pondered the peculiar course his life had taken. With the recent surgery seemingly successful in eradicating the cancer, he mused that perhaps he had eluded the grasp of death yet again. But life, with its unpredictable and often harsh narratives, had a different end in store. Despite the initial success of the surgery, Rene's condition deteriorated swiftly as the cancer returned, more aggressive than before, leading to his untimely passing just weeks later. This final encounter with mortality underscored the fragile and unpredictable nature of existence, leaving behind a legacy of tales that blur the lines between chance, fate, and the inexorable march of time. Rene's life, marked by remarkable escapes and losses, serves as a testament to the enigmatic forces that guide our paths through this world.

The impact of ancestors on our lives extends beyond their physical presence, a truth I've come to recognize as undeniable. This concept resonates deeply with me, particularly in the context of my German grandfather, John, whom I never had the chance to meet because of his untimely death three years before I was born. Despite the absence of direct interaction or shared memories, I've grown to understand and appreciate the profound ways in which he has influenced my life.

My reflections on family history and the stories passed down to me have revealed striking similarities between my grandfather and myself, serving as a testament to the invisible threads that connect generations. It's fascinating to consider that despite the passage of time and the barrier of death, there is a tangible legacy that manifests in physical and intellectual traits that persist through families. In our case, it's not just the shared physical characteristics of blond hair and blue eyes, uncommon within our broader family lineage, but also our identical height of five feet eight inches.

This realization brings to light the mysterious and powerful nature of genetics, but it goes beyond mere physical resemblance. The idea that certain attributes, preferences, and even ways of thinking can be passed down through generations is compelling. It suggests that our ancestors continue to live on through us, not just in our appearances but also in subtler aspects of our beings, such as our talents, inclinations, and perhaps even our dreams.

Understanding that I am, in many ways, a reflection of my grandfather John has led me to a deeper appreciation of my heritage and a stronger sense of identity. It prompts a reevaluation of what it means to be an individual, as I realize that my very existence is tied to a rich tapestry of family history. This insight has inspired me to delve deeper into my roots, to understand not only who I am but also where I come from, and to recognize the indelible mark that those who came before me have left on my life.

ERIC KOSLOWSKI

My Parents (1926–1954)

(Note: it's now March 9, 2024, and I just turned seventy years old when I wrote this section "My Parents.")

On a spring day in 1926, specifically May 12, the Cherries family of Fitchburg, Massachusetts, welcomed a new member: my mother, Rose. Her life, spanning nearly eight decades until her passing in 2003, was deeply rooted in this quintessential New England town. As the second youngest child in a bustling household of four sisters and three brothers, Rose's early life was undoubtedly filled with the joys and chaos that come with a large family. Her experiences, growing up during a time of significant societal changes and personal family challenges, shaped her into a resilient and compassionate individual. Rose Cherries emerged as a pioneering figure within her family, setting a significant precedent by becoming the first among her siblings to receive a high school diploma. This educational achievement marked a defining moment for the Cherries household, illustrating a break from the tradition that had seen the elder children leave their academic pursuits prematurely to contribute to the family's income. Rose's accomplishment was not just a personal triumph but also served as an inspiration for her younger sister, Fay, who followed in her footsteps, making them the only two in a family of nine to complete high school.

Three years subsequent to my mother's birth, in the urban landscapes of the Bronx, New York, my father, Leo Koslowski, entered the world. His life took a turn from the bustling city to the more serene environment of Leominster, Massachusetts, following personal losses that left him seeking the comfort of family. It was his sister Margaret who provided him with this refuge, offering him a new home and a chance to start anew.

Meanwhile, nestled in the nearby town of Lunenburg, where I have lived for over forty years and still reside, was Whalom Park. This local hot spot was known for its amusement attractions and community gatherings. Among its many features was a roller skat-

ing rink, a venue that became the backdrop for a fateful encounter between my parents. It's intriguing to think of this chance meeting, set against the backdrop of laughter and music, where my mother, Rose, from Fitchburg, and my father, Leo, from the Bronx, first crossed paths at Whalom Skating Rink. The initial spark ignited in this vibrant setting led to a blossoming relationship.

Their courtship, emblematic of post-war America's optimism and growth, culminated in marriage in July of 1949. This union marked the beginning of a new chapter as they decided to lay down their roots in Leominster, Massachusetts, close to both their families and the memories of their initial encounter. The story of how they met and married, set against the backdrop of mid-twentieth-century America, filled with its own challenges and changes, reflects the enduring themes of love, resilience, and the intertwining of destinies.

Despite the societal and economic challenges that often came with managing a large household, Rose's academic achievements set a foundation for her future. Her education opened doors to various professional opportunities, allowing her to contribute significantly to her community and family. Throughout her career, Rose demonstrated remarkable versatility and dedication, balancing her role as a mother to three children with her professional responsibilities. She held positions as a secretary for notable institutions such as the General Electric Company, Burbank Hospital, and Fitchburg State College, showcasing her skills and work ethic in each role.

Rose was well-known in her community for her infectious sense of humor and her unwavering willingness to help others. Her vibrant personality and innate kindness made her a cherished figure among neighbors and friends alike. In addition to her caring nature, she was also known for her striking beauty, an attribute that drew admiration and attention. Her Italian roots contributed to her distinctive and attractive appearance, which left a lasting impression not only on those around her but also on me as a child.

Her sociability and approachability meant that she had a wide circle of male friends, which became a source of tension in her marriage. I believe this contributed to my father's feelings of frustration, and it may have played a part in his subsequent struggles with alcohol. Despite the personal difficulties and family challenges that arose from these circumstances, Rose's commitment to her children never wavered. She was a pillar of strength and devotion, always there to support her family in times of need.

My recollections of my mother, Rose, are filled with warmth and affection. Her presence brought light and laughter to our home, making my childhood memories predominantly happy and comforting. Despite any familial struggles or personal hardships she faced, Rose's love for her children and her commitment to their well-being remained unwavering, defining her in my eyes as an exemplary mother and a remarkable woman.

Following the unexpected and early demise of my father in the 1990s, Rose entered retirement. This period of her life was characterized by a quieter existence, focused on her personal well-being and spending time with her family. She remained in Fitchburg, Massachusetts, the town that had become her home and the backdrop to her rich life story. Rose passed away at the respectable age of eighty-one, leaving behind a legacy of resilience, education, and love, her life serving as a beacon and testament to the enduring spirit of the Cherries family.

Leo, my father, was a man whose character was deeply influenced by the societal ethos of the post–World War II era, embodying the characteristics esteemed by his generation. His life was a testament to integrity and resilience, qualities that defined him as the archetypal head of the household during that period. He upheld the family as his paramount concern, dedicating himself to providing stability and support for his loved ones. Hard work and honesty were not just values he believed in; they were principles he lived by, guiding his decisions and interactions. His intelligence was evident not only in his problem-solving skills but also in his pragmatic, forward-looking approach to life, always considering the next steps and best paths forward for his family.

Growing up in the Bronx during the tumultuous 1930s, Leo's early years were marked by the widespread economic struggles of the Great Depression. This challenging environment served as a crucible for his character, shaping him into a person of formidable determination and tenacity. The hardship and scarcity he witnessed and experienced did not embitter him; instead, they fostered a robust sense of responsibility and an unwavering resolve to improve his circumstances and those of his family.

These experiences in his youth did not merely create a survivor; they forged a man who understood the value of perseverance, the importance of community, and the virtue of looking out for others. As he navigated through the various hurdles and societal expectations of his time, Leo's actions and life choices reflected the internalization of these lessons, making him a steadfast provider and a reliable pillar for his family through changing times. His life story, marked by overcoming adversity through strength and integrity, serves as a poignant narrative of the post-war American patriarch.

Transitioning into adulthood, Leo secured employment as a papermaker, a testament to his steadfast work ethic. The job, with its demanding schedules and tough working conditions, became the metronome of his existence: a repetitive cycle of work, drink, and sleep, interspersed with rare moments dedicated to family excursions. One cherished memory stands out vividly against this backdrop of routine: a family drive along the scenic Mohawk Trail, Route 2, culminating at the French King Bridge over the Connecticut River.

It was there, in the midst of nature's tranquility, that he shared his aspiration to one day captain a motorboat down the river's expanse. Sadly, this dream, like many others, lingered unfulfilled, a silent testament to the dreams deferred of a hardworking man.

Reflecting on this, the root of his unfulfilled aspirations becomes apparent: a constant deferment, a perpetual postponement of dreams. Leo's life was a series of "tomorrows" that never seemed to dawn. His was a paradox of quicksilver enthusiasm that frustratingly faded before morphing into concrete actions. This cycle of enthusiasm and inaction was no doubt exacerbated by the physical toll extracted by his laborious occupation at the paper mill. The ceaseless rotating shifts sapped not only his physical energy but also, insidiously, his spirit and drive, leaving little room for the pursuit of personal passions or the realization of dreams.

My father was a man of integrity shaped by the virtues of honesty and perseverance, which he upheld in the face of life's relentless challenges. He was once a soldier in the National Guard and later an auxiliary police officer for the city of Fitchburg. He was a testament to resilience, often found in solitude at our kitchen table, confronting his troubles head-on. Amid these silent battles, he would mutter in disbelief at the adversities we faced, seeking solace in the temporary escape that alcohol provided, allowing a momentary peace for him and our beleaguered family. His temper, a fierce adversary, often clouded his judgment, making it difficult to navigate the complexities of life with calm and rational strategies.

Despite his struggles, he imparted to me the invaluable lesson that life's true challenge lies not in the inevitability of death but in the rigorous test of living. "Dying is easy, living is hard. Don't ever give up," he would say, embedding in me a creed of relentless pursuit and resilience. These words, born of his profound belief in facing life head-on, served as a guiding beacon through my own trials.

One autumn day, marked by the crisp air and the fall of leaves, presented a somber scene at my family home. I found my father isolated, seated in his car parked in the driveway, lost in a deep, vacant stare. Joining him in the passenger seat, I was met with an unsettling silence before inquiring about his state of mind. His instructions were unexpected and grave; he asked me to retrieve the loaded gun from under my seat, ensure it was unloaded, and securely lock it away. Without questioning, I complied, understanding the weight of the moment. Returning to the car, I found him still ensnared in his contemplation, staring into the emptiness before him. It was then he shared a raw and vulnerable truth. Despite the despair that gripped him, he confessed his inability to end his life, driven by a profound sense of duty and love toward us, his children. He expressed an overwhelming responsibility, refusing to leave us prematurely, burdened by the thought of our lives without his presence. This moment of honesty revealed the depth of his turmoil and the strength of his commitment to family, illustrating the complex layers of his character and the silent battles he fought within.

In his late fifties, after enduring a challenging period, he encountered a critical turning point. Deciding to stop his downward spiral into self-pity and destructive behavior, he chose to make significant changes to his life. Motivated by a desire to pursue the dreams he had previously set aside, he recognized the need for a concrete strategy to facilitate this transformation. With renewed determination, he began to outline a comprehensive plan, marking a shift toward a more positive and proactive approach to life. This plan was not just about avoiding past mistakes; it was a blueprint for actively pursuing happiness and fulfillment. He identified key areas for improvement, including his physical health, emotional well-being, and professional life, setting realistic and measurable goals for each. Moreover, he committed to breaking old habits and forming new healthier ones. This involved adopting a balanced diet, incorporating regular exercise into his daily routine, and seeking out activities that brought him joy and relaxation. He also made a conscious effort to nurture and repair relationships that had suffered because of his past behaviors, reaching out to friends and family members to rebuild bridges and create a stronger support network.

In addition to these personal changes, he explored opportunities for growth and learning, considering new career paths that aligned with his interests and values and taking up hobbies that he had always wanted to try but never had the time for. This comprehensive approach to revamping his life demonstrated his commitment to not only escaping the negative cycle he found himself in but also to building a more meaningful and satisfying future. By embarking on this new journey of self-improvement, he illustrated the power of resilience and the potential for change at any stage of life. His actions served as a reminder that, while it's never too late to alter one's path, it requires intention, effort, and perseverance to turn dreams into reality.

His decision to quit drinking and smoking was a significant turning point, challenging yet crucial for the profound transformation he sought. This abrupt cessation was a testament to his commitment to change, a tangible first step away from self-destruction and toward self-improvement. The immediate benefits of this decision were manifold; not only did his physical health begin to improve, but his mental clarity and emotional well-being also saw significant enhancements. This positive shift allowed him to transition from a mindset of victimhood to one of achievement and possibility.

Embracing this new chapter, he immersed himself in activities that fostered both personal growth and joy. Bicycling became a way to explore his surroundings while improving his fitness. Chess offered a mental challenge, sharpening his strategic thinking. Reading opened new worlds and perspectives, enriching his understanding and empathy. Golfing provided a peaceful escape into nature and an opportunity for social interaction and networking. However, his journey of transformation extended beyond personal hobbies and health; it deeply touched his familial relationships. He actively worked to repair and rejuvenate bonds with his family members that had been strained or neglected. He initiated conversations, spent quality time with loved ones, and expressed his regrets and intentions for a better future. These efforts were not just about making amends; they were also about rebuilding trust, understanding, and love—rekindling connections that had once been vibrant.

Now with a revitalized outlook on life, he approached each day with a sense of purpose and optimism, believing in his heart that there was still plenty of time to achieve fulfillment and happiness. Yet despite this newfound positivity, a niggling doubt remained at the back of his mind—a whisper questioning the reality of the time he had left. Was it as expansive as he hoped, or was it more finite than he wanted to admit? This uncertainty did not deter his spirit; instead, it fueled a sense of urgency to make the most of every moment, to live fully and love deeply, embracing the present while hopeful for the future.

Just as he was beginning to embrace this new chapter in his life, around his sixtieth birthday, an unexpected twist occurred. His routine health checks, part of his new commitment to well-being, led to a concerning discovery—a tumor in his bladder. This news was particularly alarming because he had been noticing minor yet unusual signs, like traces of blood in his urine, which he had initially brushed off as minor issues. Now faced with the potential gravity of his situation, he regretted ignoring these symptoms earlier. However, instead of succumbing to panic or denial, he approached the situation with the same resolve and clarity he had applied to his recent life changes. He sought comprehensive medical evaluations, determined to understand and confront whatever health challenges lay ahead. The results from the advanced examinations brought a harsh reality into focus; the tumor was cancerous. The ambiguity surrounding the cancer's origin and whether it had spread beyond the bladder added layers of complexity and urgency to his situation. Despite the shock and fear this diagnosis provoked, he found solace in the fact that there were still options available. The treatment paths were laid out before him: chemotherapy and radiation, surgical removal of the tumor and bladder, or a cautious approach of watchful waiting—each carried its own risks and potential outcomes.

Faced with these choices, he took the time to reflect on the life he had begun to rebuild and the dreams he still yearned to fulfill. This contemplation was not just about choosing a medical treatment; it was about deciding how he wanted to live in the face of uncertainty and adversity. With the support of his revitalized relationships and a deeper understanding of his own resilience, he prepared to make an informed decision.

This critical health scare underscored the importance of the changes he had already made and the value of the time he had. It reinforced his commitment to living deliberately and meaningfully regardless of the challenges. With incomplete information but a heart full of hope, he was ready to face the next steps, balancing the practical considerations of his medical condition with his renewed desire to embrace life fully regardless of its unpredictability.

The day that remains vivid in my memory, casting a long shadow over my thoughts, began like any other but quickly morphed into one of profound significance. It was just a few days following my father's grim diagnosis, and the weight of his decision on how to proceed with treatment loomed largely over us. I visited him, intending to offer support and help him navigate the overwhelming sea of medical options laid before him. As we sat in the quiet familiarity of his living room, he shared his deep-seated fears and uncertainties. He articulated the dilemma he faced: initiating treatment with chemotherapy and radiation, which might incapacitate him for an unknown duration without the assurance of diminishing the tumor, or opting for the surgery, which, while potentially curative, would alter his life irreversibly. The stark reality of the chemotherapy and radiation's potential side effects—prolonged debilitation, risk to other organs, and the lingering possibility of inevitable surgery—was daunting. Meanwhile, the surgical removal of his bladder, though possibly curative, carried the heavy price of living with a permanent external urine collection bag, a constant reminder of his battle with cancer and a significant change to his quality of life.

In that moment of vulnerability, he looked to me for guidance, his eyes seeking more than just advice—they sought comfort, reassurance, and validation. The responsibility of influencing such a critical decision weighed heavily on me. My response, formed from a blend of logic, emotion, and the desire to see him free from suffering, emerged with a gravity I had never before experienced. The advice I gave, formed under the pressure of the moment and my own emotional turmoil, remains a significant burden, echoing in my mind with persistent clarity.

I ponder often on that day, replaying our conversation, questioning the wisdom of my counsel, and grappling with the profound impact of our choices. It was a moment that transcended the usual dynamics of our relationship, one that has since been imprinted on my conscience, shaping my reflections on responsibility, love, and the intricate dance between life and death.

At thirty-six years old, I was at a point in my life where I felt secure in my capabilities and decisions. With a college education under my belt and the success of my entrepreneurial endeavors, I had cultivated a strong sense of self-assurance and believed in the soundness of my judgment. This self-confidence, coupled with a history of making calculated, successful choices, made me feel prepared to offer meaningful advice, even in situations as grave as my father's health crisis.

COULD HAVE BEEN; SHOULD HAVE BEEN; HERE I AM

In that moment, my father looked to me not just as his child but also as a trusted adviser, someone whose opinions he respected and valued deeply. He was adrift in a sea of uncertainty, grappling with a life-altering decision, and he turned to me for the clarity and support he so desperately needed. Understanding the magnitude of his trust and the depth of his vulnerability, I took on the responsibility with a solemn sense of duty. As we discussed his options, I meticulously considered the potential outcomes of each path. We both understood the aggressive nature of his illness, visualizing the tumor as a malevolent force poised to wreak havoc on his body. This perception drove us to lean toward immediate, definitive action. With the facts at hand and the urgency the situation demanded, the option of surgery appeared to be the most pragmatic approach. It promised the removal of the immediate threat, the cancer, potentially offering a direct route to eliminating the disease from his body.

In advocating for the surgical option, I believed we were choosing the path with the most tangible benefit, aiming to excise the source of his suffering and thereby grant him a fighting chance at a cancer-free life. The radical nature of the procedure, while daunting, seemed a necessary sacrifice to forestall the cancer's insidious progression. This decision was guided by the desire to protect him, to preemptively strike against the disease that threatened to undermine the new lease on life he had only recently begun to explore.

Reflecting on that period, I recognize the weight of the advice I offered. It was a decision made from a place of love, concern, and a fervent wish to see my father overcome his illness. However, the complexity of such a decision, made under the shadow of fear and the pressure of time, remains a reminder of the intricate interplay between knowledge, intuition, and the profound desire to do what is best for those we hold dear. Following thorough discussions and contemplation, the consensus was to proceed with the surgical removal of my father's bladder and the insidious tumor within. This decision, monumental in its consequences, led to the necessity of living with an external bladder bag—a significant adjustment but one deemed essential for his survival. His medical team, after careful review and agreement with our decision, moved quickly to schedule the operation, understanding the urgency of the situation.

The surgery was conducted with haste but precision. I awaited the outcome with a blend of apprehension and hope, a tumultuous mix that seemed to define this entire ordeal. The subsequent conversation with his doctor provided a sigh of relief; the surgery had been successful. Yet this relief was tempered by the revelation that the cancer had infiltrated the muscle of the nearby abdominal wall, necessitating additional excisions. Despite this complication, the medical team was confident in the thoroughness of their intervention, believing they had eradicated all traces of cancer from the bladder area. Their optimism offered a beacon of hope in the murky waters of postoperative recovery.

The next day, seeing my father, his spirit unbroken, was both uplifting and heart-wrenching. Despite the physical toll, he radiated a sense of survival, as if he had dodged a lethal blow. He openly expressed regret for the lifestyle choices that had led to his condition, acknowledging the harsh toll of decades of neglect. Yet there was no trace of self-pity in his voice, only resolve. He was determined to use this second chance to foster a healthier life, to honor the body that had carried him through so much, and to rectify the years of harm with a newfound commitment to well-being.

This shift toward health and self-care was inspiring, marking the beginning of what we hoped would be a revitalized chapter in his life. But life, as it often does, held unforeseen twists. Just as we were adjusting to the new normal and embracing this wave of positive change, we were blindsided by an unexpected turn of events. What happened next was something no one could have predicted, casting a shadow over our budding hope and testing our resilience in ways we never imagined.

Three weeks post-operation, a follow-up examination was scheduled to evaluate his postsurgical recovery, which we approached with cautious optimism. Initially, the checkup proceeded without incident, painting a picture of a standard, albeit slow, recovery. However, this semblance of normalcy was shattered when the results of a routine chest X-ray were unveiled. The images revealed the presence of numerous dime-sized tumors scattered across both lungs, a shocking development given that no such signs had been evident in the presurgical scans. The sudden appearance of these tumors was as mystifying as it was alarming.

In the days that followed, further medical evaluations confirmed our worst fears; the tumors were proliferating rapidly, now the size of quarters, betraying a virulent and unyielding progression. The surgical team hypothesized that microscopic cancer cells, perhaps dislodged during the initial operation, had found their way into his lungs, where they found fertile ground to develop into multiple, formidable tumors. Confronted with this dire turn of events, there was no choice but to commence immediate chemotherapy despite the well-documented severe side effects and the toll it could take on his already weakened state.

The ensuing weeks were marked by an aggressive chemotherapy regimen, a period fraught with intense physical and psychological suffering for him. The chemicals, while aimed at eradicating the cancer, wreaked havoc on his body, draining his vitality and casting a shadow over his spirit. The aftermath of this arduous battle was heartbreakingly clear in the follow-up examination. The relentless tumors, far from being eradicated, had not only endured but had also begun their merciless spread to other regions of his body. Faced with this grim reality, the doctors, having exhausted all conventional medical avenues, delivered the crushing verdict: there were no further treatments to pursue. They recommended he return home to make the most of the time he had left and to arrange his final affairs.

The impact of this news was devastating. Amid the turmoil, I vividly recall my father's resigned words, "So this will be my end, from a disease." His voice, tinged with a mixture of disbelief and acceptance, echoed the profound injustice of his fate. It was a moment of stark reality, confronting the cruel, indiscriminate nature of illness and the fragility of life itself. The journey from a hopeful recovery to the brink of farewell was harrowing, leaving us to grapple with the impending loss and the harsh, unyielding course of his disease.

His physical and mental deterioration advanced rapidly. He often described feeling like a prisoner on death row, tormented by the abundance of time to contemplate his fate. Every morning, he greeted the day with a childlike wonder, asking, "I'm still alive for another day?" fully aware that the time would come when he could no longer utter those words. I witnessed his journey through disbelief, anger, hope, and finally acceptance, each phase marked by distinct behaviors. For instance, during disbelief, he struggled to understand how, despite abandoning alcohol and cigarettes, cancer still ravaged his body. This confusion rendered him a victim to the illness. This stage is perilous as the affected may underestimate the severity of their condition and opt for inadequate medical consultation. In his case, failing to seek a second opinion and relying solely on the limited expertise of a small-town doctor for such a severe illness was absurd. Merely fifty miles from his home stood Dana-Farber Cancer Institute, a leading entity in cancer research and treatment. Regrettably, his doctors did not recommend he seek a second opinion or explore innovative treatments unavailable at their facility but rather encouraged him to persist with conventional methods such as chemotherapy, radiation, and surgery.

As the cancer within him grew more aggressive, he was starkly confronted with the mortality his illness imposed. In an act of desperation and hope, he opted for chemotherapy, fully aware of its dim prospects for success. Yet in this dark hour, he found solace in faith and prayer, clinging to the slender hope that perhaps his body harbored an innate capacity for healing. However, this hope was shadowed by a nagging question: had the years of self-neglect and indulgence irreparably harmed his body's natural repair mechanisms? Deep down, he recognized the brutal truth that there is a limit to the physical abuse a body can withstand before it relinquishes the will to fight back. His years of heavy drinking and smoking, he feared, might have pushed his body past this critical point. Desperate for redemption, he vowed to reform his lifestyle, pleading for just one more chance to prove he could change. Alas, it was too late. The cancer had mercilessly spread, ravaging his body from within. His spirit, once buoyed by a fragile hope, now sank into the somber depths of acceptance. As his physical functions waned, his doctor prescribed palliative care medications to ease his final days at home, a solemn acknowledgment of his imminent departure from this world.

The day came when my mother, bearing a weight of sorrow, informed me that he could no longer swallow his pain medication. The cruel reality was that he needed hospitalization for a morphine intravenous drip to manage his excruciating pain. Prompted by her call, I summoned an ambulance. As they wheeled him out, halfway down the stairs, he locked eyes with me, a silent plea etched in his gaze, questioning why he must leave the sanctuary of his home. I explained the necessity, the inability to manage his pain at home, and the relief the hospital could provide. Yet with a piercing look, he uttered, "Only the living can feel pain, I prefer the pain." His words struck a chord, a profound acceptance of his condition and a defiance of the life that was slipping away. I understood his yearning to remain amid the familiar, even in pain, yet the sight of his suffering, the groans and moans of his torment, were unbearable. Despite his wishes, we had to act; the hospital, with its promise of pain relief, seemed our only recourse to ease his agonizing final journey.

My mother and I followed the ambulance to the hospital, where my father was swiftly admitted and placed in a patient care room. Around the same time, my sister Carol arrived. To ease his discomfort, the medical team started a morphine drip, which gently alleviated his pain and induced a semiconscious state, reminiscent of a deep, tranquil sleep.

In a quiet moment, the attending nurse requested that Carol and I step outside for a private conversation in the hallway. She shared with us, in gentle terms, that our father's time was limited—perhaps a day or two at most. She inquired about our consent to adjust the morphine to whatever level was necessary to ensure his comfort. When I questioned whether this might accelerate his departure from us, she acknowledged that the increased dosage, while alleviating his suffering, could indeed hasten his passing in a dignified and painless manner.

After a heart-wrenching discussion, Carol and I, recognizing our father's critical condition and prioritizing his peace, gave our consent for the medical team to administer the necessary level of care to maintain his comfort even if it meant facing the inevitable sooner. My father was peacefully asleep when we all agreed it was best to return home and come back to visit him during the evening to monitor his condition.

Around 7:00 p.m. that same day, I, along with our close family friend Frank, whom my father greatly enjoyed spending time with during his occasional visits, arrived at the hospital. To my surprise, upon entering the room, I found my father awake, sitting up and watching television, radiating a sense of cheerfulness and expressing his joy at seeing us. Curiously, I asked him, "Are you feeling okay?"

His response took me by surprise as he humorously remarked, "If I had known the relief that morphine could provide, I might have become an addict years ago." We shared a brief moment of laughter, but then the atmosphere shifted when he firmly grasped my right hand and arm, looking into my eyes with a grave expression. He began to apologize, regretting that he had never given me anything of significant value.

I immediately countered his apology, emphasizing how mistaken he was. I explained, "No, Dad, you're so wrong. You've imparted countless lessons about life. You've given me your sense of humor, strength, intelligence, and even your honest, sometimes fiery, temper. But above all, you've given me the most precious gift a father could offer his son—the gift of life itself." I continued to express how his existence made mine possible and that I carry within me half of his genetic legacy, which I would pass on to my own children, thereby extending his presence into the future, potentially for generations to come. "Through your descendants, carrying pieces of your essence, you'll live on," I assured him.

He looked at me for a few silent, intense seconds before softly responding, "Eric, nobody wants to face their end, but I know my time is drawing close. Your words bring me comfort, making the thought of passing a bit easier." Releasing his grip, he gently fell back into sleep.

I leaned forward, kissed his forehead, and whispered a promise to see him in the morning. Little did I know, that conversation would be our final one before he passed away at two the following morning, quietly in his sleep, and alone. At around the same time, I was in my own bed, sleeping, when I was suddenly and violently shaken awake. I tumbled out of bed, and within moments, the telephone rang. It was my sister informing me that our father had just passed away, and she asked if I wanted to meet her at the hospital to see him one last time. I declined, feeling a profound sense of his presence, as if he had just visited me. "He was just here," I told her.

For many in my family, that night is remembered with sorrow, but for me, it carries a different significance. In that unexpected moment, my father imparted one final lesson: to live life fully and without hesitation. In his own way, through our last conversation and his departure, he underscored the importance of seizing life's moments. I've come to understand that in his final hours, he truly embodied this principle.

Let's rewind to the year 1954.

CHAPTER 2

Starting with My First Breath

March 9, 1954

Here I stand, a quintessential member of the "baby boomer" generation. My journey began on March 9, 1954, entering this world not in the typical fashion but feetfirst—eager and practically sprinting from my very first breath. As the first son in my family, I arrived as a robust newborn, tipping the scales at eight pounds and five ounces, adorned with blond hair and piercing blue eyes. It didn't take long for my parents to recognize they had more than they bargained for with me.

Growing up in the energetic post-war era, I was a spirited child from the start. My early years were marked by a boundless curiosity and an insatiable appetite for adventure. My family, steeped in the values and traditions of the time, quickly found their hands full as I explored every nook and cranny of our home and the surrounding neighborhood. My laughter filled the air, and my boundless energy kept everyone on their toes. As a baby boomer, I was part of a generation that experienced unprecedented change. I watched as the world around me transformed with the advent of television, rock and roll, and later, the Civil Rights Movement. These changes shaped my worldview, instilling in me a sense of possibility and a desire for progress.

School years brought new challenges and opportunities. I was a curious student, eager to learn but often more interested in the stories behind the facts. My teachers noted my creative mind and my knack for asking probing questions. I wasn't just content with the what; I needed to know the why and the how. This thirst for knowledge led me to explore various interests, from science to literature, each subject offering a new lens through which to view the world. As a teenager, I embodied the quintessential boomer spirit of rebellion and innovation. I questioned authority, sought to break the mold, and dreamed of making a difference. The music of the Beatles and Bob Dylan provided the soundtrack to my adolescence, their lyrics echoing my own thoughts and aspirations.

Now as I look back, I see how those early years were a prologue to a life lived with zeal and a constant pursuit of understanding. From that very first day, feetfirst into the world, I've never stopped moving forward, always with an eye on the horizon, eager to see what lies beyond. My early memories are tinged with my father's stern admonitions, his voice echoing, "Stop crying, son, or I'll really give you something to cry about." It seemed I was perpetually challenging his patience, forever the proverbial thorn in his side.

But what of the world into which I was born? The year 1954 held its own dramas and developments, setting the backdrop for my grand entrance. Let's delve into the events and cultural shifts that were unfolding at the time, painting a picture of the world as it greeted one more spirited baby boomer.

Major Events of 1954

- The United States Supreme Court made a landmark decision, ruling that race-based segregation in schools was unconstitutional, marking a significant step forward in the Civil Rights Movement.
- Senator Joseph McCarthy's nationally televised inquiries into communist infiltration of the Army reached their zenith, sparking a backlash and leading to his eventual

condemnation by the Senate, signaling the waning of his influence.
- International tensions were high as the Soviet Union rejected proposals to reunify Germany, keeping the Cold War temperature elevated.
- In a covert operation, the CIA intervened in Guatemala, aiding in the overthrow of the government and shaping the political landscape of Central America.
- The establishment of the Southeast Asia Treaty Organization (SEATO) by the US and Southeast Asian and Pacific nations reflected the expanding global strategy against communist expansion.
- A shocking incident occurred when radical Puerto Rican nationalists attacked the House of Representatives, injuring five congressmen, highlighting the extremes of political activism.
- The US and Canada began constructing an early-warning radar system in Northern Canada, a response to the increasing threat of Soviet missiles.

Business and economy

- The New York Stock Exchange prices soared, reaching their highest level since the crash of 1929, indicating a booming economy.

Science and technology

- The increasing global concern about nuclear fallout and radioactive waste disposal underscored the darker aspects of atomic energy.
- Dr. Jonas Salk made a monumental stride in public health by beginning to inoculate schoolchildren with his newly developed polio vaccine.
- The dismissal of physicist and nuclear pioneer J. Robert Oppenheimer from government projects because of his

political beliefs, marked a chilling effect on scientific freedom during the Red Scare.
- Medical science achieved a significant milestone with the first successful kidney transplant, paving the way for future organ transplants.

Sports

- The World Series saw the New York Giants triumph over the Cleveland Indians with a clean sweep of 4–0.
- The relocation of the Philadelphia Athletics to Kansas City reflected the shifting landscape of American sports.
- The debut of *Sports Illustrated* magazine indicated a growing interest in sports journalism.
- Roger Bannister of UK made history by becoming the first person to run a mile in under four minutes, breaking one of the most iconic barriers in athletics.

Arts and entertainment

- Cinematic achievements included the release of classics such as *On the Waterfront* and *Rear Window*, along with Akira Kurosawa's *Seven Samurai*.
- The music scene was enriched by hits like "Hernando's Hideaway" and "Mister Sandman."
- Television entertainment was dominated by shows like the *Jack Benny Show* and *The Adventures of Rin-Tin-Tin*.
- Notable literary works included *The Lord of the Rings* by J. R. R. Tolkien and *Lord of the Flies* by William Golding, which would go on to become classics.
- The inaugural of Newport Jazz Festival was held, signifying the growing popularity of jazz music.
- Bill Haley and His Comets' recording of "Rock Around the Clock" signaled the birth of rock and roll.

Everyday life

- The rapid increase in television ownership, with twenty-nine million US households owning sets, changed the landscape of American entertainment and culture.
- The emergence of Billy Graham as a leading figure sparked a renewed interest in Christian revival meetings.
- The Davy Crockett fad swept the nation, with sales of "coonskin" caps skyrocketing, showcasing the power of television marketing.
- Going to the movies was a popular pastime, with a ticket costing only seventy cents.

Fun facts

- The comic book industry was thriving, with sales reaching twenty million copies a month.
- The phrase "under God" was added to the Pledge of Allegiance, reflecting the era's intertwining of patriotism and religious sentiment.

This rich tapestry of events and cultural shifts provides a vivid backdrop to the world that welcomed a new generation, setting the stage for the changes and challenges that would come with the growth and maturation of the baby boomer generation.

I was born in a quaint town named Leominster, nestled somewhere in Central Massachusetts. This town is notably recognized as the birthplace of John Chapman, more famously known as Johnny Appleseed. Born on September 26, 1774, in Leominster, and passing away around March 18, 1845, near Fort Wayne, Indiana, Johnny Appleseed was an American missionary nurseryman. He played a significant role on the North American frontier, aiding the preparation for nineteenth-century pioneers by distributing apple tree nursery stock across the Midwest.

While the legendary figure of "Johnny Appleseed" is predominantly a product of folklore, John Chapman was indeed a real and committed nurseryman, who aimed to profit from his apple seedlings. Around the year 1800, he began gathering apple seeds from cider presses in Western Pennsylvania. Embarking on a westward journey, he established a sequence of apple nurseries spanning from the Alleghenies to Central Ohio and beyond. He distributed thousands of seedlings, either selling them or giving them away for free to pioneers, who then cultivated acres of productive apple orchards, thereby creating a living tribute to Chapman's enthusiastic missionary work.

So that's where my life began: in a small town called Leominster, nestled somewhere in Central Massachusetts, famously known as the birthplace of Johnny Appleseed. After spending my first year there, my family moved to the neighboring town of Fitchburg, where I would spend the next twenty-one years of my life. Those years between birth and adulthood were formative, shaping me into the person I am today.

As a child, I was driven by a relentless curiosity about how things worked. This obsession often drove my father to the brink of insanity, as I dismantled many of his personal tools and favorite items, simply to peer into their mysterious workings. Regrettably, my undeveloped young brain was not yet skilled in reassembling what I had taken apart, leaving many household items inoperative or falling apart prematurely because of my "investigations." This habit of mine drove my parents to despair, as they found themselves surrounded by malfunctioning hardware. Invariably, whenever something broke in the house, I was the prime suspect and, more often than not, rightly so. It was in this environment of curiosity-induced chaos that my journey truly began. I was compelled to understand how the universe worked, no matter what the cost to my father's personal possessions.

The need to know at any cost has been the driving force throughout my life's journey. It's hard to articulate or even control this drive; all I knew was that I had an insatiable need to understand. Some might call it curiosity or simply being nosy, but I believe it's more about unraveling mysteries and seeking deep meaning and understanding in everything around me. It's said that there are three stages of intellectual development in one's life. The first stage, from birth to the age of twenty-one, is when the brain acts like a sponge, absorbing information from the world and storing it in our memory for future use. The second stage spans from twenty-one to sixty-five, during which we use this amassed knowledge to perform a variety of high-level cognitive and managerial tasks. The final stage, from sixty-five until death, is considered the give-back years. This phase might involve teaching, offering guidance, or leaving behind something beneficial for future generations to utilize.

My School Years (1961–1972)

The voyage of life is characterized by a series of pivotal changes, each propelling us into unfamiliar territories, testing our adaptability, and molding our sense of self. One particularly significant and lasting change I encountered occurred when I was merely seven years old, a time still vivid in my mind after sixty-two years. This was my inaugural day at school, a day that stood in stark contrast to all my parents who had previously warned me about interacting with strangers. On this significant day, my mother led me to a room brimming with strangers and left me amid them, a scenario not unlike other children's experiences, akin to how one might leave clothes at a dry cleaner. This practice was customary in the 1960s, a time when the societal norm saw most mothers as homemakers while fathers, the main breadwinners, dedicated themselves to long hours and sometimes held several jobs to make ends meet.

The duty of overseeing educational matters, especially the challenging initial day, traditionally rested upon the mothers. My early arrival granted me the opportunity to observe as my soon-to-be classmates were left one by one in this new setting. Back then, class sizes were considerable, hosting around forty students per teacher, which nearly exceeded the classroom's capacity. Numerous children grappled with separation anxiety, manifesting their distress through visible discomfort as their mothers left. A boy named Phillip particularly stood out in my recollection; his tears and screams for his mother, along with his repeated attempts to chase after her until she disappeared from view, left a lasting impression on me.

Initially, a wave of loneliness washed over me when my mother departed, leaving me isolated in this new environment. However, this feeling was quickly replaced by the recognition that I was embarking on a novel journey, one that required me to forge my own path without the immediate guidance of my parents. This epiphany instilled in me a fresh sense of autonomy and duty. I was aware that my parents had faith in me to act properly in their absence, which was a significant shift in my young life. This change sparked an enthusiasm for learning and a fondness for school life, emotions that stayed strong and unchallenged until the moment I was confronted with the results of my first report card.

First grade was a pivotal juncture in my journey, brimming with eye-opening truths. Throughout my early years, I was consistently lauded by adults, described as a handsome, well-mannered child with a bright future ahead. However, this rosy perception crumbled when I encountered my first academic evaluation. Contrary to the glowing reviews from relatives and caregivers, my report card painted a different picture; it described me as a slow learner with occasional behavioral issues, a revelation that starkly contradicted the positive image cultivated in my infancy. This assessment acted as an alarm for my parents, especially my father, who was profoundly let down by the news. He quickly labeled me as indolent and ineffectual, a reaction that starkly diverged from the encouragement I had grown accustomed to. On the other hand, my mother maintained her support, urging for patience and holding onto the belief in my latent abilities, hoping I would eventually disprove my father's harsh judgment.

This situation was a heavy burden for a seven-year-old. I was caught between a disheartening report card, a sympathetic mother, and the daunting task of disproving my father's harsh judgment. In hindsight, my first-grade teacher's assessment and my father's disappointment were grounded in truth. Despite my best efforts, I consistently performed below average throughout my schooling. Even in subjects I enjoyed, excellence eluded me, leading to a heartbreakingly challenging twelve years of education. However, the true lesson came not from academic success but from resilience. I managed to complete all twelve years of schooling, defying my own doubts and external expectations. Despite not having the best grades, I never succumbed to the temptation to quit. The most important lesson I learned, which I would grade myself an A in, was the value of perseverance. I could have been a dropout, perhaps should have been by some standards, but instead, I emerged as a graduate. This journey taught me the power of determination and the importance of never giving up regardless of the odds.

Finally, the long-awaited graduation day from high school had arrived. This day marked a significant milestone, one I had been earnestly looking forward to ever since receiving my first unsatisfactory report card years ago. The determination to turn my academic performance around had fueled my journey through high school, making this moment all the more momentous. Now it was time to close this chapter of my life, a chapter filled with twelve years of classical education, personal growth, and countless memories with classmates who had become more like family.

Me, 1972

As the ceremony commenced, I was engulfed by a mix of emotions: excitement for the future mingled with a sense of nostalgia. The familiarity of school hallways, the routine of classes, and the daily interactions with friends and teachers were all about to become part of my past. The realization that I was about to leave behind the world I had known for so long was both thrilling and daunting.

The climax of the ceremony was the moment my name was called, and I walked across the stage to receive my high school diploma. It was a surreal experience, a tangible recognition of all the hard work, challenges overcome, and achievements earned. However, as I held the diploma in my hands, an unexpected wave of sadness enveloped me. It was a profound sense of separation, akin to walking into a dark enveloping cloud. The finality of the moment hit me—this was not just an end to my high school years but also possibly the last time I would see many of my classmates.

This transition, from the structured environment of high school to the vast, open possibilities of the future, was a significant turning point. While I was stepping into a new chapter filled with opportunities and challenges, I was also leaving behind a familiar and comforting world. The sweet-sour mix of excitement for the future and sadness for what was being left behind marked the end of an era in my life, encapsulating the bittersweet nature of growth and change.

My feelings toward school oscillated between enjoyment and deep affection, yet it seemed as if I could never fully grasp the educational process that tantalized me with intriguing information but consistently failed me when it came to achieving high marks. My academic journey resembled an unending roller coaster, creating a vast loop from first to twelfth grade, where I occasionally neared success only to predominantly earn below-average grades. I concluded that traditional schooling was not suited for me. Reflecting on this period, I understand that my primary obstacle was a failure to make the necessary "connection" with the educational material.

Shortly after high school graduation, armed with my diploma, I was eager to embark on the next chapter of my life: entering the workforce. The common path for high school graduates seemed to bifurcate into two distinct directions: entering a trade, such as becoming a factory or construction worker, or pursuing further education in college toward a professional career. Given my less-than-stellar academic performance, a career in trades seemed the logical choice. My father, having dedicated his life to working shifts in a paper mill, perhaps had unwittingly set a precedent for what appeared to be my impending career trajectory.

Becoming an Adult

The transition from childhood to adulthood is a nuanced and deeply personal journey that varies significantly from one individual to another. As a child, I vividly remember yearning for the independence and autonomy associated with adulthood; the wait seemed endless. Yet I often encountered adults who expressed a desire to return to their childhood, armed with their current knowledge and experience. This concept puzzled me. Why would anyone wish to revert to a stage of life with more restrictions, less freedom? From my perspective back then, adulthood symbolized a liberation from parental oversight and an opportunity to make my own choices and carve out my own path. The idea of regressing back to childhood, with its inherent limitations, seemed counterintuitive. I couldn't comprehend why anyone would forsake the apparent benefits of adulthood for the perceived simplicity of childhood. This dichotomy highlighted the complexities of growing up and the contrasting perspectives on what it means to be a child versus an adult.

Young minds often dwell almost entirely in the present, focusing only on what seems possible at the moment without considering the future. During my youth, my perspective was mainly inward, marked by a keen self-awareness and concern about how others might perceive me. I constantly faced demands regarding how I should behave and what it meant to become the man society expected. However, I was at a loss as the examples around me were varied and conflicting. I encountered quiet men, loud and obnoxious ones, men displaying what could be seen as feminine traits, gamblers, schemers, professionals, authoritarians, and those who seemed perpetually childish. This array of models was bewildering. What does it truly mean to be a man upon reaching adulthood? I believe it boils down to responsibility and the freedom of choice.

The notion that one possesses the freedom to shape their own destiny is an empowering concept. However, as I've navigated through life's myriad experiences, I've come to understand that destiny often seems to exert its own influence, almost as if it's choosing us rather than the other way around. This realization begins at the very onset of life. Consider the act of being born; it wasn't a choice we made but rather a decision made by God and our parents, setting us on our initial path—a path where destiny seemed to have the upper hand. From there, life appears to unfold in a series of events and opportunities, some of which seem orchestrated by forces beyond our control, much like parental decisions in our early years. These forces could be societal expectations, unforeseen circumstances, or the family and culture we are born into. While we navigate through these, we face various opportunities, some seized and others ignored, influenced by the context and conditions laid before us.

However, amid this interplay of choice and chance, there emerges a concept of "true calling." This can be understood as the unique purpose or path that aligns with one's deepest passions, talents, and circumstances. It's where our individual choices and external influences converge, leading us to fulfill roles that feel inherently right. The journey to discovering this calling can be complex, influenced by both our decisions and the paths that destiny seems to steer us onto. This interconnection between choice and destiny continues to shape our journey, guiding us toward what we might consider our true calling in life.

A true calling imbues life with passion, purpose, and direction, transforming daily activities into sources of satisfaction and joy. This calling shapes not just what we do but also who we are, fostering a life that feels meaningful and driven. From early childhood, the question arises: is our destiny to evolve into purposeful adults, or do we linger in a perpetual state of childhood, dependent on others for guidance and unable to forge our own paths?

Opportunities for growth, both physical and mental, present themselves throughout our lives, challenging us to embrace them and mature. Our pace of development often hinges on our reactions to life's varied experiences. Each experience, whether positive or negative, offers valuable lessons that contribute to our growth and understanding. Deviating from this path of learning and growth invites trouble, potentially derailing us from our true calling.

Life is in constant motion; it waits for no one, and neither should we. Our journey should be one of continual advancement, leveraging our past experiences to navigate a more informed and fulfilling path forward. Clinging to the past traps us in a cycle of stagnation, akin to an aircraft in a holding pattern, constantly moving but making no real progress. This metaphorical holding pattern can persist until we, or an external influence, decide to chart a new forward-moving course. Thus, living in the past can maintain us in a state of suspended development, preventing us from reaching the full potential of adulthood. Breaking free from this cycle requires acknowledging our past while making deliberate choices to move forward, steering our lives toward our true calling and the fulfillment of our potential as mature, purposeful individuals.

My progression from childhood to adulthood seemed influenced by an unseen force, guiding me along a predetermined path. The key lay in my ability to choose: to step onto a new path as it unfolded before me or to stay in the comfort of what was familiar, essentially remaining in a childlike state. This dilemma often led me to ponder the nature of these guiding forces. Were they sociological, rooted in the societal pressures to conform and adhere to communal norms? Were they biological, stemming from our genetic makeup and the innate defenses passed down through generations? Or were they spiritual, influenced by a divine presence guiding us toward our destined path?

I've come to understand that these forces could originate from any one of these sources, a combination of two, or even all three. Societal pressure, for example, plays a significant role in shaping our journey to adulthood, urging us to follow established norms to maintain our place within the community. Biologically, we inherit traits and defenses that shape our physical and mental growth, with our immune system serving as a prime example of inherited protection that also adapts through social interactions. Spiritually, the belief in a higher power offers guidance and purpose, but it remains our responsibility to interpret and act upon this guidance, making conscious choices to fulfill our destiny.

Life, in its essence, is not a rehearsal but a live performance, continuously unfolding with each decision we make, visible to those around us and impacting the world in various ways. The choices we make not only shape our individual journeys but also have the potential to influence future generations. Hence, it's crucial to navigate life with mindfulness and consideration, understanding that our actions and decisions may echo beyond our immediate presence, affecting our descendants and the broader tapestry of humanity.

So far, my life's journey has unfolded from the innocent explorations of childhood to the complex realities of adulthood. Along this continuum, I've discovered that maturing—gaining experience and wisdom—inevitably opens up an expanding array of opportunities and callings. Indeed, my life seemed to branch into myriad of potential paths, each intriguing in its own right, presenting a spectrum of possibilities for what my future could hold.

Faced with this vast landscape of choices, I understood that it was imperative for me to select one direction and dedicate myself wholeheartedly to it, lest time slip away unchecked. The reality is, life is composed of critical junctures and pivotal moments that are bound by specific temporal windows. These opportunities are not perpetual; they arise at particular phases of our lives, waiting to be seized. If not acted upon within the right time frame, they may elude us indefinitely, retreating back into the cosmos, rendering them increasingly difficult, if not impossible, to grasp later on. This understanding has guided my decisions, pushing me to act decisively and with purpose, aware of the fleeting nature of life's many opportunities.

In the following sections, I will delve into the various callings that have shaped my life, exploring how I embraced each one and the profound impacts they've had on my journey. These callings often manifested as an overwhelming urge or yearning that unexpectedly swept over me during different phases of my life. Intriguingly, these callings usually emerged spontaneously, often surprising me with their intensity and the incongruence with my current stage of life or capabilities.

Despite the clarity and force with which these callings presented themselves, acting on them was not always straightforward. My age, financial constraints, or other circumstantial limitations frequently meant that these intense desires had to be postponed or shelved, awaiting a more opportune moment to pursue them. This conflict between my inner desires and external realities has been a recurring theme in my life, yet it has also fueled my resilience and adaptability.

One of the most profound of these callings was the aspiration to become a commercial pilot. This ambition was not just a fleeting fancy but a deep-seated passion that resonated with my core. However, the path to achieving this dream was fraught with obstacles, not least of which were the financial and educational requirements, which seemed insurmountable at times. In the next part, I will recount the journey of how this calling emerged, the challenges it presented, and the ways in which I navigated the complex landscape of pursuing a career in aviation. For now, I really need a job to support my future endeavors.

It's Now Time to Work

The day following graduation, I applied to various factories in town, optimistic about securing a well-paying job that could eventually support a future family. However, reality quickly set in as I faced rejection after rejection; it seemed that employers favored more experienced, mature candidates over an eighteen-year-old with no practical skills. Even an attempt to follow in my father's footsteps at his factory ended in disappointment. My initial confidence waned as I struggled to find my footing in the adult world.

In my escalating desperation, I reached out to anyone who might assist me in finding employment. It was during this time of uncertainty that a stroke of serendipity occurred, completely altering the course of my job search. The turning point came unexpectedly during a casual conversation with my neighbor Albert. Upon hearing about my challenging situation, he generously offered me a position working under his guidance in the machine shop department of a well-known lock manufacturing company. Although the job was based on piecework, it promised decent pay and the stability of regular daytime hours. With a sense of profound gratitude and relief, I eagerly accepted the offer, thankful to have finally found a foothold in the workforce.

However, it wasn't long before I began to understand that life within the confines of a factory setting was not conducive to my well-being or career aspirations. The relentless monotony of machining identical parts, performing the same motions and tasks day after day, soon evolved into a soul-crushing routine that weighed heavily on me. Just two months into the job, the stark realization hit me like a wave of cold water. I could not, under any circumstances, envision spending the remainder of my professional life trapped in such a cycle of repetitive drudgery. It became clear that what I desperately needed was a change—a significant shift in direction that could rekindle my enthusiasm and provide a sense of purpose and fulfillment.

In the midst of my dissatisfaction with the daily grind, I accidentally discovered an old deserted room within the boundaries of the plant, nestled right next to the noisy environment of the machine shop. Driven by a strong sense of curiosity, I made my way through the mess, stepping over clutter and maneuvering around discarded furniture, to unveil the secrets of this neglected area. To my astonishment, this overlooked space, shrouded in a thick layer of dust and silence, revealed its past identity; it was once a laboratory. This revelation unfolded as I observed the remnants of scientific exploration and inquiry that had been left behind, providing a stark contrast to the monotonous mechanical world I had grown accustomed to.

In the old neglected corner of the plant, I stumbled upon an abandoned laboratory. It was like stepping back in time: benches laden with dusty glassware, silent hoods, and various equipment all sat as if waiting for their operators to return. Curious, I inquired about its history with Albert, my boss. He shared that during World War II, the lab was bustling, used for quality control of special military equipment manufactured in the plant. But as the war concluded, the need for the lab vanished, and it was subsequently forgotten.

Every morning before my shift, I'd sneak into the lab, enveloped by a sense of wonder and mystery. Who had worked here? What had their days been like? There was an inexplicable pull to this place, as if I were somehow linked to its past despite the impossibility of that notion—I was born nearly a decade after the war's end. Yet I felt a profound connection, as if the lab's history and my own were intertwined, a sentiment that felt more spiritual than rational.

This enigmatic bond sparked a realization within me, a calling that I couldn't ignore. Despite the unlikelihood of transitioning from a factory worker with mediocre academic records to a college student, the mundane repetition of factory life was no longer bearable. The lab represented a path not taken, a life of inquiry and discovery that could be mine if only I dared to reach for it. Driven by this newfound inspiration, I resolved to leave the predictable confines of the factory behind and venture into the unknown realm of higher education. The odds were stacked against me, given my lackluster high school performance and lack of formal scientific training, yet the pull of a different future, a different destiny, was too strong to resist. I had to try, driven by the belief that there was more to my story than the factory floor.

Moving on to Higher Learning

In a nearby town where I grew up, there was a highly respected two-year state community college that was actively recruiting students for a novel college entrance program. This unique program was designed particularly for high school graduates who hadn't performed to their full potential but who harbored aspirations of obtaining a college degree in the liberal arts. The aim of this program was clear and purposeful: to establish a robust foundation of knowledge in key areas such as English language, literature, reading comprehension, essay writing, mathematical skills, and interpersonal and social skills. By doing so, the program intended to prepare students thoroughly for higher level academic challenges and studies. This initiative represented a significant opportunity for underachieving students to redefine their educational trajectories and pursue more ambitious academic goals.

Remarkably, the program was designed with inclusivity in mind, as it did not necessitate entrance exams or a minimum high school GPA for admission. This feature made it a perfect fit for someone in my situation. It was akin to being thrown a lifeline, offering a rare opportunity to completely redefine the direction of my academic journey. Seizing this opportunity felt like being given a second chance—a chance not only to rectify my previous academic inadequacies but also to lay the groundwork for a future brimming with potential and promise. Engaging in this program was like opening a new chapter where past academic failures no longer dictated my capabilities or my destiny. It was an empowering moment, filled with the possibility of transformation and growth, guiding me toward a brighter, more successful future.

This unique opportunity reignited a spark of excitement for learning within me, a sensation that took me back to the unbridled enthusiasm I experienced at the onset of my educational journey, akin to the joy and anticipation of starting first grade. Now as I embarked on this new chapter in my academic career, that feeling was revitalized; I was once again imbued with a profound sense of possibility and purpose. This wasn't just about attending classes; it was about embarking on an intellectual voyage, filled with the promise of discovery and personal growth. Eager to delve into this new academic environment, I looked forward to exploring the diverse paths that lay ahead, each one offering a unique avenue for learning and self-discovery. This moment marked a significant transition, as I was not just revisiting the thrill of learning but also embracing the vast opportunities that this college journey presented.

It was only during my first year at community college that I finally established the "connection" crucial for attaining any form of higher knowledge. In that year, my curriculum mandated completion of College Math 1 and College Math 2. My instructor for Math 1, Mr. Burba, was a middle-aged individual whose jovial nature and multifaceted personality quickly fostered a deep sense of trust and rapport among the students. He had an exceptional way of narrating mathematical theories as if they were stories, thereby maintaining the students' engagement through a method he referred to as "depth of perception learning."

Mr. Burba's approach was founded on a unique analogy; he compared understanding mathematical concepts to examining the world globe. He pointed out that within the globe, there are layers—lands and oceans, countries and cities, streets and houses, and finally, individuals within those houses. He suggested that one could delve deeper into the components of a person or, conversely, explore the broader context of Earth's relationship with other celestial bodies. He always started his lessons by outlining the overarching concept, akin to sketching out the universe, before zooming in on the intricate details that constitute that larger picture. This educational strategy aimed to provide students with a comprehensive perspective, facilitating the formation of connections with familiar concepts such as the earth, oceans, and land. By establishing these initial connections, Mr. Burba could then guide us through the more complex details, which now seemed more approachable and understandable. He essentially make complex matters simple with his teaching methods.

I still vividly remember the first day of class when Mr. Burba, with a mysterious smile, etched a daunting mathematical equation on the chalkboard. The class fell silent, each of us wrestling with the intimidating string of symbols and numbers, our minds echoing the same sentiment: "This is impossible." Yet within moments, Mr. Burba began to deconstruct the equation with an ease that bordered on artistry. He segmented the complex formula into multiple manageable parts, turning the indecipherable into something palpably approachable. Then with the same calm demeanor, he posed the question again, "Can anyone solve it now?" This time, a surge of hands shot up—a testament to the shift from perplexed students to eager learners. Witnessing him transform what seemed an insurmountable challenge into a series of simple, solvable problems was nothing short of magical. It wasn't just an equation that he simplified; he unraveled the complexities of a problem that had seemed beyond our comprehension.

This experience was transformative for me. Mr. Burba's methodical breakdown taught me a valuable life lesson: to confront what seems incomprehensible by dissecting it into smaller understandable pieces. This approach has enabled me to navigate through numerous challenges, turning "impossible" tasks into sets of manageable actions. His teachings extended beyond mathematics; they were lessons in perseverance, problem-solving, and the power of perspective.

From Mr. Burba's teachings, I want to share a tool that has immensely clarified complex concepts for me. This tool, known as slice and dice, acts as a visual aid, breaking down comprehensive ideas into manageable, individual components and then presenting them in a graphical format. This method allows for focused analysis of each part in isolation, minimizing distractions and enabling a clearer understanding of the whole. To illustrate, consider the process of producing a mineral water product to the end user. Here are four simple steps one can use.

First step: define the main idea. This is where we set the stage for our endeavor, constructing a product from its initial concept all the way to its ultimate usage. In this instance, our product will be a "bottle of mineral water." This serves as our initial point of focus and the basis from which we'll proceed.

Bottle of Mineral Water

Second step: identify the end point. In this phase, we establish the final goal or outcome that we aim to achieve with our product. For our example, the end point would be the "use" of the bottled mineral water by the consumer.

Third step: determined the "process" between the starting point (water bottle) to final use (consumption).

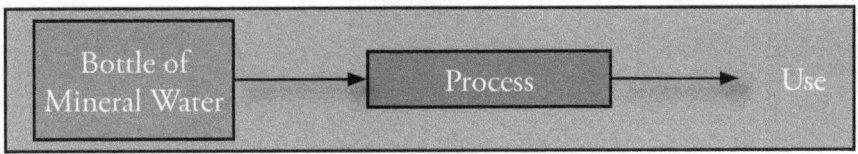

Fourth step: what additional components are needed to complete the starting point, process, and final use?

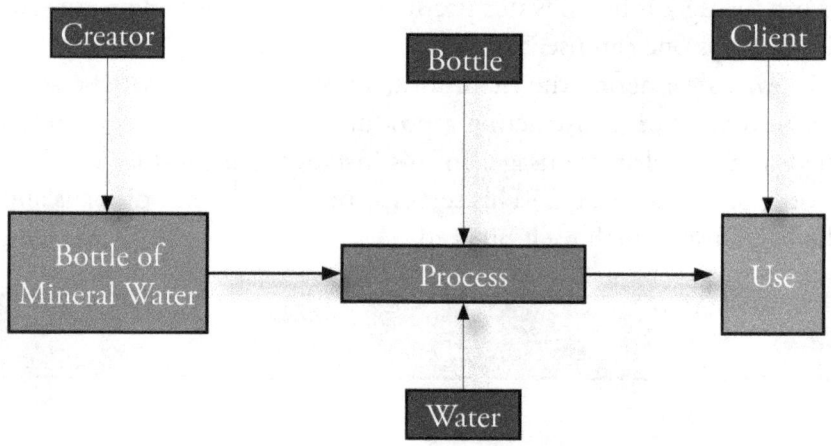

Reviewing the slice and dice flow diagram, it becomes clear that the concept of the bottle of mineral water originated from an individual, and throughout the process, bottles filled with water are prepared for final consumption by a client. Each component within the diagram can be individually examined, acted upon and free from any interference by other elements. This focused approach sharpens the ability to analyze and enhance any single component effectively. Similarly, this diagram could metaphorically represent a person's entire lifespan, from the first breath to the last, outlining the various paths taken throughout their life.

To Mr. Burba, wherever life may have taken you, I hope this message finds you well and happy. I want to express my deepest gratitude for the indelible impact you have made on my life. Your lessons transcended the confines of the classroom, becoming a beacon of guidance in the tumultuous sea of life. Thank you for teaching me the invaluable skill of breaking down what initially seemed impossible into manageable parts, allowing me to tackle challenges with confidence and poise. Your wisdom went beyond academic instruction; it was a masterclass in navigating life's complexities. You showed me that within the heart of chaos lies the potential for clarity and order, a lesson that has illuminated my path time and again. Your teachings have instilled in me a mindset that sees beyond the surface turbulence, seeking out the underlying structure and solutions. The influence you wield over my approach to life's hurdles is profound. Because of you, I confront both significant and trivial challenges with a renewed perspective, applying the critical thinking and problem-solving skills you so diligently honed in us. Your lessons have become a part of who I am, influencing my decisions and actions in countless ways. So, Mr. Burba, thank you from the bottom of my heart.

Completing my first year at the community college was not just a significant milestone in my academic journey; it also led to an unexpected and remarkable achievement. I made the dean's list for both semesters. This accomplishment was not merely a line on my academic record; it was transformative, providing me with a profound sense of encouragement and validation that had been conspicuously absent from my academic life prior to this point. The recognition of my hard work and dedication served as a powerful affirmation of my capabilities and potential, which had often gone unrecognized or doubted. Now as I faced just one more year before I could earn my associate degree in liberal arts, my determination was stronger and more unyielding than ever before. This newfound sense of confidence and purpose fueled my commitment to my studies and my future goals, reinforcing my resolve to continue excelling and proving to myself what I was truly capable of achieving in the academic realm.

The academic success I had recently achieved sparked within me a powerful passion, kindling a deep-seated desire for further knowledge, new challenges, and continued personal growth. This newfound intellectual curiosity was intense, nearly overwhelming, yet it lacked a precise direction. It was during this period of introspection and searching that I experienced a moment of clarity, a sudden revelation about my true aspirations. I wanted to pursue a career in science. While I was still unsure of the specific discipline that would captivate my interest, the general direction of my future was now crystal clear. This epiphany made me realize that my educational pursuits were far from complete. It signaled a time for substantial change—a time to transition to a new academic environment better suited to nurturing my burgeoning interest in science. This meant transferring to a college with the resources, programs, and faculty to help me channel my renewed academic zeal into a solid, tangible career path in the scientific field.

The community college where I had dedicated the past year of my academic life was renowned for its exceptional liberal arts education. However, it unfortunately fell short in providing programs in the scientific fields. Continuing with the second year of their program, while beneficial in other contexts, would only serve to delay my newfound aspiration to delve into the realm of science. This realization prompted a significant decision. Fortuitously, residing within the same town was a state college well-known for its extensive array of four-year degrees across various scientific disciplines, providing a more suitable pathway for my academic and career ambitions.

My decision to apply to this institution was driven by the urge to align my educational pursuits with my burgeoning passion for science. The application process was filled with anticipation and hope, reflecting my desire for a transition that could better serve my academic and professional objectives. To my immense relief and excitement, my application was accepted, signifying the beginning of a thrilling new chapter in my life. This acceptance was not just a change in educational institutions; it was also a pivotal moment that marked the transition from a period of exploration and self-discovery in the liberal arts to a focused journey toward a career in the sciences. With this new opportunity at the state college, I was poised to embark on a path that promised to be rich with exploration, learning, and personal growth, fully embracing my passion for science.

Scheduled for an introductory meeting with my new academic adviser, Dr. Condike, I approached this initial encounter filled with a combination of anticipation for what was to come and a strong sense of determination to make the most of this new educational path. I was keen to push my limits and fully immerse myself in the scientific studies that lay ahead. With this eagerness to challenge myself and carve out a significant academic and career trajectory, I inquired of him which scientific discipline within the college was considered the most challenging and rewarding. Dr. Condike, considering my question, directed my attention toward the bachelor of science degree in chemistry, highlighting its reputation for rigor and depth.

Without a moment's hesitation, fueled by a blend of naivety and enthusiasm, I declared my intention to enroll in the chemistry program. At that moment, I was blissfully unaware of the demanding and rigorous journey that lay ahead in pursuing such a challenging field. This decision marked a significant commitment on my part, one that I made with determination but without a full understanding of the complexities and challenges that would accompany a rigorous study in chemistry. Yet this initial decision to embark on what was reputed to be the most demanding program the college offered was a testament to my desire for growth and my willingness to venture into new, uncharted academic territories.

The chemistry curriculum I embarked upon proved to be exceptionally challenging, indeed more so than I had initially anticipated. The comprehensive and demanding nature of the courses stretched my academic endeavors beyond the typical four-year trajectory, extending it to five years to complete all the necessary coursework effectively and to fulfill the requirements for securing my degree. Alongside this, I chose to enrich my scientific understanding further by pursuing a minor in biology, adding another layer of complexity and breadth to my studies. This decision, while enriching, contributed to the extended duration of my academic journey as it required a careful balance and integration of two demanding scientific fields.

CHAPTER 3

Family Hood

Family Ties

Growing up, family was the epicenter of my world. My mother hailed from a vibrant large family of Italian descent, brimming with traditions and gatherings that knit us tightly together. Our calendar was perennially marked with weddings, Christmas parties, card game nights, vacations, and, on somber occasions, funerals. I was surrounded by numerous aunts, uncles, and cousins, creating a bustling extended family. Life within this close-knit group was a continuous cycle of mutual assistance and shared experiences. Whether it was collaborating on home improvement projects, offering advice on purchasing a used car, or engaging in sports like group golf outings, there was always a sense of communal effort.

We often rented a lakeside camp where everyone congregated for cookouts, swimming, boating, and sheer enjoyment, ensuring that there was never a dull moment. Clothing for the kids was never a problem; hand-me-downs were circulated among us cousins so frequently that our clothes seemed timeless, never going out of fashion. It was not unusual to find a cousin or two in the same classroom during my school years, a testament to the size and closeness of our family network.

I had always assumed that such large family circles were commonplace until I met the Fungs, my new neighbors. They were a family of just three with no other relatives in the country.

Encountering their small family unit was a shock; they appeared so isolated at times. It was then that I realized not every family enjoyed the bustling, intertwined lives that I had grown up with, and it gave me a new perspective on the diverse shapes that families can take.

Even within my father's German lineage, which comprised solely of his sister, I found familial connection through three cousins on that side. Thus, the concept of having a family felt like a natural progression for me. It was quite common and widely accepted in our community to marry right after high school graduation, often to a sweetheart whom one had known throughout those formative years. My sister Carol, for example, maintained a steady relationship with her boyfriend from high school well into their college years, both nurturing hopes of eventual marriage. Sadly, their plans did not materialize, but the intention was sincere. In the context of the 1960s and '70s, societal pressures and the looming presence of the Vietnam War often hastened young people into early marriages, perhaps also influenced by perceptions of a shorter average lifespan.

In the early 1960s, the average life expectancy was notably lower than it is today, with men living to about sixty-six years and women to seventy-three. Unfortunately, many spent their later years battling debilitating diseases. I vividly remember this period through the lens of personal tragedy—my uncle Eddie's untimely death at just forty-six. He suffered from an aggressive form of cancer that had spread throughout his body. At that time, medical understanding of cancer, particularly its early detection, was limited. The predominant method for diagnosing and attempting to treat cancer involved exploratory surgery, which was crudely akin to performing an autopsy on a living person. Common belief held that once "opened up," exposure to air could hasten a patient's demise, and there was some truth to this. We later learned that such invasive procedures could indeed disperse micro cancer cells to other parts of the body.

My uncle underwent this harrowing exploratory surgery, and his condition deteriorated rapidly afterward. I was only five years old when he passed away, and his death was my first confrontation with mortality. At his wake, his appearance profoundly shocked me. Lying in the casket, he looked nothing like the robust curly-blond-haired man I remembered, who was always quick to smile. Instead, he appeared as a gaunt, frail figure with ghostly white hair and dark sunken eyes encircled by stark black rings. I was terrified and confused by the sight, unable to reconcile it with the uncle I had known. When I asked my mother why we couldn't just wake him up and nourish him back to health, she had no answers that could ease my fears.

This experience left an indelible mark on me, shaping my perceptions of death and dying. Even decades later, the haunting memory of that day lingers, fueling a deep-seated fear of witnessing death firsthand. My aunt Mary, now a widow, tried to comfort me by saying Eddie was merely sleeping and would soon awaken to be with Jesus. She encouraged me to approach and bid him farewell, but as I walked up to the casket, the disparity between my memories of Uncle Eddie and the reality before me was overwhelming. I turned away and dashed to the back of the room, searching for a place to hide from this nightmare. This early encounter with death, framed by the limitations of medical science at the time and the stark finality of the wake, profoundly influenced my understanding of life's fragility.

In the mid-twentieth century, given the comparatively shorter life expectancies, many people felt a pressing urgency to marry young, often before the age of twenty-one. This early commitment was driven by the desire to be young and healthy enough to raise a family and to witness their children grow into adulthood, hopefully even seeing them marry. The societal norm strongly favored early marriages, as those past their early twenties were quickly approaching what was perceived as a closing window of opportunity. Indeed, by the ages of forty or fifty, if one had not yet married, societal labels such as "bachelor for life" for men and "old maid" for women were commonly assigned. These terms, laden with negative connotations, reflected the strong cultural expectations and pressures of the time.

Despite the harsh judgment faced by those who remained single, a significant number of individuals chose this path, either by circumstance or by choice, leading lives focused on personal pursuits, careers, or community involvement rather than traditional family structures. For myself, the goal was clear from an early age: to marry as soon as possible. This personal objective was not just about adhering to societal expectations; it was also about securing a partner with whom to build a life and family, ensuring that together we could enjoy the milestones and experiences of our children's lives without the shadow of shortened years hanging over us. This mindset shaped much of the social fabric of the era, where the race against time was a pervasive element in the personal decisions and societal norms of the day.

Marriage Years

During my second year of college, I entered into marriage with my first wife, Dorothy, a union that was short-lived, spanning less than two years. This period of my life is characterized by its lack of significant events, a statement I make not out of bitterness but as a simple reflection of the truth. The relationship, in retrospect, lacked depth and did not leave a lasting imprint on the course of my life. This acknowledgment is not to cast shadows but to recognize, with the benefit of hindsight, that the decision to marry was ill-advised.

It's important to understand that we were both young, merely twenty-one, an age at which many decisions reflect the era's norms rather than personal readiness for lifelong commitments. This was particularly true in the 1970s, a time marked by different social expectations and personal explorations. The dissolution of this first marriage came rapidly, yet it was a stepping stone to greater self-awareness and future endeavors.

Having learned from this early experience, I transitioned into the next chapter of my life with my second wife, Yong Ok Chon. This move symbolized not just a change in partners but also a shift in understanding and expectations from life and relationships. In addressing the delicate subject of cross-cultural relationships, my intention is not to provoke or upset but rather to offer a candid account of my personal experiences, highlighting the challenges and insights that can emerge from such unions. My narrative takes us to my second marriage, which introduced a new set of dynamics into my life because of the differing cultural backgrounds involved.

My second wife was born and raised in South Korea and relocated to the United States in her midtwenties in search of new opportunities and experiences. Our paths crossed when she was thirty-two years old and I was six years her junior, at twenty-six. At the time of our meeting, she was navigating life in a new country with limited English proficiency, which naturally presented communication barriers between us and impacted our day-to-day interactions. Additionally, she was in the United States as a green card holder, which denotes she was a permanent resident but not yet a citizen.

One of the defining aspects of our relationship before we decided to marry was her focused pursuit of US citizenship. This goal was of paramount importance to her, shaping much of her life's direction and decisions at the time. While this objective is understandable from the perspective of someone seeking stability and belonging in a new country, it also introduced a complex layer to our relationship, intertwining personal matters with legal and bureaucratic ones.

The backdrop of our union, marked by these unique circumstances, underscored the multifaceted nature of cross-cultural relationships. These unions can be rich and rewarding, offering a tapestry of shared experiences and learnings. However, they can also be fraught with challenges, from language barriers and cultural misunderstandings to differing expectations and objectives. In our case, these complexities were an integral part of our journey together, shaping the contours of our shared life and interactions.

After our wedding, our family grew quickly with the arrival of two children within a span of four years: first our daughter, Tammy, and then our son, Jay. These additions to our family brought joy and new responsibilities. However, our marriage began to strain under the weight of numerous challenges. The language barriers that initially marked our communication continued to pose difficulties, complicating our ability to discuss and resolve everyday issues as well as deeper relationship concerns. Cultural differences further compounded these challenges as we navigated distinct customs, traditions, and expectations that often clashed, making mutual understanding and compromise more difficult.

These stresses, rooted in fundamental differences and misunderstandings, became insurmountable over time, contributing to an increasingly tense and discordant household environment. The cumulative effect of these pressures eventually led to the breakdown of our marriage, a painful and complex process that was not initiated lightly.

The separation marked a significant turning point in my life. Following our split, my wife, with the assistance of her lawyer, initiated legal proceedings that had profound implications for my future. The outcome of these proceedings was devastating. I was left without my family, as custody arrangements separated me from my children. I lost my home, a place I had associated with personal security and family life. My financial stability was shattered, leaving me to navigate uncertain economic waters, and I was stripped of personal belongings, which carried not only practical value but also sentimental significance. This series of losses marked a period of immense personal upheaval, challenging my resilience and forcing me to confront and adapt to a drastically altered life landscape.

Years later, I learned from an email that my second wife, Yong, had passed away two years prior because of a prolonged illness. At only seventy-three, she died alone in a nursing facility. Yong had no immediate family in the US, only her three children: Danny from her first marriage and Tammy and Jay from ours. When the news reached me, I reached out to the funeral home and spoke with the director who had managed her final arrangements. He revealed that Yong had visited him a year before her death to meticulously plan and prepay for her funeral, opting for a modest ceremony. Her final wish was to be cremated, with her ashes scattered in the ocean, in hopes that they might drift back to her native Korea. She had requested that no one be contacted when she passed away. It was heartrending to learn that she chose not to say goodbye to her children who were nearby. To Yong, I am grateful for the life we shared and the wonderful children you gave me. I know it was challenging for you, adapting to a foreign land, but you persevered. Rest in peace, Yong. Your journey here is complete.

Then came the time for my third marriage, a decision that unfolded nearly four decades after my second union had ended. Over those years, my life had undergone significant transformations. Both of my children had grown into independent adults, and the allure of single life had gradually faded. As I approached the twilight years, I felt a stirring within me—a recognition of the need for monogamous companionship and the comfort it brings. With this newfound clarity, I knew it was time to embark on this journey once again, to tie the knot in what I hoped would be my final and lasting commitment.

I first met Lori through the secretarial staff at the laboratory where we worked. She had recently been hired as a sample log-in person and reported directly to the laboratories office manager, Nick. At that time, I had no inkling of the significant role she would soon play in my life; her arrival caught me completely off guard. Lori was already married, living with her spouse, her three teenage daughters, and his two adolescent children. Our professional interactions were initially limited. Meaning, we only knew each other superficially until circumstances changed.

One day, Lori was assigned to assist me with presentations I was preparing for local boards of health. These presentations focused on issues concerning the quality of private drinking well water—an area of increasing concern and relevance. I was so invested in the subject that I later published a book titled *Wellwaterology*, which thoroughly explored the complete topic of private drinking water wells. This new collaboration allowed us to work closely together, gradually paving the way for a deeper connection that neither of us had anticipated.

For about a year, Lori and I traveled locally together for work projects, a circumstance that allowed us to develop a much closer personal bond. Unbeknownst to me, during this time, Lori was harboring feelings for me and was even considering a divorce from her husband. I had always adhered to a strict work policy of not fraternizing with colleagues, yet, inexplicably, I found myself making an exception with Lori. Our relationship began to extend beyond professional boundaries, and we started meeting secretly in discreet locations. Eventually, our secret was exposed. Once our relationship came to light, Lori felt compelled to accelerate her divorce proceedings. Personally, I had never intended to remarry because of my negative experiences from my previous two marriages. However, Lori was different; there was something uniquely captivating about her.

Despite the potential challenges posed by our age difference—Lori being fifteen years younger than me—our connection deepened over time. When I graduated from high school, she was merely three years old, a fact which initially seemed daunting, yet it became insignificant as we grew older together. I longed for a tranquil, drama-free life, a sharp contrast to the hectic pace I had maintained for the last four decades. Remarkably, Lori shared my desire for a peaceful lifestyle, albeit sprinkled with occasional adventures.

It's fascinating how life unfolds. I am profoundly grateful for the way things have turned out. Lori is the kindest, most loving person I know. She cares for me in countless ways, and I reciprocate that care deeply. Within two years, we were married, building a life together that we both cherish. Now, eight years later, our bond continues to strengthen and flourish. An added joy of our union is the extended family I have gained: new parents-in-law, two brothers-in-law, and three additional children. This expanded family circle has enriched our lives immeasurably, bringing new relationships and experiences that continue to enhance our shared journey.

CHAPTER 4

Could Have Been, Should Have Been

So what exactly do I mean when I say, "I could have been and should have been"? I came to understand that one's life is not merely a series of random paths and directions. Instead, these paths are deliberately chosen by the individual to align with their specific lifestyle. The choices we make are a reflection of our unique individuality and personality, which are continually shaped and refined throughout our lifespan. This realization underscores the profound impact of personal decisions in crafting the narrative of our lives. In the following discussion, I will explore some of the paths I chose and how they influenced my life for better or worse. The key point is that I made these choices consciously. I decided to either integrate them into my life or set them aside for a later time, depending on how they aligned with my goals and values at different stages of my journey. This introspection offers insight into the power of personal agency in shaping our destiny.

Medical Doctor

As I neared the completion of my strenuous yet rewarding journey toward obtaining a chemistry degree, an unexpected proposal was presented to me. My sister Carol's boyfriend, whom she dated throughout high school and college, had a brother named Biff who was attending medical school in Mexico. Over the years, Biff and I developed a friendship based on common interests such as waterskiing, leather coats, and science. I also became close to his parents and found additional shared interests.

Biff invited me to accompany him to New York City to attend a fashion convention where his father, the owner of a leather coat factory in Mexico, was showcasing his latest line for the first time. These coats were handmade, durable, and stylish. We flew from Boston Logan Airport to New York City and attended the two-day event. Initially, I was unsure about the purpose of the trip, but it became clear on the first evening when I met his parents at an upscale restaurant near the convention center.

His mother, always interested in my gymnastic background, asked for private tumbling lessons, marking the start of my brief stint as a gymnastics instructor. The dinner provided enjoyable conversations about the convention and the future of their leather coat line.

Biff's father, a dentist with a diverse business portfolio, had recently bought an old pharmacy dating back to the late 1800s, planning to convert it into a medical complex. He suggested I consider joining this complex as a doctor after learning of my impending college graduation with degrees in chemistry and biology. The family offered to support my medical education in Mexico in exchange for my commitment to the complex. After discussing this proposal with my father, whose cautionary advice was, "If you take the offer, he will own you for a long time," I decided to decline. This decision led to years of lost contact with Biff's family, only reuniting briefly at his mother's funeral.

Unfortunately, the medical center failed to thrive and closed shortly after Biff's father passed away.

A "Fix It" Man

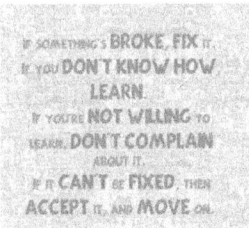

I discovered that I had a knack for repairing broken items. This epiphany first dawned on me around the age of ten. My mother's vacuum cleaner hose had detached from the metal connecting end—and for once, I swear,

I was not the culprit. Consequently, she took it to a local "fix it" shop situated in a bustling area that blended commercial and residential spaces. The shop was run by a single individual, Edsel Weirder, an elderly Finnish gentleman from the old country. He assessed the damaged vacuum cleaner hose and managed to fix it effortlessly within minutes, charging only a fraction of what a new one would cost. This experience was eye-opening for me; it was incredible to watch him work, fixing the hose while we waited, showcasing his adept skills right before our eyes.

Back in the early '60s, the neighborhoods in my surrounding towns were often defined by specific ethnic groups who gathered together, sharing cultural and specialized skills passed down from the "old country" into their new generational communities. For instance, areas predominantly inhabited by Italian descendants were filled with restaurants, social clubs, stoneware art products, and corner grocery stores, all reflecting Italian culture and making residents feel at home in their community.

The "fix it" shop where my mother took the vacuum cleaner hose was situated in the heart of a Finnish-populated community in Fitchburg, Massachusetts, a testament to the area's cultural diversity and heritage. I had the privilege of growing up in a Finnish/Swedish neighborhood, where most of my childhood friends were first-generation Americans. Their families, including grandparents, had migrated from the old country to America, seeking a better life, especially during the late 1940s and early 1950s. This period saw many Europeans from countries like Finland and Sweden, ravaged by the aftermaths of World Wars I and II, emigrating to the USA in search of improved conditions. A significant number of these Nordic migrants settled in the Northeastern United States, in sparsely populated areas such as farms and fruit orchards, bringing with them specialized skills like carpentry and livestock farming, thereby creating new employment opportunities for future immigrants.

Perhaps because of their hands-on professions, they seemed to possess a natural aptitude for repairing things. To me, this ability was akin to a magician conjuring a rabbit from a hat, leaving the audience in a state of "how did he do that" amazement. I recognized this power to fix the broken as something I desired for myself, but I was unsure how to acquire such a skill. However, I noticed that the repairman had two essential things: tools and a workshop. Much like a magician requires props and a stage, I realized I needed my own set of tools and a space to work.

At ten years old, my resources were scarce, so I turned to what I called a "nonvoluntary investor"—my parents. Unbeknownst to them, they provided the initial tools, which my father would mysteriously lose, and the cellar in our house became my makeshift workshop. This setup marked the beginning of my journey. Now all I needed were some paying customers to truly kick-start my venture into the world of repairs.

I found my inaugural paying customer thanks to my sister Carol. Her friend had a broken record player, and as fate would have it, I had recently acquired a set of tools and a workshop ready for such a challenge. However, there was a hitch—I was clueless about how to repair it, let alone understand how it functioned. My strategy was to bring the record player to my makeshift shop and, armed with a mix of luck, prayer, and persistence, attempt to fix it.

Upon disassembling the turntable, I discovered the issue: a glob of grease had contaminated the drive wheel, causing the audio playback table to slip. I meticulously cleaned the drive mechanism and reassembled the unit, and with a figurative "abracadabra," it worked perfectly again. I returned the repaired record player to its grateful owner and earned my first fee: two dollars. This incident, though seemingly minor, taught me an invaluable lesson: never shy away from a new challenge. Instead of saying "I can't," I learned to ask "How can I?" This philosophy has been a guiding principle in my life, especially when it comes to solving problems.

My father always said that with a long and strong enough lever, one could move the world. I adopted this belief; with the right knowledge and tools, anything broken could be fixed. This realization steered me onto my life's path—repairing what was broken. However, I was left pondering whether this was the path I wanted to follow forever. The short answer? No.

I could have been a "fix it" man, should have been a "fix it" man, but ultimately, I chose a different path and ventured into my next life-altering endeavor.

Mechanics and Science

My two close friends from high school, Bob and Peter, pursued vastly different careers, yet both were drawn to professions that revolved around repair and maintenance. Peter was determined to become a medical doctor, leading him to enroll in a local college where he studied biology and premed. In contrast, Bob followed his passion for automobiles and joined a mechanic apprentice program at a local dealership, specifically for General Motors. Their career choices intrigued me immensely; they were both essentially "fixers," albeit in very different contexts—Bob fixed vehicles while Peter aimed to heal the human body.

These friends profoundly influenced my own career trajectory. At the time, my own professional inclinations were undefined and shrouded in uncertainty. Being young and impressionable, I was easily swayed by the allure of a profession, especially if it promised a title, a touch of prestige, or a decent salary. I was keen to establish a career path that resonated with my interests and aspirations even as I grappled with indecision. Bob's and Peter's dedication and clarity in their chosen fields served as a beacon for me, guiding me through my own journey of self-discovery and career exploration.

I'd like to share a captivating tale about my adventurous friends, Bob and Peter, and our shared escapade after high school. We all signed up for a scuba diving course at the local YMCA, where we eagerly earned our diving certifications. In the rugged northeast coast, particularly around the Gloucester and Rockport areas, diving for lobsters was a popular activity, and we quickly joined in. Every weekend, the three of us would gear up and head out to sea, plunging into the ocean to hunt lobsters on the seabed. Our dives typically lasted between two to three hours in a shallow cove, employing both snorkeling and scuba diving techniques.

Starting with snorkeling, we skimmed over the water's surface, covering a broad area to spot the lobsters ambling along the ocean floor. Once a lobster was in sight, we would switch to our air tanks, allowing us to dive deeper. We would then stealthily descend toward the unsuspecting lobsters and skillfully scoop them up into our catch bags. This routine repeated until we had secured a respectable haul. With our day's adventure complete, we would pack up our gear and head to a local restaurant, where we relished bowls of creamy chowder and cold beer, recounting the day's exploits and planning our next dive.

Our weekly escapade of diving for lobsters and visiting our favorite local restaurant for chowder and beer became a cherished ritual during the spring, summer, and fall months. Over time, we grew quite familiar with all the waitstaff, who came to expect our jovial trio every weekend, but one particular day stood out when we encountered a change in the routine. Upon arriving at the restaurant after a successful dive, we were greeted by a new waitress who had just started her job. She was assigned to serve us, bringing a fresh face to our usual setting.

My personal post-dive ritual involved a predictable sequence as soon as we settled at our table. I would promptly place my order with the waitress—a bowl of clam chowder and a large cold beer. Immediately after, I would excuse myself for a much-needed bathroom break, a routine born out of the urgency that often follows hours spent in the ocean. This particular day, with the new waitress taking our orders, marked the beginning of a slight twist in our post-dive tradition, adding a new layer of interaction and novelty to our cherished weekends.

After a long and grueling dive, I found myself somewhat disheveled, my gear and clothes bearing the salty remnants of the ocean as I made my way to the restroom to freshen up a bit. Upon my return to the table, I noticed something unusual; instead of the cold beer I usually enjoyed, there was a Coca-Cola and a bowl of clam chowder waiting for me. Puzzled, I asked the new waitress about the unexpected change in my drink order.

She informed me, somewhat apologetically, that all I could have was Coca-Cola, not beer. I tried to maintain my composure and politely requested that she bring me a beer instead. In an unexpected move, she insisted I stick with the Coke, handed me a lollipop, and advised me to calm down, firmly stating that beer was out of the question. Her peculiar approach took me by surprise, and in a moment of frustration, I retorted, "You're not my mother. Would you please get me a beer right now!"

She simply smiled politely and walked away, leaving me with her final words: "Only Coke for you." Her actions were oddly maternal and confusing, adding a layer of unexpected humor to the situation. This unusual interaction became a talking point among us for the rest of the ride home, as I tried to make sense of the new waitress's unorthodox methods.

Just before they dropped me off at my house, Bob and Peter finally confessed about the waitress's strange behavior. They admitted they had orchestrated a prank during our time at the restaurant. While I was in the bathroom, they approached the waitress and misleadingly informed her that I was mentally handicapped and extremely unstable with alcohol, warning her not to serve me any, even something as mild as a beer. They explained that I might request a beer and might behave unusually, but she should firmly offer me only a Coke. Additionally, they whimsically suggested that a lollipop would help calm me down. The waitress complied, believing she was helping manage a sensitive situation. Realizing the deception, I couldn't help but acknowledge the elaborate setup. Although I took it in good spirits, I reminded them jokingly that they still owed me a beer for their antics.

Bob and Peter's friendship profoundly influenced my career trajectory, introducing me to two new career possibilities. Bob, in particular, played a pivotal role. He generously spent time with me, teaching me the intricacies of vehicle repair through hands-on experience. Together, we tackled the challenge of repairing the front end of his Volkswagen Beetle, which had been damaged in an accident. This project was a significant learning curve for me, and it inspired me to dive deeper into the world of mechanics.

Encouraged by my newfound interest, I approached Bob about rebuilding my ninety-horsepower Mercury outboard engine, which had major operational issues. Bob's response was characteristically enthusiastic: "Not a problem." We embarked on the project together and successfully restored the engine to its original functioning state. This experience was a catalyst for me, sparking a deeper passion for mechanical engineering.

Bob continued to mentor me, teaching me how to rebuild brakes and conduct minor body repairs.

His guidance was invaluable as I rebuilt an eight-cylinder car engine and constructed two Harley Davidson–style motorcycles from scratch. These motorcycles have served me well for the past twenty-five years.

I owe a great deal of my mechanical skills and success to Bob's mentorship. He not only imparted practical skills but also inspired confidence in my abilities, and despite the infamous beer-and-chowder prank, I hold nothing but gratitude for him. Thanks to Bob, I forged a path in a field I now excel in.

Peter, on the other hand, was the driving force behind my pursuit of higher education. Among our group of friends, he was the only one who attended college, with a lofty goal of becoming a medical doctor. Inspired by his ambition, I, too, was drawn to the idea of a career in medicine, and together we embarked on the journey to earn our undergraduate degrees.

As we progressed through our college years, there emerged an unspoken competition between us, each striving to be the first to don the white coat of a doctor. Peter majored in biology while I pursued chemistry, complementing it with a minor in biology. His academic journey was streamlined, enabling him to graduate in four years, whereas it took me five years to complete my courses because of the added complexity of my minor.

In the end, neither of us entered medical school, yet we both remained in the field of science. I established a career as a research chemist, immersing myself in the fascinating world of chemical reactions and solutions. Peter found his niche in pharmaceutical sales, where he leveraged his extensive knowledge of biology to excel. Both of us found fulfillment and success in our respective paths, which might not have been possible without each other's influence and the initial shared dream of medicine.

I am immensely grateful to Peter for his role in steering me toward a rewarding career in the sciences. Just like with Bob, despite the memorable prank that Peter pulled, my appreciation for his influence remains undiminished. Thank you, Peter, for the inspiration and camaraderie during those formative years.

Tradesman

During the Vietnam War era from the 1950s to the 1970s, America found itself embroiled in significant conflict. This period was marked by the looming threat of involuntary military draft for young American men, which led many to seek various avenues to avoid conscription. One such method was obtaining a college deferment. This provision allowed individuals to delay their military service usually until their educational pursuits were completed or until the deferment policies changed. Prior to 1971, a substantial number of young men opted for college primarily to gain a deferment that would otherwise have led them into vocational or trade schools. However, the deferment program came to an end in 1971, and the draft itself was abolished in 1973. Consequently, there was a noticeable shift as more individuals began pursuing trade schools once the incentive of college deferments disappeared. This change significantly influenced the educational and career choices of that generation, highlighting how sociopolitical factors can steer personal and professional decisions.

During my high school years, I initially had little interest in pursuing a trade education. The Vietnam War was drawing to a close, and with the end of the draft, students like me were faced with a wider array of career choices without the pressure of military service. One of the curriculum requirements at my high school was to take a woodworking shop class. This course piqued my interest in how simple pieces of wood could be transformed into functional objects such as furniture or shelving.

I embarked on multiple woodworking projects, starting with an overly heavy baseball bat, followed by a coffee table and a corner shelf. While these items were not particularly well-crafted, they served as valuable learning experiences. They taught me how to handle various woodworking tools and techniques, from measuring and cutting to sanding and finishing. This exposure not only improved my practical skills but also deepened my appreciation for craftsmanship and the creative process involved in building something tangible from raw materials.

Years later, when I purchased my first house, I found myself in need of additional space, prompting the decision to add a garage with a second-floor living area that included a bedroom, living room, and a small bathroom. The cost estimates for this project were daunting, making it clear that it would only be financially feasible if I undertook the labor myself. Fortunately, I had a friend, Charley, who was a retired carpenter. He generously offered to help me with the construction for minimal pay, sharing his expertise and experience.

Together, we built the entire structure from the ground up, starting with the foundation and progressing through framing, roofing, and finishing. The project was completed in less than a year, a testament to his skill and our combined efforts. What proved most invaluable, however, were the lessons he imparted during the build. He taught me the fundamentals of carpentry, from reading blueprints and selecting the right materials to mastering joinery techniques and ensuring structural integrity. These lessons went beyond mere instruction; they were practical, hands-on experiences that have significantly shaped my approach to DIY projects. I still employ his methods to this day. Each time I work on a new project, I am reminded of the craftsmanship and precision he instilled in me.

My second major project began shortly after I acquired my second house. This property also required a sizable addition—a three-car garage with an upstairs living area. Unfortunately, my mentor and friend Charley had passed away, leaving me to tackle this more ambitious project on my own. This new endeavor was not only larger in scale but also more complex, involving intricate electrical and plumbing work that I had yet to master.

Determined to succeed, I began the project with basic materials, starting with a single nail and a piece of wood. I methodically worked through each phase, from framing to installing electrical circuits and plumbing systems. I educated myself on these new trades, utilizing resources such as DIY books, online tutorials, and advice from local tradespeople. Over the course of the year, I progressed from the initial structural work to the final touches, including the last coat of paint.

By the end of the year, I had single-handedly completed the project, a testament to the skills I had acquired and refined. Both garage structures still stand today in excellent condition, serving as enduring reminders of the joys and challenges of learning and applying tradesman skills. The experience reinforced a valuable lesson. Regardless of one's profession, taking the time to learn some trade skills can be immensely beneficial. These skills have served me well throughout my life, enhancing both my capabilities and my confidence in handling a variety of practical challenges.

Stand-up Comedian

Laughter is not only a universal language but also a powerful tool for maintaining well-being. Numerous studies have confirmed that a good sense of humor can significantly enhance mental and physical health, increase one's appeal to others, and improve leadership skills. Engaging in laughter involves taking in oxygen-rich air, which stimulates the heart, lungs, and muscles while simultaneously triggering the release of endorphins by the brain. This not only activates the stress response system but also helps to mitigate it effectively.

Moreover, the act of smiling, which often accompanies laughter, has been shown to offer additional health benefits. These include lowering blood sugar and blood pressure, reducing stress, boosting the immune system, and promoting the release of natural painkillers and serotonin. These effects collectively contribute to a healthier, more resilient body.

Socially, laughter and smiling can make individuals more approachable and attractive, fostering connections and enhancing interpersonal relationships. The simple act of laughing can diffuse tension and create an atmosphere of shared joy and understanding. In essence, humor serves as a crucial mechanism that not only alleviates stress but also resets our perspective, bringing us closer to reality and to each other. Thus, incorporating more humor into daily life could be a simple yet effective strategy for enhancing personal and collective well-being.

My introduction to humor came from my father, who was a natural-born comedian. Regardless of the gravity of a situation, he always found a way to see the humorous side. For example, after a serious car accident that completely totaled his car, he could glance at the wreckage and quip, "I never liked the color of that car anyway. I think I'll buy a blue one next." His ability to lighten the mood was unparalleled.

I vividly remember a day we went golfing. He was struggling to hit the ball off the tee, missing the ball entirely on his first, second, and even third swing. Instead of growing frustrated, he looked down at the ball and deadpanned, "Stop moving around. You're making me look bad." We both burst out laughing. That moment of levity seemed to dissolve all the tension, and his next swing sent the ball rocketing down the fairway. It was a perfect illustration of how humor could cut through stress and make any challenge seem more manageable. This lesson, that laughter can realign our perspective and simplify our actions, has stuck with me ever since.

I first realized that I, too, possessed a sense of humor during particularly challenging times when problems seemed insurmountable. This trait, I believe, was a direct genetic inheritance from my father. No matter how tough a situation became, I instinctively searched for the humorous angle, using laughter as a tool to clear the air and facilitate resolution. This ability to diffuse tension with humor is a valuable asset in my personal tool kit.

Humor has become my go-to strategy, not just in personal life but professionally as well. It's a precious gift from my father, and I am committed to using it at every opportunity. My approach has shaped how others perceive me. In meetings or during casual conversations, I am known for looking to evoke a laugh or a smile. This doesn't just happen; it requires a specific technique that I've honed over time. Such a humanistic approach to interacting with others has not only made me approachable but also helped in building rapport and easing difficult discussions.

The technique I use to create humor in conversations is much like playing volleyball, a sport I learned much from. In volleyball, the play starts with a serve to the opposing team, followed by a receive, then a set, and finally, the spike where the ball is driven to an unexpected spot on the court. Crafting a humorous situation follows a similar sequence: listen, set up, then deliver.

Listening is the initial phase where I gather all pertinent information about the situation. This involves paying close attention to the context and the emotions of those involved. Just as in volleyball where you need to observe the opponents' positioning and readiness, in humor, understanding the setting is crucial.

Next is the *setup*. This phase requires imagination and impeccable timing. I create a story, closely related to the actual situation but with a twist—I usually make myself the main character. The believability of the story hinges on effective body language that conceals the impending punch line. It's crucial to maintain focus and avoid distractions during this phase as any misstep can dismantle the setup.

Finally, the *spike*—the delivery of the punch line. At the precisely right moment, and again without distractions, I reveal the truth. The effectiveness of the punch line depends on how convincingly the setup was delivered. If the audience believed the story, the revelation that it was all a setup usually results in a bigger laugh. The more they were convinced, the greater the payoff in laughter and smiles.

This method of humor—receive, set, and spike—proves effective time and again, not just in lightening the mood but also in making memorable moments.

I make it a point to incorporate humor into my daily life to make it more bearable and engaging. This has led me to seriously consider trying my hand at stand-up comedy at least once in my life. To prepare, I frequently purchase joke books and study them diligently, hoping to recall the right joke at the perfect moment. I still have plenty of time to fulfill this dream, and the prospect excites me—there's no telling the joy it could bring to others and myself.

Thank you, Dad, for this incredible gift of humor. It has not only enriched my life but also allowed me to bring a smile to the faces of those around me. Whether it's a well-timed joke in a tense room or a funny anecdote shared among friends, humor has been a priceless tool in connecting with others and seeing the lighter side of life. Pursuing stand-up comedy might just be the next step in exploring this gift further, potentially spreading even more happiness and laughter.

Rock Star

It was 1964, and the landscape of American entertainment was about to change forever. *The Ed Sullivan Show*, affectionately referred to by its host as "a really big shew," had become the cultural zeitgeist of the time, a beacon for anyone who aspired to make their mark in the realms of film, comedy, magic, and especially music.

Me at sixty-five

This wasn't just another variety show; it was the pinnacle of exposure, a coveted stage where an appearance could catapult an unknown artist to stardom overnight. The summer of that year was memorable for a myriad of reasons, but one moment stood out distinctly in the collective memory of the nation: the introduction of the Beatles to the American public. Ed Sullivan, with his knack for spotting transformative talent, brought the British quartet from London to the forefront of the American music scene. Their debut was scheduled for eight o'clock on the evening of February 9, a date that would go down in history as a monumental moment in television and music history.

America, in all its sprawling diversity, came to a standstill that night, tuning into CBS to catch a glimpse of the Liverpool lads on *The Ed Sullivan Show*. An unprecedented seventy-three million viewers, a record-breaking audience at the time, huddled around their television sets, drawn by the buzz of anticipation and the allure of witnessing history in the making. Families, friends, and curious onlookers across the nation were united by a single event, a testament to the unifying power of music and television.

There I was, a young spectator among millions, my eyes wide with anticipation, glued to the screen as if nothing else in the world mattered. I, too, was about to be swept up in Beatle mania, unknowingly standing on the cusp of a cultural revolution. As the opening chords of their performance filled the living room, I felt as if I were being transported, ushered into a new era of music and youth culture. That night, without fully realizing it, I, along with the rest of America, was stepping into a new chapter of my childhood, one that would be forever marked by the melodies and mania of the Beatles.

Then suddenly, the Beatles appeared on the screen, a sight unlike any musical group before them. The distinct setup immediately caught everyone's attention. Ringo, the charismatic drummer, was elevated on a drum podium, a good six feet above, setting him visually apart from the rest of the group. Below him were the three guitarists/singers—Paul, George, and John—each poised with their instruments, ready to make history. The studio audience's reaction was explosive, an outpouring of energy and hysteria that seemed to shake the very foundations of the theater. This was "Beatle mania" in its purest form, a level of fan fervor that was utterly unprecedented on live television.

The moment John Lennon counted off "one, two, three, four," the studio, and indeed America, was swept up in the tidal wave of Beatle music. They launched into "I Saw Her Standing There," and the audience's enthusiasm reached new heights. The screams and cheers were so loud that the song itself was barely discernible over the television broadcast. However, the quality of the audio mattered little to me; I was captivated by the energy, the charisma, and the sheer coolness of the Beatles. Watching them, I couldn't help but imagine myself in their shoes, strumming a guitar and eliciting that same wild response from an audience. At that moment, I knew I wanted to be up there with them, living the dream of being a rock star, particularly emulating one of those iconic guitarists.

COULD HAVE BEEN; SHOULD HAVE BEEN; HERE I AM

How could four musicians, whimsically named after an insect, ignite such a synergistic phenomenon that revolutionized the music world? The answer is glaringly obvious once examined: they excelled at their craft. But saying they were merely "great" would be an understatement; they were phenomenal performers. Their allure was not just in their music but in their entire presentation. The Beatles had a distinct look and style that set them apart, their mop-top haircuts becoming as emblematic of the '60s as their music. Their songwriting—penning lyrics that ranged from the deeply personal to the whimsically surreal—broke new ground in what could be explored in popular music. Musically, they blended different genres with an inventive prowess that was unheard of at the time, from the jangling cheer of pop to the introspective depth of rock and the experimental echoes of psychedelia.

The Beatles didn't just stand out; they were the proverbial white elephants in the music room, impossible to overlook and mesmerizing to observe. Their rise to fame underscored a pivotal lesson; embracing uniqueness, coupled with genuine talent and innovation, can carve paths to unprecedented greatness. They demonstrated that being different, when allied with hard work and creativity, was not just good—it was revolutionary.

From an early age, I grasped the concept that aligning with the majority offered a form of security, a collective movement along a well-marked, familiar path toward the future. Yet this conventional route, trodden by so many, struck me as overly predictable and lacking in depth. My soul was restless, craving something beyond the ordinary, a desire to forge a new path, solitary and uncharted yet guided by the rich tapestry of my own life's lessons and errors. This aspiration was to shape my individuality and to mold a distinct identity in a world of conformity.

This ambition mirrored the journey of the Beatles. Their transformation into the icons that captivated millions on *The Ed Sullivan Show* was not an overnight occurrence; it was the culmination of years of evolution, a continuous shaping process honed by unique talents, personal trials, and collective experiences. They ventured beyond the safety of the familiar, embracing the risks of individuality and innovation. Their story taught me a valuable lesson; greatness and authenticity stem from the courage to be distinct, to learn from every fall, and to treat each success as a step, not a destination. They were indeed a work in progress, a testament to the power of growth and personal development in the journey to success.

The realization dawned on me that carving out my own unique path could well mean stepping into the world of music—creating melodies, mastering an instrument, and unveiling my abilities to the world. Fueled by ambition, I entertained visions of rock and roll stardom, of captivating audiences with my lyrical and musical expressions. However, this aspiration, though fervent, clashed with reality—I was a novice in the truest sense, lacking knowledge in songwriting, instrumental proficiency, and stage presence.

Acknowledging these gaps, I understood that my dream required more than mere enthusiasm; it demanded dedicated practice, learning, and acquisition of the necessary tools. I needed to immerse myself in music to understand its language and nuances. I was faced with the daunting task of learning from scratch—how to craft a song that resonates, how to bring melodies to life with an instrument, and how to connect with an audience from the vulnerability of the stage. This journey, I realized, would require patience, perseverance, and the right resources. I was on the brink of a new adventure, a quest to transform from a dreamer into a musician, equipped with the resolve to navigate the challenges ahead.

At ten years old, there was only one place to start: my parents. However, they quickly dismissed my request for an electric guitar and music lessons to become the next Beatles member. So naturally, the next best source of support was my best friend at the time, "Chipper."

Chipper, officially named Lynwood, resided just two houses down from mine and was a year older than me. He, too, was captivated by the Beatles and harbored dreams of rock stardom. However, much like my situation, his parents firmly responded with a "not a chance in hell" to his musical ambitions. Perfect—I had found the second member of my nascent rock band.

COULD HAVE BEEN; SHOULD HAVE BEEN; HERE I AM

At the time, England was exporting numerous duo acts like Chad and Jeremy and Peter and Gordon. "Eric and Chip" sounded good to me, but Chip argued that "Chip and Eric" had a better ring to it. Fine, we had settled on a name; now all we needed was an act. *Look out, ladies, we'll be hitting the scene in no time*, I thought. Oh, but then I remembered, we had no instruments, no knowledge of how to play them, couldn't sing, and hadn't written a note of music.

Logically, the first step was to obtain instruments and learn how to play them, followed by practicing singing and writing songs. We had a plan but lacked the funds to buy guitars, so we decided to build them ourselves. Chip's father was a carpenter and had an abundance of scrap wood and the necessary tools. However, our youthful enthusiasm was not matched by our carpentry skills. We attempted to construct guitars: cutting a piece of plywood into the shape of a guitar body, attaching a two-by-four for the neck, and stringing transformer wire across twelve-penny nails. As one might guess, the result was far from a functional musical instrument. Despite all our efforts, we found ourselves back at square one, still without any real instruments.

While Chip and I were diligently assembling our unique Frankenstein guitar, Chip's father observed our efforts with great interest, impressed by our dedication to the project. A few days later, Chip's father surprised him with a brand-new electric guitar to encourage his aspirations of becoming a rock star. This was a significant advancement for our band as we now had a guitar for Chip to play. This development left me on a quest to find a guitar for myself.

Chip and I, both members of Boy Scouts Troop Number 41 in Fitchburg, Massachusetts, received a monthly magazine titled *Boys' Life* as part of our membership benefits. In the back of this magazine, there was an advertisement that caught my eye. It offered various gifts to Scouts who sold Christmas cards. Among the array of rewards was an electric guitar with an amplifier—a prize for selling thirty-six boxes of cards. The boxes, each containing twelve cards, could be ordered in batches of twelve boxes. The allure of obtaining the guitar and amplifier was irresistible, especially since the advertisement featured a captivating sketch of the set rather than a photograph—a common advertising technique in the 1960s. Despite it being a drawing, it looked perfect to me, and I was determined to sell those thirty-six boxes to make the guitar and amplifier mine.

To initiate my order for the first twelve boxes of Christmas cards, the company required my parents' consent and signature. My mother gave her approval, and we received the first twelve boxes from the card company three weeks later. It took me about a week to sell all twelve boxes to neighbors and friends. The next set of twelve boxes proved to be a bit more challenging, requiring two weeks to sell, and the final twelve were even more difficult, taking four weeks to sell, but eventually, all were sold. Then came the waiting period for my new guitar and amplifier to arrive. The anticipation was immense, but I felt incredibly proud and satisfied, knowing that my hard work selling thirty-six boxes of Christmas cards would soon be rewarded with a beautiful guitar and amplifier.

Four weeks after placing the order, my mother received a notification from the local post office that a package had arrived for us. I was brimming with excitement about the arrival of my hard-earned instrument and couldn't wait to play it. The next day, while I was at school, my mother picked up the package. When I returned home, I found it waiting for me: a cardboard box approximately three feet long and four inches wide. My excitement waned slightly, puzzled by the size—how could the amplifier possibly fit in there with the guitar?

Upon opening the box, the first item I encountered was a dark plastic box, about three inches by eight inches, which turned out to be the amplifier. Then I pulled out the guitar, which was entirely made of plastic and resembled more of a child's toy than the instrument I had envisioned. Despite the initial disappointment from the toylike quality of the guitar, I noted it was strung with nylon strings and could hold a tune, an upgrade from the plywood Frankenstein guitar I had built with Chip.

Determined to improve its sound quality, I began modifying the guitar. I replaced the nylon strings with real electric guitar metal strings and added a volume knob with a detachable phone jack, which made it look more like a real instrument. However, it still sounded like a toy. But what happened next was entirely unexpected and would set me on the path of becoming a musician.

I devotedly played that plastic guitar every day for months, gradually making progress as I learned simple tunes or just experimented with sounds. Observing my persistent efforts and struggles with the toylike instrument, my mother decided it was time for a change. She understood my passion and the limitations I faced with the current guitar. Taking matters into her own hands, she visited the local five-and-dime department store and placed one of their Japanese-made guitars on layaway. This guitar was to be my Christmas gift, still six months away. The news filled me with indescribable joy and disbelief; I was over the moon knowing that I would eventually own a real guitar.

Every day after school, I made it a point to walk past the store, gazing longingly at the guitars displayed in the front window, dreaming of the day the one on layaway would be mine. The anticipation of that day fueled my excitement and my dreams of becoming a musician.

The long-awaited day arrived when I finally acquired a semi-professional electric guitar, yet one significant challenge remained: I lacked an amplifier. Ingeniously, I modified the plastic amplifier from my toy guitar, allowing my new instrument to connect and produce sound. Admittedly, the audio quality was far from perfect, but it was functional. Now armed with my guitar and makeshift amp, my next step was to seek out fellow musicians to form a band.

It's peculiar how life unfolds; not long after I got my new guitar, I stumbled upon two guys from the neighborhood in quite an unexpected manner. It was a warm summer day, and from behind my house, I could hear music drifting from the wooded area beyond our backyard. Curious, I ventured out and discovered two youths, Paul and Mike, perched on a boulder, both strumming guitars and singing. They seemed a bit older than me, and at my tender age, even a small age gap translated into a significant difference in maturity. They were playing "Two Silhouettes on the Shade" by Herman's Hermits, a hit from a popular English band of that era. The song's lead guitar riffs were notoriously challenging, but Mike executed them flawlessly, mirroring the original recording. Paul complemented him well, handling the rhythm guitar with ease. I was thoroughly impressed.

As I approached them, their music ceased, and they looked up with a mix of surprise and inquiry, essentially asking, "Who the hell are you?" I can't recall my exact response; their musical prowess had left me rather intimidated. It's a common reaction, I suppose, to feel diminished or even paralyzed in the presence of those who awe us. I felt decidedly out of place and, without another word, retreated back to the safety of my home, engulfed in a mix of emotions. Was I letting a golden musical opportunity slip through my fingers? Or were Paul and Mike simply out of my league, unlikely to be interested in a friendship with someone of my younger age?

A week or two after our initial encounter, I was taken aback when Paul appeared from the woods and approached me in my backyard. He apologized for the brusqueness of our first meeting, explaining that the wooded area was actually part of his family's property and that he and Mike used it as a secluded spot for band practice. Their quest for privacy made sense to me; I often faced similar challenges at home. Countless times, my parents had half-jokingly suggested I take my guitar practice somewhere far from their ears, ideally as distant as the moon. It appeared that what was melodious to me was merely a cacophony to them.

Meeting Paul may have been a pivotal, life-altering moment for me. He wasn't the typical teenager flowing with societal currents; instead, he was a deep thinker with aspirations for significant achievements. His exceptional skills spanned mathematics, chess, electronics, and music. Although I never confirmed it, his intellect suggested a remarkably high IQ, often making him the most knowledgeable individual in any setting. Unlike Paul, my circle of friends, including myself, hovered around average or slightly below in terms of academic or technical prowess. For me, mastering new, especially technical, subjects required considerable effort, repetition, and motivation. Paul, on the other hand, possessed an innate ability to quickly understand and retain complex concepts. His memory was astonishingly accurate, enabling him to remember phone numbers and names and recall them flawlessly even after years. His multifaceted talents were undeniable.

What truly set Paul apart was his willingness to share his knowledge. He patiently taught me how to play the guitar, the basics of electronics, and, importantly, the strategies for playing a fierce game of chess. We spent countless days discussing various topics and honing our guitar skills. Eventually, our collaboration, along with Mike and Don, led to the formation of a rock band that performed locally, bringing joy to our neighborhood. From Paul, I learned the immense value of knowledge and its power to unlock doors that previously seemed closed. The idea of becoming a professional musician became less of an end goal, and I found myself driven by a thirst for knowledge. This new aspiration made me ponder my future. What path should I take next? In what field should I specialize? This decision would shape the course of my life, prompting me to consider where I could acquire the breadth of knowledge I now sought and whether I was capable of assimilating it.

A Pilot

From an early age, I was captivated by the world of aviation, a fascination particularly ignited by my passion for model gas planes. This hobby, which became a significant part of my life, has its origins deep-rooted in my childhood memories from the mid-'60s. Even now, I can vividly recall the unique, distinctive buzzing noise that would gradually fade in and out, a mysterious yet familiar sound that piqued my curiosity and excitement. This noise wasn't coming from just anywhere; it originated from the local baseball field, which was situated at least a quarter mile away from where I lived. Despite the considerable distance, on quiet days, I could still catch the faint yet unmistakably intriguing sound of someone flying a model gas plane.

This distant hum of engines became a siren call for me, drawing me toward the field with a sense of wonder and an insatiable desire to discover more. It was more than just a sound; it was an invitation to explore, to learn, and to immerse myself in a world that seemed both fascinating and out of reach. Each time the sound reached my ears, it sparked a deep-seated yearning to be a part of that distant but captivating world. The experience was about more than just the planes themselves; it was about the freedom they represented, the skill and precision required to navigate them, and the endless possibilities they symbolized in the vast expanse of the sky. This early exposure to the wonders of flight and aerodynamics laid the groundwork for what would become a lifelong passion and a calling that I would struggle to ignore.

Baseball field

The moment the distinctive sound reached my ears, an instinctive reaction kicked in; I immediately seized my bicycle and embarked on a brisk journey toward the source. With determined pedaling, I made my way to the baseball field, covering the distance in a matter of five to ten minutes, propelled by a mix of eagerness and anticipation. Upon arriving, I was greeted by the sight of pilots, their figures poised with concentration and skill, expertly maneuvering their model planes through the clear sky. They performed a mesmerizing series of acrobatic stunts that captivated my attention completely. These stunts included flying upside down in a show of daring defiance against gravity, executing perfect, tight loops that painted invisible circles in the air and executing steep, heart-stopping climbs followed by thrilling, rapid dives toward the ground, only to skillfully level off at the last moment.

As the model airplanes zipped and darted back and forth, a faint sweet petroleum odor wafted through the air, a unique scent that was strangely pleasant and intrinsically linked to the model engines. This odor was accompanied by a visible vapor trail, a ghostly white line that hung in the air, delineating the path of their flight. This visual and olfactory backdrop added an almost surreal quality to the experience, enhancing the sense of awe and wonder that washed over me. Standing there, amid the sounds, smells, and the skilled display of control and freedom, I felt an overwhelming sense of belonging and a deep yearning to join the ranks of those pilots, to take control of a plane myself, and to carve my own trails in the sky.

Back in those days, the realm of radio-controlled model airplanes was almost a luxurious hobby largely because of their prohibitive cost and the complex technology that powered them. Such advancements were not commonplace and were typically reserved for 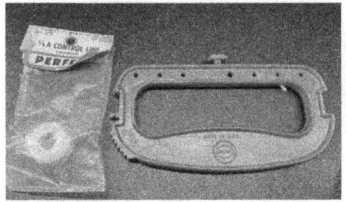 the most avid or well-funded enthusiasts. Instead, the predominant type of model planes we encountered were those operated using a more rudimentary system: two tether lines that connected the plane to a handheld controller. This setup allowed the pilot, through simple motions, to directly influence the plane's altitude. By pulling up or pushing down on the controller, one could command the airplane to climb or descend respectively. However, this method inherently restricted the planes to only fly in circles around the pilot, a limitation when compared to the freedom of radio-controlled counterparts.

Despite this limitation, the tethered model planes carried their own charm and challenge, providing a hands-on approach to understanding aerodynamics and control. However, the simplicity of these hand-built models was somewhat deceptive; they were often beyond the financial reach of many families at the time. The components required for these model planes, from the engines to the durable materials needed for construction, were quite expensive, reflecting a significant investment. This economic barrier added an extra layer of exclusivity to the hobby, making it a coveted yet elusive pastime for many young enthusiasts like me.

In our childhood, the world of model planes was far more modest than the elaborate radio-controlled or tethered varieties that filled our dreams. Our access was primarily limited to those quaint models crafted from balsa wood, known for its lightweight and easy-to-shape properties, ideal for the hands of eager yet inexperienced young aviators. These balsa wood planes came predominantly in two distinct varieties, each offering a unique approach to flight. The first type was equipped with a lead weight strategically positioned on the nose. This simple modification transformed the model into a glider, allowing it to harness the wind and soar through the air with a silent grace. The concept of balance and aerodynamics became tangible lessons as we adjusted the weight and threw our gliders, watching them navigate the invisible currents above. The second variety offered a different kind of thrill: powered flight, albeit on a very modest scale. This type was engineered with an elastic band that extended from the rear end of the fuselage to a plastic propeller mounted at the front. By winding the propeller, we stored potential energy in the elastic band, which, when released, spun the propeller rapidly and propelled the plane forward into brief but exhilarating flights. This process not only provided endless fun but also introduced us to basic principles of propulsion and energy conversion.

Though essentially toys, these balsa wood models were our first foray into the vast world of aviation. They were more than mere playthings; they were our initial tangible lessons in the fundamentals of flight. Through trial and error, we learned about lift, thrust, drag, and gravity. We began to understand how altering the shape of the wings or the weight distribution could affect flight patterns. These early experiences, as rudimentary as they were, planted the seeds of curiosity and passion for aviation that would grow and evolve with us over time.

In my childhood, one of the most anticipated events each week was the arrival of a new volume from a mail-order *Golden Book Encyclopedia* set that my family had subscribed to. This was not just any collection of books but a comprehensive set of thirty-six volumes, each meticulously organized to cover a broad spectrum of knowledge across various subjects in alphabetical order. This expansive encyclopedia set was a treasure trove of information, systematically arranged to guide a curious mind through the labyrinth of human knowledge and discovery. The first volume of the series, covering topics from A to B, held within its pages a particularly fascinating section dedicated to the theory of airplane flight and controls. This section spanned twenty pages and was an enlightening introduction to the principles of aviation. It captivated my imagination and expanded my understanding significantly. The explanation of how airplanes achieve flight was detailed and engaging, breaking down complex concepts into understandable segments.

One explanation that remains vividly etched in my memory is that of thrust, a critical force enabling airplanes to move through the air. The encyclopedia provided an analogy that was both intriguing and enlightening; it likened the action of a screw being driven into a piece of wood to that of a propeller slicing through the air. This comparison made the concept of thrust tangible and relatable, transforming an abstract principle into something I could visualize and comprehend.

The encyclopedia went further, illustrating this concept with a diagram showing a thrust control knob connected to a throttle cable. This cable, in turn, was linked to the carburetor, a crucial component responsible for mixing air and fuel in the engine. By adjusting this knob, a pilot could control the engine's power output, varying it from idle to full throttle. This detailed explanation not only shed light on how pilots manage the power of their aircraft but also instilled in me a deeper appreciation for the intricacies of airplane controls and the delicate balance required to navigate the skies. Through this encyclopedia, aviation was no longer just an abstract fascination but a field rich with detailed mechanics, principles, and inspiring possibilities. It became a cornerstone in my education, fueling my curiosity and providing a solid foundation in the basics of flight, which I would continue to build upon in the years to come.

The concept of how an airplane achieves lift and remains suspended in the sky was a complex puzzle for my young inquisitive mind. I knew intuitively that the wings were central to this process, but the detailed physics behind it were not easily comprehensible. Eager for clarity, I turned to my father, hoping he could shed light on the enigmatic principles of flight, particularly in relation to our model gas planes, which seemed to defy gravity with ease. My father, understanding the complexity of my query, simplified the explanation to suit my level of understanding. He elucidated, "What goes up must come down when the engine stops turning." This fundamental notion captured the essence of flight in the most elementary terms; the plane remains aloft because of the thrust generated by its engine. Once the engine depletes its fuel supply, it ceases to produce thrust, and consequently, the plane can no longer sustain its flight and begins to transition into a glide, eventually descending back to its point of origin.

This explanation, while simplified, encapsulated a fundamental principle that is well understood among pilots and aviation enthusiasts: the importance of the engine in maintaining flight and the inevitable return to earth once its power is exhausted. It was a critical lesson that instilled in me an early respect for the laws of physics and the unforgiving nature of gravity. This basic understanding served as a crucial foundation, a sort of mental runway, from which my curiosity and knowledge about aviation could take off and soar. It was a reminder of the delicate balance between the forces of lift, thrust, drag, and gravity that pilots must navigate to keep their aircraft safely in the air.

The Christmas when I turned eleven years old marked a significant milestone in my childhood, as my father presented me with a special gift: a model gas plane manufactured by the renowned Cox company. This wasn't just any toy; it was a carefully designed entry-level model airplane, constructed entirely from flexible plastic. The design was intuitive, with the plane's wings and motor ingeniously secured to the fuselage using multiple elastic bands. This unique feature played a crucial safety role; in the event of an unforeseen crash, the parts were designed to detach safely from each other. This meant that instead of breaking upon impact, the components would simply separate, significantly reducing the risk of irreparable damage and extending the lifespan of the model.

This thoughtful design was particularly suited for beginners like me, who had little to no experience in piloting model aircraft. It allowed for a learning curve that was forgiving, encouraging trial and error without the constant fear of destroying a cherished gift. The Cox model gas plane was more than a toy; it was a teaching tool that allowed my father and me to bond over shared flights and failures, gradually improving our skills and understanding of the mechanics of flight. This gift was a perfect match for our novice status, providing endless hours of enjoyment and learning, laying down a foundation for a hobby that we both cherished deeply.

Our inaugural flight with the Cox model gas plane was a momentous occasion, and we chose the parking lot of a nearby airport as the stage for this significant event. The decision to select this particular location was strategic; it was not only spacious enough to accommodate the initial uncertain maneuvers of novice pilots like us but also surrounded by large fields. These expansive areas provided a safety net, ensuring that if the plane were to veer off course, we could easily retrieve it without much difficulty, minimizing the risk of loss or damage.

The day we chose for our inaugural flight was marked by an unmistakable chill, characteristic of the cold season at the New England airport. I can still recall how the biting cold seemed to freeze time, numbing my face, hands, and feet as we stood in the expansive parking lot, preparing for what was meant to be a momentous occasion. Despite the frigid temperatures, my enthusiasm remained fiery and hot, a stark contrast to the icy air surrounding us. My father, with steady hands numbed by the cold, meticulously set up the airplane's control lines, a process that felt like an eternity to my impatient young self. However, the biting cold did little to dampen my spirits as the excitement of flying our model plane for the first time overshadowed the discomfort.

Once the airplane was assembled and ready, the next crucial step was to breathe life into it by starting the engine. My father, ever the patient teacher, carefully filled the tiny fuel tank, primed the engine, and connected the battery to the glow plug. He then attempted to kick-start the engine into action by deftly spinning the propeller with a practiced finger. However, despite our persistent efforts and hopeful attempts, the cold weather proved to be a formidable adversary. The little engine, unaccustomed to such frigid conditions, stubbornly refused to cooperate, denying us the satisfaction of a successful start. After more than an hour of trying in vain, with the cold gnawing relentlessly at our resolve, we were forced to accept defeat for the day. Disheartened and cold, we packed up our gear, vowing to return when the weather was more forgiving.

As the months rolled by, each passing day seemed to dash our hopes further. December's chill gave way to January's frost, followed by February's blizzards and March's lingering cold snaps. The ground remained a blanket of snow, an insurmountable barrier to the maiden flight of our little airplane. The delays were not just a test of patience but of resolve, and as the cold months dragged on, I sensed a growing disinterest in my father. By the time spring's warmth finally melted away the last remnants of winter in late April, the enthusiasm we once shared had cooled significantly. To my recollection, that model airplane, the symbol of our shared ambition and excitement, never did take to the skies.

This initial setback in my journey toward the skies was disheartening, yet it failed to extinguish the flame of my dream. Despite the cold start and the unfulfilled maiden voyage, my aspiration to become a pilot, to soar above the clouds and conquer the skies, remained as strong and determined as ever.

Several years after the initial disappointment of that failed first flight, when I was around sixteen years old, my life took an unexpected and fortuitous turn with the arrival of a new kid in the neighborhood. His name was Armand, and although he was slightly older than me, we quickly discovered a shared wavelength that transcended our age difference. We bonded over a variety of common interests that were pivotal during those formative years: music, which was our universal language; sports, where we challenged and cheered for each other; and the topic of girls, which, at that age, was a constant source of mystery and fascination. This mutual understanding and shared set of interests paved the way for a robust friendship that would endure the many changes that life threw our way, remaining steadfast until we both eventually moved away from our childhood neighborhood.

Armand brought with him not just companionship but also a connection to a world that reignited my dormant passion for aviation. He was a part of an intriguing and admirable organization known as the Civil Air Patrol (CAP), a nonprofit that serves as the civilian auxiliary of the US Air Force. This affiliation was not just a title; it offered him experiences and responsibilities that were both mature and adventurous. As a cadet in the CAP, Armand had the chance to engage in activities that were both critical and exciting, such as participating in local search and rescue missions. These missions were not only vital to the community but also provided real-world applications of teamwork, leadership, and problem-solving skills. Moreover, his involvement with the Civil Air Patrol provided him with an opportunity to learn basic aviation skills. This aspect of his life was particularly fascinating to me, reigniting the spark of my childhood dream of flying.

Through Armand, I glimpsed a structured path toward the world of aviation, one that combined the thrill of flying with the discipline of formal training and the honor of contributing to public service. His stories and experiences served as a beacon, guiding my renewed interest in aviation and offering a glimpse into the possibilities that lay in the discipline and structure provided by organizations like the CAP. This new friendship not only enriched my teenage years with camaraderie and shared adventures but also rekindled my aspiration toward the sky, providing a clearer vision of how I could turn my long-held dreams into achievable goals.

In the late '60s, the pathways to becoming a pilot, especially through civilian routes, were steeped in financial barriers that made them inaccessible to many aspiring aviators like me. The alternative, joining the Air Force, offered a more financially viable route as the government would bear the cost of flight training. However, this option required enlistment, something that was not immediately possible for me because of my young age and, admittedly, a degree of apprehension regarding military commitment at that stage of my life.

In this context, the Civil Air Patrol presented itself as a potential middle ground. It was an avenue that, while not directly leading to a pilot's license, offered a foray into the world of aviation that was less prohibitive in terms of both age and finances. Armand, my friend and mentor in many ways, was a strong advocate for the CAP, highlighting its benefits not just for advancing aviation knowledge but also for building character and leadership skills through its cadet program.

Despite Armand's genuine encouragement and the clear opportunities that the Civil Air Patrol represented, I found myself hesitating. My interest in the CAP itself was tepid at best. While the idea of flying continued to enchant me, the structured, disciplined environment of the cadet program, along with its broader focus beyond just aviation, didn't quite align with the romanticized image of flying I harbored. This dissonance led me to sideline this opportunity, making it the second instance where I let a potential gateway to the skies pass me by.

This period of my life underscored a recurring theme: a persistent dream of flight juxtaposed against the realities of my circumstances and youthful indecisions. Despite the allure of the skies, I hadn't yet found the path that resonated deeply enough to compel me to overcome the barriers before me. It wasn't until a third opportunity presented itself later on that my journey toward aviation would take a more definitive turn. This evolving narrative of missed chances and continued longing played a crucial role in shaping my resolve and understanding of what it truly meant to chase a dream.

The Christmas of 1976 marked a distinctive period in my life, one that stands out vividly in my memory. During this time, I resided in a duplex ranch-style home, sharing the building with Warren and Ruth, who were not only my neighbors but also my landlords. The couple was kind and industrious, adding a sense of community and warmth to our shared living environment. Warren, in particular, was a man of diverse talents and interests. By trade, he worked as an emergency vehicle fabricator, a profession that involved the meticulous building and modifying of ambulance-type trucks, ensuring they met the critical needs of emergency services. However, it was his unique hobby and side job that caught my attention and reignited my latent passion for aviation.

Aside from his main occupation, Warren had an intriguing avocation; he was involved in towing gliders at a nearby local airport. This was no casual pastime. Warren was a commercial pilot, holding a specific rating for towing gliders, a niche within the aviation community that required skill, precision, and a deep understanding of both powered and unpowered flight dynamics.

On weekends, Warren transformed from a fabricator of emergency vehicles to a pilot, operating a single-engine Cessna 188 AG wagon. This aircraft, known for its robustness and reliability, was specially adapted for the task of towing gliders. I learned from Warren that the process was both methodical and exhilarating. He would taxi the plane onto the runway, attach it to a glider via a long cable, and then take off, gradually lifting the unpowered glider to approximately two thousand feet above ground level. At this predetermined height, a crucial moment occurred—the cable would be released, allowing the two aircraft to part ways. The glider would then float gracefully into the thermals, seeking currents of air to sustain its flight, while Warren executed a steep, swift descent back to the airport, preparing for the next tow.

This aspect of Warren's life fascinated me. It was a blend of technical skill, airborne adventure, and a unique form of camaraderie among pilots and glider enthusiasts. Observing his weekend activities and listening to his stories provided me with a different perspective on aviation, one that was less about speed and more about the beauty of controlled, silent flight. This experience with Warren broadened my understanding of the aviation field and subtly steered me toward reevaluating my own aspirations and the multitude of pathways within the world of flight.

That particular Christmas, amid the usual exchange of holiday cheer and gifts, Warren presented me with something unexpected and incredibly special—a gift that would pivot the direction of my life toward the skies. He gifted me a one-hour introductory flight at the very airport where he spent his weekends towing gliders. This was not merely a gift but a gateway, an opening to a realm I had long fantasized about but had considered beyond my reach because of financial constraints.

Until that moment, I had held onto the belief that the path to becoming a pilot was lined with insurmountable financial barriers, accessible only to those who could afford the significant up-front costs associated with flight training. The very notion of an introductory flight—a concept designed to provide novices with a tangible experience of flying at a minimal cost—was foreign to me. It was an eye-opener, revealing that there were accessible entry points into the world of aviation that I had not previously considered.

The opportunity presented by Warren's gift was exhilarating. Here was a chance to step into the cockpit, to feel the controls under my hands, and to view the world from an entirely new perspective. It was an invitation to dip my toes into the vast ocean of aviation and to see firsthand whether the dream that had been simmering within me matched the reality of piloting an aircraft.

Motivated by a blend of intrigue, excitement, and a dash of apprehension, I accepted Warren's challenge. This was not a decision made lightly; it was a conscious step toward a dream deferred, an acknowledgment of the flame of aspiration that still burned within me. The gift of an introductory flight was the push I needed to transition from dreamer to doer, from an onlooker to an active participant in the aviation world.

This experience, as I would later realize, was the catalyst that propelled me toward earning my pilot's wings. It was the moment that transformed aviation from a distant dream into a tangible, achievable goal. Warren's thoughtful gift didn't just offer me the experience of flight; it opened the door to a new chapter in my life, one where the skies were not a limit but a playground.

The opportunity before me represented more than just another entry in my life's diary; it was my third chance at following a dream that had been simmering within me since childhood—the dream of soaring above the clouds as a pilot. After previous attempts had been thwarted by life's unpredictable winds, this time felt different, charged with a sense of promise and urgency.

January's frosty embrace was the backdrop against which this chapter of my journey would begin. I was instructed to arrive at the airport on a day that seemed custom-made for new beginnings, with the clear winter sky as my welcoming committee. My anticipation was mixed with a hint of nervousness as I approached the hangar, knowing that the decisions made today could steer the course of my entire future.

COULD HAVE BEEN; SHOULD HAVE BEEN; HERE I AM

Tony, my assigned instructor, was the personification of experience and encouragement, hailing from Ireland with a personality as inviting as the rolling green hills of his homeland. His approach to teaching was anchored in simplicity and depth, emphasizing the sacred trinity of flying skills: aviate, navigate, and communicate. Tony explained that in the air, as in life, priorities matter, especially in moments of emergency crisis. "Aviate" stood for the art of controlling the aircraft, the fundamental task without which all else becomes moot. "Navigate" was the strategy, the plotting of one's course through the vast skies. Lastly, "communicate" represented the essential need to maintain contact with the outside world, ensuring safety through cooperation and clarity.

Our first flight together was not about dazzling aerial stunts or venturing into distant horizons but about laying the foundational stones of these three principles. Tony assured me that while today we would only scratch the surface, the path to mastery was a journey we would take together, step by step, flight by flight. With every maneuver and every piece of advice, I felt my childhood dreams intertwining with the tangible reality of the cockpit, the controls slowly becoming extensions of my own aspirations.

This introductory flight was more than just a lesson; it was a bridge between the person I had been and the pilot I aspired to become. Under Tony's guidance, I began to understand that flying, much like life, is an endless learning curve, where each challenge is a doorway to new heights and insights. As we glided back to earth, I knew that no matter how vast the sky, the journey would always lead me to discover more about the world and about myself.

We started our session with a discussion on the fundamental physics of flight, delving into how various forces act upon the aircraft and how the controls can be used to manage these forces effectively. Tony illustrated these principles with simple yet vivid examples, ensuring I understood how each movement of the controls would impact the airplane's behavior in the air. Following the theoretical part, we transitioned to a hands-on experience with a thorough pre-flight inspection of the aircraft. This critical step was not just about following a checklist; it was about engaging with the airplane, understanding its parts, and respecting its limits. Tony guided me through each element of the inspection, from the tip of the propeller to the end of the tail, teaching me to look for signs of wear, damage, or any irregularities that could compromise safety.

He stressed the importance of this preflight ritual, emphasizing that being meticulous on the ground can prevent dire situations in the air. He pointed out that finding issues like empty fuel tanks, oil leaks, or mechanical faults while still on the ground was far preferable to encountering them midflight. Tony's thoroughness and attention to detail highlighted the critical balance between trust in the machinery and the constant vigilance required for safe flight. The lesson was clear; preparation and precaution are as integral to flying as the act itself. By taking the time to inspect the aircraft meticulously before taking off, we not only ensure our safety but also deepen our connection and understanding of the machine that allows us to touch the skies. This hands-on approach instilled in me a sense of responsibility and respect for the complexities of aviation, laying a solid foundation for the many flights ahead.

After the thorough preflight check confirmed that every aspect of the aircraft was functioning correctly, Tony and I secured ourselves into the cockpit, adjusting our harnesses for a snug fit, ensuring our safety and comfort for the journey ahead. The cockpit, with its array of instruments and controls, was a hub of potential waiting to be unleashed. We initiated the engine start-up, a process met with the hum of the engine coming to life, a testament to the machine's readiness and our impending ascent.

With the engine running smoothly, we proceeded to taxi toward the active runway. This phase was not merely a transfer from point A to point B; it was an integral part of our preflight process, allowing us to feel the aircraft's response to our inputs and to spot any potential issues on the ground, all guided by the methodical progression through our detailed checklist. The act of taxiing, with its precise movements and attention to detail, prepared us mentally and physically for the flight. As we approached the runway, a final series of checks were performed to ensure that all systems were go. With a mutual nod of readiness, I reached for the radio and communicated our intentions to take off, ensuring that any nearby aircraft were informed of our intentions. This step, critical for ensuring safety and coordination, was executed with clarity and confidence.

Then came the moment of truth. With the runway clear and our aircraft primed, we gradually increased the throttle, feeling the engine's power translate into forward momentum. The runway lights zipped by faster and faster as the aircraft gathered speed, a physical manifestation of our rising adrenaline and anticipation. The moment the wheels relinquished their grip on the tarmac, our transition from terrestrial beings to aviators was complete. We were no longer bound by the constraints of the ground as we lifted off into the open sky, embarking on a journey that was as much about discovery in the air as it was about rediscovering ourselves.

As we ventured away from the immediate surroundings of the airport, Tony introduced me to the foundational dead-reckoning techniques. He emphasized the importance of always being aware of our position relative to the airport, a key aspect of our navigation duty. This skill, though basic, was crucial for understanding and maintaining our course.

Once we reached our predetermined altitude of three thousand feet, Tony transitioned the lesson to the practical aspects of flying. He began by explaining and demonstrating basic maneuvering techniques essential for any pilot to master. The first task he introduced was holding a steady course, a fundamental skill that involves maintaining a constant heading, which is crucial for navigating between points. Next, Tony demonstrated coordinated turns, a maneuver that requires simultaneous use of the ailerons and rudder to ensure the aircraft turns smoothly without slipping or skidding. He emphasized the importance of balance and timing, guiding me through the nuances of executing such turns with precision. We then focused on maintaining level flight, a condition where the aircraft is neither climbing nor descending. Tony explained how to use the horizon and aircraft instruments to keep the plane steady, a critical skill for ensuring comfort and safety during flight.

Finally, we practiced ascents and descents, where Tony showed me how to change altitude while keeping the aircraft under control and stable. He taught me how to initiate a climb by increasing power and pitching up and then how to descend by reducing power and pitching down, all while monitoring speed and engine settings. Each of these maneuvers was a building block in understanding how to control the aircraft effectively. Tony's guidance through these fundamental procedures was not only about learning to fly but also about understanding the behavior of the aircraft in response to pilot inputs and external conditions.

The concluding segment of our flight lesson centered on the intricate procedure of landing, which is arguably the most complex aspect of flying. Tony carefully guided me through the process, which involved configuring the aircraft correctly for the approach, ensuring clear and constant communication with the airport's traffic controllers, and achieving precise alignment with the runway for a safe touchdown. He made it clear that the measure of a successful landing is the safety and well-being of everyone on board. This initial flight, filled with learning and hands-on experience, was a remarkable milestone, truly initiating my journey into the vast and challenging world of aviation.

As we approached the airport runway, Tony guided the plane into the landing configuration with methodical precision, highlighting the necessity of exactitude in aviation. This phase underscored the serious nature of piloting; I understood that safely returning to the ground was a matter heavily reliant on adept skill and unwavering focus, as any deviation or oversight could lead to severe consequences. Our first and only landing of the day was performed with such smoothness and adherence to protocol, it could only be described as textbook perfect. In that exhilarating moment, the allure of flying fully enveloped me. I experienced an unparalleled bond with the aircraft, and a vivid, unshakable vision for my future emerged. I was meant to be an airline pilot. This inaugural flight transcended a mere instructional session; it was the definitive moment when I realized that flying was not just a dream but my true calling.

Within a span of two years, I had reached a significant milestone. I earned my private pilot's certificate. This achievement was the fruit of my dedication and passion for aviation. By the subsequent year, I had furthered my skills and qualifications by securing a multi-engine rating, a step that expanded my flying capabilities and opened new horizons. Progress didn't stop there; a few years on, I attained an instrument rating, which allowed me to fly under a wider range of conditions, and successfully completed my commercial written exam, marking my transition from an amateur to a professional mindset in aviation.

In an interesting twist of fate, I also acquired a twin-engine Piper Seneca during this period. This aircraft, which represented a significant personal and financial investment, somewhat ironically ended up being donated to my ex-wife and her lawyer a few years later, following life's unpredictable ebbs and flows.

Two decades after those early steps, I made another notable addition to my aviation journey by purchasing a Beech Bonanza A36. This aircraft, known for its reliability and performance, reignited my passion for flying and allowed me to continue enjoying the skies for many additional years, reinforcing my lifelong dedication to aviation.

So did I ever fulfill the dream of becoming an airline pilot? The answer is no, I did not. Despite possessing the potential and the necessary qualifications, life took me along a different pathway, and that specific aspiration never materialized for me.

An Electronics Engineer

As a young child, I found myself captivated by the enigmatic concept known as the "black box." This term sparked a deep curiosity within me, leaving me yearning to uncover the secrets held by these mysterious devices. I wondered about their inner workings, the principles that governed their operation, and the minds behind their creation. In my youthful interpretation, the term "black box" extended beyond its conventional aviation connotation to encompass any electronic device that played a role in human life and required electricity to function.

This broad definition included devices as simple as a light switch, which offered the straightforward function of turning devices on and off, to more intricate apparatuses like radios or televisions. Despite the varying levels of complexity, I recognized that all these devices shared a crucial commonality: they were powered by electricity. In the following sections, let me share the insights and understanding I garnered about electricity from the innocent and exploratory perspective of a young boy.

My earliest notable experience with electricity traces back to when I was around three years old, during the Christmas season. My mother had adorned each window of our apartment with a single white electric candlestick. These decorations lacked on-off switches, so she would activate or deactivate them by manually tightening or loosening the bulbs, serving as makeshift switches. She believed these to be secure decorations, not foreseeing the curious actions of her toddler son.

One day, my sister Carol, who was six at the time, unscrewed one of the candle bulbs and persuaded me to place my index finger into the now-vacant socket. Naively trusting her, I did as she suggested and experienced an unforgettable shock. It was my initial confrontation with electrocution, and I was entirely unaware of the potential dangers involved. Questions flooded my mind: could this incident make me ill, lead to death, or, perhaps worst of all, result in a stern reprimand from our parents? Despite the alarming experience, my sister consoled me with her laughter, assuring me that there was no need for worry. Ultimately, she was right; everything turned out to be fine.

Nonetheless, this shocking event sparked a deep and enduring fascination within me regarding the enigmas of electricity. I began to see it as a "black box" filled with mysteries waiting to be deciphered. This childhood incident inadvertently set me on a path filled with curiosity and a desire to explore and understand the intricacies of electrical phenomena.

Curiosity is an innate and powerful force that permeates the essence of all living beings. It is my belief that the learning process for every creature, from the smallest insect to the most intelligent humans, is fundamentally propelled by curiosity. This inquisitive nature often leads to a methodology of learning that involves experimenting through trial and error. Take, for instance, the illustrative scenario where an individual faces the challenge of inserting their finger into an electrical socket, only to be met with a sharp, immediate physical shock. The outcome from such a risky experiment? An unforgettable lesson has been learned: never to insert a finger into a light bulb socket again. I hope my sister doesn't give me a kite and convince me to fly it during an electrical storm.

This incident begs the question: how much knowledge about the "black box" of electricity is necessary to satisfy one's curiosity? The response to this query, I propose, is not universal but rather subjective, varying greatly with the maturity and experience of the individual. In the context of my own experience with electrocution at the tender age of three, my brain's development was in its very early stages, not yet capable of fully processing or understanding the gravity of the event. As a result, my initial curiosity about the dangers and mechanics of electricity was temporarily quelled. However, this was not the end of my journey with curiosity. As I grew older and my mental faculties developed, my interest evolved. It shifted from a mere focus on the dangers of electricity to a broader and more profound fascination with its capabilities, especially in the intriguing realm of radio technology. This transition reflects the dynamic nature of curiosity as it grows and changes with our understanding and life experiences.

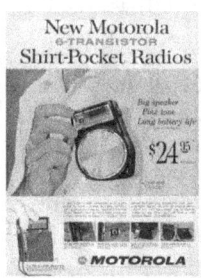

During the early 1960s, the Motorola radio company found itself leading a technological revolution with the introduction of some of the earliest pocket-size transistor radios that were made accessible to the general public. These cutting-edge devices represented significant advancements, standing in sharp contrast to the previous generation's bulky, cumbersome, battery-consuming, and heat-generating portable tube radios. The innovative design of these new transistor radios meant that they could be effortlessly carried around, fitting snugly into a shirt pocket, thus revolutionizing the way people listened to music and news on the go.

These pocket-size wonders typically came equipped with a single earphone, allowing for private listening experiences without disturbing others. Additionally, a distinctive feature of these radios was the inclusion of a kickstand on the rear of the device. This clever addition allowed the radio to be positioned upright on a flat surface, making it possible for a small group to listen to the broadcasts together through the compact yet effective two-inch speaker. Although these pioneering devices initially supported only the AM band, this limitation did not detract from their appeal as the AM band was predominantly used for general broadcasts and was the primary source of news, entertainment, and music for many listeners during all times.

The introduction of these transistor radios marked a significant leap forward in portable technology, providing unprecedented convenience and mobility in radio listening, reflecting Motorola's role in propelling the portable electronics revolution. What truly distinguished these radios and placed them at the forefront of the technological frontier was their incorporation of transistor technology, which was considered a groundbreaking innovation during that era. Advertisements boasted the number of transistors each radio contained, a tactic that turned the transistor count into a notable feature despite its enigmatic nature to the average consumer. The radios themselves also flaunted this detail, proudly displaying the number of transistors as a badge of advanced technology and quality.

To most people, the specifics of why the transistor count was important remained a mystery. The technical aspects of how transistors improved radio performance—such as their contribution to reducing size, enhancing sound quality, and increasing reliability—were beyond the understanding of the typical user. Despite this lack of comprehension, there was a widespread and somewhat paradoxical fascination with acquiring models boasting higher transistor counts. Consumers, influenced by marketing and the allure of owning a piece of cutting-edge technology, were naturally drawn to these higher-numbered models, equating more transistors with superior functionality and status even without grasping the technical rationale behind it. This phenomenon reflected a broader trend in consumer behavior where advancements in technology, even if not fully understood, were coveted for the perceived benefits and prestige they brought. The transistor count became a simple, quantifiable measure of a radio's sophistication and potential performance, making it an easy selling point for manufacturers despite the general public's unclear understanding of the technology's intricacies. This focus on transistor numbers in marketing strategies not only fueled sales but also spurred an increased interest in portable electronics, setting the stage for future innovations in consumer technology.

This phenomenon intrigued me greatly, to the point that it became a persistent question in my mind. The collective obsession over higher transistor counts in radios, without a clear understanding of its significance, led me to seek explanations from various adults around me, including my father. However, their responses were invariably the same: "I don't know." This uniform lack of clarity and understanding among the adults in my life only deepened the mystery and heightened my curiosity. Even when I turned to the family encyclopedias, which I hoped would shed light on this technological enigma, I was met with disappointment. The volumes, brimming with knowledge on countless other subjects, offered no clear answers regarding the importance of transistor count in radios. This void of information did not deter me; instead, it acted as a catalyst, propelling my desire to delve deeper into the matter.

Fueled by an insatiable thirst for understanding, I became more determined than ever to uncover the truth behind the transistor count's significance. This quest for knowledge led me on a journey of self-education and discovery, pushing me to seek out more specialized books, magazines, and eventually experts who could demystify the technology for me. My initial bewilderment and the lack of readily available explanations only served to make the quest more enticing and the eventual understanding more rewarding.

It wasn't until several years later, once my comprehension of basic electronic circuitry had become more sophisticated, that I truly began to understand the critical importance of the transistor phenomenon. This enlightening journey served to underscore a pivotal lesson about the intrinsic nature of brain maturity and its profound impact on our ability to grasp intricate concepts. It starkly highlighted how our level of understanding is intricately bound not only by the developmental stage of our brain but also equally by the availability and accessibility of information. The Motorola six-transistor AM radio emerged as my inaugural "black box," a compelling mystery that I was resolutely determined to solve. This represented the commencement of what would become a lifelong journey, a dedicated quest to unravel and decode the hidden secrets of electronics enclosed within its unassuming plastic casing.

Embarking on this newfound mission, I set my sights on mastering the field of electronics, harboring the ambition to one day be the innovator behind these "black boxes." The idea of designing and creating devices that could captivate and mystify others just as the transistor radio had done for me filled me with an unparalleled sense of purpose and excitement. Despite this clear vision for my future, the path forward was anything but clear. I was at a crossroads, unsure of where to start or how to obtain the requisite knowledge and skills needed to achieve my ambitions. Nevertheless, this uncertainty did not deter my determination; instead, it fueled my resolve. This pursuit had transformed into more than just a passing interest—it had become my new vocation, a calling that I felt compelled to follow. I knew that the journey would be long and fraught with challenges, but the prospect of unraveling the mysteries of electronics and contributing my own innovations to the world provided an irresistible allure.

With this resolve, I began to seek out resources, reaching for anything that could further my understanding and skills in electronics. I looked for books, joined clubs, and sought guidance from knowledgeable individuals, immersing myself in the subject with unwavering commitment. Each step, no matter how small, was a step closer to achieving my dream of becoming a creator of technological marvels, shaping the future one "black box" at a time.

Looking back on my formative years, the allure of electronic devices to my youthful curiosity becomes increasingly clear. Gadgets like televisions, radios, and electric motors were more than mere objects; they represented enigmatic forms of artificial life to me. In my youthful perception, electricity acted akin to a vital force for these mysterious "black boxes"—though devoid of life in the traditional sense associated with humans or animals, they possessed the remarkable ability to perform various useful tasks. These ranged from emitting sounds and projecting images to executing physical labor. Intriguingly, these devices could be "awakened" from a state of inactivity, springing to life to perform their designated roles, and then "returned to rest" once their purpose was served, all without the need for constant attention or maintenance. This nuanced perspective on electronics spurred a deep-seated intrigue and respect for their capabilities, further deepening my fascination and driving my ambition to understand and eventually contribute to the field of electronics.

This fascinating concept of artificial life, while intriguing, inherently came with its distinct limitations. While electronic devices did not resist being turned off and could be reactivated time and again, they lacked the capability for self-repair. Any malfunction or failure within their components could leave them partially or entirely nonfunctional for an indefinite period. This stands in stark contrast to living organisms, which not only can produce sound, create visual signals, and perform physical tasks but also possess the remarkable ability to heal and recover from injuries. However, living beings cannot be completely powered down and restarted like machines; for them, an absolute shutdown, akin to death, is final and irreversible. Unlike the constructs of technology, living entities actively resist complete cessation and instinctively navigate away from threats, aiming to preserve their existence. This intrinsic drive, the inherent will to live, starkly sets living beings apart from the man-made marvels of technology, highlighting the profound differences between organic life and its artificial counterparts.

My fascination with electronic devices not only persisted but also deepened as I transitioned from my childhood into my adolescence. This stage of life became a crucial turning point for me, a time when I started to unlock the secrets of the enigmatic "black box" that had captivated my imagination for so long. My mind, now more mature and ready, was eager to absorb the principles of electronic theory. However, I encountered a significant obstacle; I found myself in a state of isolation with this interest. None of my immediate social circle, including my parents, relatives, or close friends, shared my passion or held any discernible knowledge about electronics or circuitry. This isolation created a tangible barrier to my burgeoning aspirations in the field of electronics.

This sense of isolation remained until the day I encountered Paul, a neighbor who was pursuing his studies in electronics at a local college. Paul was four years my senior, and he quickly assumed the role of an elder brother figure in my life. He provided much-needed guidance and mentorship, bridging the gap between my solitary interest and the communal knowledge necessary for advancement. Through Paul, a whole new realm of possibilities in the field of electronics unfolded before me, significantly altering the trajectory of my educational and professional pursuits.

One of the most transformative and enlightening aspects of my relationship with Paul was the hands-on, real-time exposure to the world of electronics that he provided while he was immersed in his college education. Until meeting him, my understanding of success and the pathway to a promising future had been somewhat skewed, heavily influenced by predetermined societal roles. I had harbored the belief that one's future was largely shaped by one's birthright. For instance, I assumed that children born into families of doctors or lawyers were naturally destined to follow in their parents' professional footsteps, continuing the family legacy in a sort of predetermined professional lineage. This belief was deeply rooted in the notion that early exposure to a specific profession or field of study naturally predisposes children to gravitate toward and excel in similar careers as they grow older.

Paul's mentorship fundamentally disrupted and reshaped this preconceived notion for me, demonstrating that targeted exposure and effective guidance have the power to set someone on an entirely new path, irrespective of their initial circumstances or familial background. His influence went beyond mere instruction; it was instrumental in stoking the flames of my burgeoning passion for electronics, propelling me toward a commitment to pursue technical training and higher education in this exciting field. This significant turning point in my life underscored a valuable lesson. While early exposure and the professions of one's family can indeed shape an individual's future to a certain extent, alternative pathways, such as mentorships and personal interests, can equally lead to equally rewarding careers and substantial personal growth.

The disparity in wealth was a striking and unavoidable aspect of life growing up in Massachusetts, creating stark distinctions among the various social groups. This division of wealth was not only recognized but widely accepted, effectively categorizing individuals into separate social echelons within the same community. It drew a line between those who were fortunate and those who aspired to attain similar fortune. In my high school, this divide was evident in the future paths chosen by my peers. Students from affluent families typically pursued higher education in prestigious Ivy League colleges like Harvard or Yale, a route perceived as a natural extension of their privileged upbringing. In contrast, those from middle- to lower-income backgrounds often opted for more accessible educational paths such as state junior colleges and trade schools, or they entered the workforce directly upon graduation.

Interestingly, possessing significant wealth did not necessarily guarantee the personal or professional success of the children from these well-to-do families. In fact, many individuals from privileged backgrounds struggled with issues such as drug addiction, alcohol abuse, criminal activities, and general rebellion against societal norms. This phenomenon underscored a lesson within my community. There was a widely held belief that personal achievement and character built through hard work and perseverance held more intrinsic value than success or status that was simply inherited or handed over without effort. This perspective influenced my understanding of success, reinforcing the idea that true accomplishment stems from one's own efforts and achievements rather than from the advantages of one's birth.

In the midst of these observations about wealth and success, I encountered Paul, who would soon become a pivotal figure in my life. Paul hailed from a socioeconomic background distinctly different from the affluence displayed by many families in our community.

Far from being surrounded by luxury, Paul's family was entrenched in financial struggle, a situation exacerbated by the premature death of his father at the age of thirty-eight. This tragic event left his widow and four sons, including Paul, in a state of economic uncertainty and emotional turmoil.

Their living conditions were a testament to their financial difficulties. Unlike the spacious and lavishly furnished homes of the more affluent, Paul's family residence was more akin to a cluttered workshop than a conventional home. It was a space where the boundaries between living areas and workspaces blurred, with every available nook crammed with parts and pieces of electronic and musical equipment. This may have seemed chaotic to an outsider, but for Paul, it was a familiar environment brimming with potential. Despite the apparent disorder, he possessed an extraordinary knack for navigating this labyrinth of components. He knew the history and precise location of each item, imbuing the clutter with a sense of order and purpose. This unique setting, far removed from the opulence and ease observed in wealthier households, contributed significantly to Paul's resilience, ingenuity, and profound understanding of electronics and mechanics.

Paul's memory was nothing short of exceptional; it was as if he had a mental catalog of every component, tool, and project he had ever encountered. He never seemed to need to jot down numbers or lists, retaining even the most intricate details with astonishing ease. This remarkable trait made me regard him not just as unusually gifted but also as bordering on the genius level despite his apparent lack of polish in social settings. His distinct combination of brilliance, coupled with his unconventional background, offered me a new lens through which to view life and the definitions of success, starkly challenging the conventional narratives that often link success solely to wealth and privilege.

Through Paul, I came to realize that lessons of substantial value and profound inspiration could emerge from the most unexpected of sources. It was a revelation that not only defied the status quo but also enriched my understanding of the world. This insight set the foundation for a journey into the realm of electronics and beyond—a path I could scarcely have envisioned prior to our meeting.

Paul's influence was a testament to the idea that true wisdom and mentorship can be found in places overlooked by a society preoccupied with material success and traditional indicators of achievement.

Paul's noticeable social awkwardness seemed to be a by-product of his upbringing and environment, which were heavily male-dominated. Growing up without the presence of sisters or female cousins and attending an all-boys Catholic school from first grade all the way through to the twelfth grade meant that his interactions with the opposite sex were exceedingly limited. This paucity of early-life experiences with women rendered social engagements with them particularly daunting for Paul. Consequently, he naturally veered toward social circles and activities that were predominantly male, such as math and chess clubs, environments in which he felt a greater sense of comfort and belonging because of their familiarity and his shared interests with other members.

In contrast to Paul, my own social experiences at the age of fourteen were markedly different. I found myself increasingly drawn to the company of female peers, actively seeking out their presence and conversation. This divergence in our social inclinations and experiences only highlighted the variety of backgrounds and personalities within our shared environment, showcasing the different ways individuals adapt to their social surroundings based on their upbringing and personal comfort zones.

Our burgeoning friendship evolved into a unique reciprocal teaching arrangement wherein we each addressed the other's "black box" mysteries. Paul, with his deep understanding and passion for electronics, guided me through the complexities of circuits, components, and the principles that make them work. In return, I shared with him my own experiences and strategies for interacting with girls, a social domain he found perplexing and challenging. This exchange, while perhaps unconventional, proved to be remarkably effective, enabling both of us to expand our respective areas of expertise and comfort. However, while the insights and personal growth facilitated by my relationship with Paul were invaluable, it is time to pivot back to my personal narrative, specifically my evolving journey within the realm of electronics. This field, once a vast and impenetrable "black box" of mysteries, began to unfold before me with increasing clarity guided by the foundational knowledge Paul provided. My fascination with electronics continued to grow, shaping my ambitions and directing my future educational and career paths.

While pursuing my college degree in chemistry, my curiosity and passion for electronics did not wane. Instead, I took proactive steps to further my knowledge in this area by enrolling in additional courses on basic electronic theory, circuit design, and practical repair techniques. Opting for these classes as electives was a deliberate choice, driven by my desire to build a robust foundational understanding of electronics. I anticipated that the skills and knowledge acquired from these courses could prove to be invaluable later in my professional and personal life. This decision to broaden my educational scope was motivated by more than just a casual interest; it was a strategic move, acknowledging the potential overlap between chemical principles and electronic applications. My intuition regarding the usefulness of this interdisciplinary approach eventually proved to be correct as the skills and knowledge I acquired from these electronic courses enriched my understanding and capabilities in the field of chemistry, illustrating the interconnectedness of these disciplines.

During the initial phase of my college years, my life was filled with a whirlwind of personal responsibilities and commitments. Having entered the bonds of marriage, I found myself grappling with the financial responsibilities of maintaining an apartment while simultaneously striving to support my family. To make ends meet and ensure the continuation of my academic pursuits, I juggled three different jobs alongside my college coursework. This period was marked by a relentless pursuit of balancing my educational goals with the demands of my personal life.

However, as I was nearing the completion of my fourth year of study in the mid-'70s, poised to enter the final fifth year required to obtain my chemistry degree, the nation began to experience significant political and economic upheaval. The election of Jimmy Carter as president marked the beginning of a period characterized by substantial challenges. The country faced an energy crisis, manifesting in scarce and costly gasoline, which in turn affected everyday life and the broader economy. Additionally, the nation was gripped by increasing job losses, contributing to a growing sense of instability and uncertainty. To compound these issues, skyrocketing interest rates led to an unprecedented surge in credit card debt, affecting countless individuals and families, plunging many into financial distress.

These tumultuous conditions had a profound impact on the fabric of American society and, by extension, on my own life and future prospects. The shifting landscape forced me to reevaluate my priorities and strategies for achieving my academic and career goals amid a time of widespread uncertainty and change.

The financial strain and market instability during this period left me with no choice but to temporarily halt my education and seek full-time employment to support my family and stabilize our economic situation. Amid this search for a viable solution, I discovered an opening at a small yet renowned electronics firm. This company specialized in the production of power supplies integral to telephone systems, a niche but crucial market. The devices they crafted were considered at the forefront of technology at the time, highly coveted by telecommunication companies across the country because of their reliability and advanced features.

Fortunately, this challenging time was mitigated somewhat by the connections I had nurtured. A good friend of mine, who was already employed at the electronics firm, became aware of my situation and my quest for employment. Recognizing the potential fit between my skills and the company's needs, he facilitated an opportunity for me by arranging an interview for me for the position of an electronic test technician. This chance was a glimmer of hope amid the economic turmoil and represented a crucial turning point, aligning my personal needs with professional opportunities and allowing me to apply the knowledge I had accrued from my elective courses in electronics.

I found myself immensely grateful for the decision to take electronic courses as electives during my college years. The comprehensive knowledge and practical skills I had acquired from these classes proved to be invaluable. When faced with the company's entrance examination, a test designed to assess the technical abilities of potential employees, I found that the questions and problems presented were familiar territory for me, thanks to my educational background in electronics. This familiarity made the examination seem less daunting and more straightforward than it might have otherwise been, enabling me to perform with a level of confidence and proficiency that ultimately helped me secure the job with relative ease.

Embarking on this new role brought with it a profound sense of fulfillment and a newfound clarity in my professional life. It was as if all the disparate pieces of my past experiences and education were finally coalescing into a clear path forward. In this position, not only was I able to apply and expand upon the electronic principles I had learned, but I also felt a strong sense of purpose and engagement that I had not fully experienced before. This transition marked a significant moment in my life. I was no longer just struggling to survive and support my family amid economic hardship; I was also pursuing a career that resonated with my deepest interests and aspirations. I was confident that I had discovered my true calling in life, cementing my passion for electronics and setting the stage for future advancements and opportunities in the field.

The new job was located thirty miles away from my apartment, translating into an hour-long commute each way under typical traffic conditions. Initially, before accepting the position, I hadn't fully accounted for the implications of such a lengthy travel time and the associated cost of gasoline, especially considering the economic challenges of the era. The daily journey seemed manageable in theory, but the practical realities of the commute began to weigh on me as I settled into the routine. However, about a month into the job, I began to adapt to the new circumstances. I learned the art of ride-sharing with three other employees who lived in my vicinity and worked similar hours. This arrangement proved to be a practical solution to several problems. Not only did it help in significantly reducing commuting expenses by splitting the cost of gasoline among us, but it also offered a sense of camaraderie and mutual support. Moreover, ride-sharing served as a small but meaningful way to mitigate the stress of the daily drive and provided an opportunity for professional networking and personal connection with colleagues. This newfound commuting strategy represented a small but significant adjustment in my daily routine, allowing me to maintain my position and continue progressing in my new career path without being overly burdened by the logistics of transportation.

Despite the inconvenience posed by the lengthy commute, the trade-offs associated with the job were undoubtedly worthwhile. The position offered more than just employment; it provided a platform for deep professional satisfaction and growth. I found immense enjoyment in the day-to-day responsibilities and challenges that came with the role, which far outweighed the drawbacks of travel. The job was not just a means to an end but also an engaging and enriching experience that allowed me to apply and extend my knowledge in the field of electronics. The hands-on learning and opportunities for skill development available through this position were invaluable. Every day presented new challenges and learning opportunities, reinforcing the practical applications of the concepts I had studied in my elective courses and expanding my understanding of electronics in real-world settings. This alignment between my job and my personal interests in electronics turned the position into a source of joy and professional fulfillment.

This period of my life highlighted the importance of flexibility and adaptability in the face of new and potentially challenging situations. It taught me to find balance and seek out the positive aspects of each circumstance, emphasizing the value of continuous professional growth and learning. The experience served as a reminder that embracing change and finding satisfaction in the process of skill acquisition and application can lead to a rewarding and fulfilling career path.

At the company, there was a distinguished engineer named O'Brien who had played a pivotal role in the development and innovation of many of the company's critical circuits. A foundational member of the organization, he was commemorating his thirty-fifth anniversary and was on the cusp of retirement. With merely two years remaining before his planned departure, O'Brien began to pivot his attention toward concluding outstanding projects and, importantly, mentoring a successor to inherit and continue his extensive body of work.

For reasons that were initially unclear to me, O'Brien took a particular interest in my professional growth and capabilities. He opted to invest his time and knowledge into my development, a decision that would significantly alter the trajectory of my career. Under his guidance, I was exposed to intricate aspects of circuit design and development, areas that went far beyond my initial role within the company.

This intense mentorship and hands-on training unexpectedly led to my rapid advancement within the company. Just six months after starting my job, I was promoted from an electronic test technician to a junior engineer and officially became O'Brien's assistant. This advancement was not just a step up in terms of title and responsibility but also a substantial leap in my understanding and involvement in the field of electronics. O'Brien's dedication to my growth not only enhanced my skills and knowledge but also entrusted me with the significant responsibility of continuing his legacy within the company. This unexpected turn of events in my professional life underscored the importance of mentorship and the profound impact it can have on an individual's career and personal development.

The first project I undertook under O'Brien's meticulous guidance was not only complex and specialized but also of critical importance to the industry at large. It involved a segment of technology that was central to the company's success and innovation strategy. Within the company, only a select group of engineers possessed the comprehensive understanding of the circuitry involved and the technical prowess necessary to undertake a redesign of such a crucial device. Our team, led by O'Brien and with me as his direct assistant, was charged with the formidable task of activating three new unit designs, a process that entailed not only technical skill but also a keen understanding of the industry's needs and future directions.

We were responsible for overseeing the initial activation of these units, ensuring that every aspect of the designs met the stringent standards required for such pivotal components in our field.

Moreover, we were tasked with expediting the production process to meet growing market demands and internal deadlines. Despite the challenges and high expectations, the project progressed smoothly under our combined efforts.

Thanks to the expertise and leadership of O'Brien, coupled with the hard work and dedication of the entire team, we successfully transitioned the new unit designs to production within a year. This achievement was not just a testament to our collective technical abilities but also marked a significant milestone in my professional development. It was a project that demonstrated my capacity to handle complex tasks and contributed substantially to my growing reputation within the company and the industry. This success under O'Brien's mentorship was a defining moment in my career, solidifying my position as a junior engineer and paving the way for future opportunities and challenges.

Following the successful completion of this initial project, my contributions were recognized, and I was invited to participate in another significant project within the company. This opportunity served to reinforce my growing belief that I was not only making substantial strides in the electronics field but also carving out a definitive niche for myself. The satisfaction and pride I felt in these achievements were profound; what once seemed like distant dreams were steadily materializing into reality. My career in electronics, once a fledgling aspiration, was blossoming, affirming my dedication and passion for the field.

However, just as I was becoming comfortable in my trajectory and the future seemed predictably bright, an unexpected development occurred that prompted me to reassess my path. I received a phone call from the Borden Chemical Corporation, a company renowned in a completely different sector than my current focus. This call was unforeseen and set the stage for a potential shift in my career trajectory, challenging the direction I had been so diligently working toward in the electronics industry. This unexpected opportunity prompted a mix of emotions and considerations as I contemplated the implications it could have on my established path and the future I had envisioned in the realm of electronics.

ERIC KOSLOWSKI

A PVC Research and Development Chemist

Just prior to my commitment to the role of electronic technician at the electronics firm, in a broad effort to secure employment, I had dispatched my résumé to various potential employers throughout the local area, one of which was Borden Chemical. This company, known for its production of polyvinyl chloride (PVC), operated one of its key production plants in my hometown. They were in search of a candidate to fill a position in their PVC research and development department, specifically aimed at a chemist role, and my qualifications had caught their attention.

The prospect of working as a chemist held a special place in my heart as it aligned with one of my earliest career aspirations. By this time, I had nearly completed my college education in chemistry, having invested three and a half years toward my degree with just one remaining. Considering my substantial progress and the alignment of this opportunity with my original career goals, I reasoned that attending the interview could be beneficial. I saw it as a no-lose situation; at worst, I would gain interview experience, and at best, a potential avenue in my initial field of study might open up. Besides, I was already employed in a stable, well-paying job that seemed to promise ample opportunities for career advancement in the electronics sector. Thus, with a mix of curiosity and a sense of opportunity, I scheduled the interview for the upcoming week, arranging to meet with Borden Chemical's human resources officer. This decision to explore an alternative yet familiar career path in chemistry, while still entrenched in the electronics field, highlighted my open-minded approach to my professional journey, embracing opportunities to explore diverse avenues in alignment with my educational background and personal interests.

Taking the morning off for the Borden interview was shaping up to be a formidable challenge. The company was deeply entrenched in a critical phase of production, necessitating the presence of every single employee, and they were notoriously strict about granting time off for reasons they deemed nonessential—interviewing with other companies being at the top of their list. I was acutely aware that I needed to concoct a convincing, legitimate-sounding excuse to evade work for the day.

With trepidation and a heavy sense of guilt, I approached my boss, Mr. John Bowens, to request the day off. I resorted to invoking the classic "family emergency" guise: "My grandmother has passed away, and I must attend her funeral." As I said this, I reminded myself of the unspoken rule: the "grandmother excuse" could feasibly be used only twice with each employer, and here I was, burning through one of those precious allowances. He responded with heartfelt condolences, and I expressed my gratitude for his empathy and understanding all the while burdened by the knowledge of my deceit and the fear that karma might exact retribution for my dishonesty in the future. *Sorry, Mr. Bowens, I truly hope you can understand and, in time, forgive me for this charade*, I thought remorsefully. He was genuinely a decent man, and it pained me to deceive him in such a manner. This job interview with Borden had to be worth the ethical compromise—I was resolved that I couldn't bring myself to fabricate another lie to my boss, who had shown nothing but kindness and generosity toward me.

The following day dawned with a sense of anticipation. I had meticulously arranged a nine o'clock interview, which was set to commence with the human resources department before transitioning to a crucial session with the research and development laboratory's director, Dr. Goldstein. Eager. Determined, I arrived at Borden's premises around eight thirty in the morning and immediately proceeded to the human resources department, strategically located on the executive office building's second floor.

The first individual to extend a greeting was the assistant HR director, a face strikingly familiar to me. She introduced herself as Ms. Knight, igniting a flash of recognition in my mind as I remembered her from my high school days as the typing teacher who had significantly honed my speed-typing skills during my senior year. Despite the passage of years, memories of her preferential treatment in class, which often made me feel somewhat favored, like a teacher's pet, lingered vividly in my mind. This unexpected reunion seemed like it might inadvertently sway my interview prospects in a favorable direction—and indeed, it did.

Ms. Knight disclosed that there was a vacancy in the research and development department for a chemist position. As she sifted through the slew of current applications, she stumbled upon mine. Her recollection of our past interaction propelled my application to a prominent position in the evaluation stack—a twist of fate I hadn't dared to hope for. During her reference checks, one name notably stood out, further fortifying my standing—Richard Caron. Serving as the executive maintenance supervisor for the Borden site for over two decades, Richard was not just a professional contact but family; his mother was my aunt. Although his endorsement was lukewarm at best—"I don't really know him that well, but he seems okay, I guess"—it was nonetheless a familial nod that worked in my favor. A silent thank-you formed in my mind for cousin Richard's nonchalant yet effective recommendation.

Now with the serendipitous encounters and familial ties subtly working to my advantage, all that remained was to confidently present myself to the laboratory director, Dr. Goldstein, and hope my credentials and demeanor would clinch the role for me.

After our conversation, Ms. Knight kindly guided me toward the research and development sector, specifically directing me to building number 10, which was distinctly situated beyond the bustling confines of the production plant. She elaborated that my initial engagement would be with Mr. Gene Duchesneau, a laboratory group leader urgently in search of a chemist to fill a gap within his team. Pending the outcome of this initial interview, a subsequent and conclusive discussion with Dr. Goldstein was scheduled.

The interactions unfolded in a positively unexpected manner. Mr. Duchesneau, with his profound knowledge and affable demeanor, made the interview process more of a scholarly dialogue than a grilling session. This not only eased my nerves but also allowed me to showcase my skills and passion for chemical research seamlessly. Following this encouraging encounter, the meeting with Dr. Goldstein proved to be equally promising. The exchange was intellectually stimulating, reinforcing my desire to become a part of their team.

Surprisingly, the culmination of these discussions was an immediate job offer for the position of an associate chemist. The role was intriguing, focusing on the development and refinement of experimental PVC formulas crucial in the production of innovative foam materials. Recognizing the complexity of transitioning from one job to another, they extended the courtesy of a week for me to deliberate and respond to their offer. This gesture was not only considerate but also reflective of the company's understanding and respect for its prospective employees.

There I was, at a pivotal moment, with a significant career opportunity laid out before me. It was a moment of reflection, contemplating the potential shifts in my professional trajectory and the implications of leaving a familiar position for uncharted territory. The decision I was about to make would undoubtedly shape my future in profound ways.

My current role at the electronics firm had been the realization of a childhood ambition, embodying my earliest aspirations to delve into the intricate world of electronics engineering. Yet the undeniable pull of my intellectual curiosity in chemistry was now steering me toward a divergent path, delineating a clear but challenging course ahead. Torn between the familiarity and comfort of my present job and the allure of embarking on a new scientific journey, I knew that a mere instinctive leap was not the approach I wanted to adopt for such a significant life decision.

Determined to approach this crossroads with thorough analysis and thoughtful consideration, I decided to create a structured comparison between the two options. I resolved to list out the pros and cons associated with each position, not just relying on emotional instinct but on a balanced evaluation of all factors involved. To facilitate this, I constructed a detailed table, akin to a weighted decision matrix, to systematically assess and compare the various attributes of each job opportunity.

This table was designed to include several categories, such as job responsibilities, growth opportunities, company culture, work-life balance, and salary, among others. For each category, I assigned a rating based on my knowledge, expectations, and priorities, hoping that this quantitative approach would illuminate the more logical and beneficial path for my career and personal development. The objective was to provide a clear visual representation of the comparative benefits and drawbacks of each position, thereby guiding me toward a decision that was not only emotionally satisfying but also aligned with my long-term professional and personal goals.

Attribute	Electronic Engineer	R&D Chemist
Position Status	5	8
College Credit	3	10
Company Stability	5	7
Growth Potential	10	10
Comfortability	6	2
Commute (Time)	2 hours	10 minutes
Income ($)	20K	30K
Future Potential	5	5
Career Calling	7	8
My Age (years)	24	24

Engaging with the comparison table I had meticulously prepared, I delved deep into each attribute, considering its relevance and impact on my ultimate decision. The factor that stood out most significantly was the investment I had made in my college education. My academic journey was heavily laden with chemistry courses, reflecting years of dedication and a substantial accumulation of credits in this field. In contrast, my experience in electronics, although deeply rooted in a childhood dream, was formally represented by just a handful of courses.

Another pivotal element that guided my decision-making process was the career-calling attribute. It became increasingly apparent that my inner voice, my genuine passion, was more aligned with the realm of chemistry than electronics. This realization was crucial; despite the comparative list containing elements of subjective reasoning, I understood the importance of staying true to myself. Honoring one's intuition and inner feelings is essential in carving out a fulfilling career path.

I acknowledged that many factors, such as salary potential, commute time, company stability, and future job market speculations, were inherently variable and, to some extent, unpredictable. These aspects might seem concrete and persuasive at a glance, but their transient nature implies that they could alter drastically because of unforeseen circumstances. I considered the wisdom in not overemphasizing these mutable factors as they could misleadingly direct one's career trajectory based on temporary conditions or unrealistic expectations.

For example, the lure of a significantly higher salary could be enticing, yet it's imperative to assess such offers critically. A salary considerably above the market average could lead to unrealistic job expectations and performance pressures, potentially setting the stage for dissatisfaction or failure. It's crucial for compensation to align realistically with the job role and one's experience level; if an offer seems too generous, it warrants a deeper examination.

After reflecting on these considerations, I found myself leaning more decisively toward embracing a future in chemistry. This decision was not made lightly but was the result of a thoughtful analysis, balancing both rational assessments and personal inclinations. It was a moment of acknowledging where my true professional interests lay, coupled with the realization of where my academic investments had been most significant.

Reflecting on the situation now, I can see that one of the real determinants in my decision-making process was my relatively young age of twenty-four. At this stage in life, there's an inherent leeway for experimentation and making errors, whether those are related to personal investments like purchasing a vehicle, deciding on housing, or choosing a career path. This period of youth is imbued with a certain degree of resilience and flexibility, permitting one to navigate through life's decisions with an understanding that not all choices are permanent and that mistakes can serve as valuable learning experiences.

After meticulously evaluating and comparing all the attributes laid out in my comparison table, I found myself at a crossroads, unable to make a definitive decision based solely on logic and facts. Therefore, in a moment that blended a touch of whimsy with my analytical process, I decided to leave part of my decision to chance. I flipped a coin: heads designated for electronics, my childhood dream, and tails for chemistry, my burgeoning academic and intellectual passion.

When the coin landed showing tails, the decision seemed almost serendipitous—it was to be a future in chemistry. Remember, at the tender age of twenty-four, life felt both overwhelming and wide-open with possibilities. While some might argue that leaving such a significant decision to the random flip of a coin was imprudent, I viewed it as a way to break through the deadlock of indecision, embracing the blend of fate and free will. With my youth as both a shield and a spear, I was ready to embark on this new chemical journey, armed with the knowledge that experiences, more than errors, shape our paths.

Within mere hours after reaching my decision, I took the decisive step of informing Borden Chemical of my acceptance of the associate chemist position, along with the terms of employment they had proposed. Their response was swift and affirmative, with instructions for me to report for work following a standard two-week notice period to my then-current employer. The wave of satisfaction that washed over me was profound; I was about to genuinely apply the skills that I had meticulously cultivated, diving into the realm that had long beckoned me with its intricate challenges and vast potential for discovery. This transition marked not just a new job but a thrilling new chapter in my professional life, a genuine career adventure.

Yet amid the excitement, a whisper of doubt threaded its way through my consciousness—was I truly ready for the magnitude of this challenge? It was a natural moment of introspection, a common crossroads where enthusiasm meets the reality of stepping into the unknown. This internal dialogue underscored the significant step I was about to take, transitioning from the familiar to the uncharted, from a long-held dream into tangible reality. It was a pivotal moment, filled with promise and a touch of apprehension, as I stood on the brink of what I hoped would be a fulfilling and illuminating journey in the field of chemistry.

Confronting the task of resigning from the electronics firm was laden with a sense of foreboding. This was an organization that had not only welcomed me despite my relatively novice status in the field of electronics but had also invested in my growth. They nurtured my potential and propelled me to professional heights I had scarcely envisioned achievable within such a condensed time frame. Moreover, the shadow of my recent deception—feigning a family emergency for the interview at Borden's—added a layer of guilt and complexity to the situation. My actions, born from a moment of immaturity, now cast a long shadow over what should have been a straightforward professional transition.

The internal turmoil I faced was akin to the emotional tumult of ending a relationship with someone who had been nothing but kind and supportive. The firm had been more than an employer; it was a mentor and a benefactor. Finding the courage to confront my supervisor, a person of immense kindness and understanding, was proving to be an arduous task. I yearned for a justifiable grievance or a fault on their part to make my departure easier, more logical—but no such reason existed. The truth was stark and unembellished; my decision to leave was motivated solely by a desire for a different career path, not out of dissatisfaction or mistreatment.

The inevitable moment arrived the following day. With rehearsed words heavy on my tongue, I approached my supervisor, this pillar of kindness and professionalism, to communicate my decision. It was a conversation I dreaded, not only because of the personal guilt I harbored but also because I was about to sever ties with an environment that had been nothing but nurturing. Yet acknowledging the necessity of this step for my personal and professional growth, I braced myself to deliver the news with as much grace and gratitude as I could muster.

My supervisor, John, was a veteran at the company, having dedicated many years to its growth and operational excellence. His role, particularly nuanced because of the small size of the organization, spanned an array of duties that typically would have been divided among several individuals in a larger firm. John was not just a supervisor; he was the linchpin of the department, overseeing human resources, conducting employee training, managing benefits, handling promotions, and addressing workplace safety issues. His extensive knowledge and experience in electronics and our specific product lines made him an invaluable asset to the team and the company at large.

John's expertise extended beyond just administrative tasks; he was a master in the field of electronics, deeply familiar with every product device that our company developed and manufactured. His troubleshooting skills were legendary within the company walls. No matter how complex the problem, John could always be counted on to provide a timely and effective solution. His ability to navigate and resolve issues, no matter how daunting, had saved our department from countless potential setbacks.

My respect and admiration for John were profound. He was not only a mentor but also a guiding force whose positive influence had a significant impact on my professional development. His balanced approach to leadership, combining wisdom, empathy, and technical prowess, made him a role model to many, including me. Facing him with the news of my resignation was a daunting task precisely because of the high regard in which I held him and the reciprocal trust and respect that had developed between us over time.

COULD HAVE BEEN; SHOULD HAVE BEEN; HERE I AM

When the moment arrived to deliver my two-week notice to John, the complexity of emotions was palpable. As I articulated my decision, I observed a fleeting expression of disappointment shadow his otherwise warm and amiable face. It was a subtle change, but it spoke volumes, reflecting his genuine care and investment in his team members. In that instant, I felt the weight of my decision not just as a personal career move but also as a departure from a mentor and a team that had become akin to a second family.

Despite the personal difficulty, I mustered the courage to provide John with a candid explanation for my departure. I expressed my deep appreciation for the opportunities he had extended to me, the skills I had acquired under his tutelage, and the invaluable experiences I had gained while working at the electronics firm. I wanted him to understand that my decision to leave was not a reflection of any dissatisfaction with the company or his leadership but a personal quest to pursue a different passion that had surfaced within me.

John's response was emblematic of his character—gracious, understanding, and supportive. He thanked me for my contributions to the team and acknowledged the pleasure it had been to work alongside me. His acknowledgment that one must heed their inner calling and explore new paths was delivered with such sincerity and wisdom. These were simple words, yet they carried an immense weight of truth and understanding. That day, I learned a crucial lesson about professionalism, respect, and the complexity of human relationships in the workplace. John's reaction to my resignation—a blend of disappointment, understanding, and support—taught me about the grace of letting go and the importance of following one's own path even when it diverges from the comfort of the familiar. His demeanor in that moment of farewell was a testament to the kind of leader he was: one who valued the growth and happiness of his employees as much as their contributions to the company. For this lesson, and for everything else, I was, and remain, profoundly thankful to John.

In the time following my departure from the company, a somber piece of news reached me that left me reeling. John, the man who had been the backbone of our department and a mentor to many, had suffered a heart attack and tragically passed away. This news struck a chord deep within me, leaving me to reflect on the impermanence of life and the unexpected nature of change. John had been more than just a supervisor; he was a guiding light, a source of wisdom and strength for the entire team. His passing marked the end of an era for the company and for everyone whose lives he had touched.

As if in a cruel twist of fate, within the year that followed John's passing, the company itself faced its demise. Decisions were made at higher levels, and the firm closed its doors, transitioning its product manufacturing overseas in a move dictated by economic pressures and shifting market dynamics. This, too, was a stark reminder of the transitory nature of businesses and the ever-changing landscape of the global economy.

The closure of the company and the loss of John were intertwined events that underscored a poignant truth: all things, indeed, come to an end. This universal law, relentless and indifferent, spares nothing and no one. While these events carried a weight of sadness, they also served as stark reminders of the importance of embracing change, pursuing one's passions, and the value of cherishing the moments and the people that make up our professional and personal lives. The lessons learned and the memories shared, particularly those involving John's leadership and kindness, would remain with me, indelible and cherished, as I continued on my own path.

The possibility of a career in electronics engineering had always lingered in the back of my mind, a path seemingly predestined and aligned with my early interests and educational pursuits. *I could have been an electronics engineer*, I often mused, reflecting on the trajectory that seemed so certain at one time. *I should have been an electronics engineer*, a part of me argued, considering the time and energy invested in that field, the dreams cultivated during my youth, and the opportunities that arose. However, life's journey is rarely linear or predictable. Now standing at the precipice of a new beginning, I find myself stepping into the world of chemistry, embracing the title of a research chemist. This transition represents more than a mere change of profession; it is a leap into a different realm of discovery and innovation, driven by an underlying passion for the sciences that has beckoned me with increasing intensity.

As I embark on this new chapter, the question looms: will this be my last and final career stop, or does the roller-coaster ride continue? The future remains a mystery, an unwritten narrative filled with potential twists and turns. Yet the essence of life's unpredictability is what makes it exhilarating. Each experience, whether as an engineer or as a chemist, contributes to my growth and understanding, shaping me into a more versatile and well-rounded individual.

So with a mixture of anticipation and resolve, I step forward into the unknown, ready to face the challenges and opportunities that await. The roller-coaster ride of my career continues, and I am eager to see where this next ascent and descent will take me. Let's find out what the future holds, embracing each moment with curiosity and an open heart.

Monday morning arrived with a fresh sense of purpose as I stepped into the new and uncharted territory of my career at Borden Chemical. Embracing the role of a chemist was stepping into a world that was not just unfamiliar but utterly alien to me. In my life up until this point, I had been surrounded primarily by individuals in more hands-on trades—mechanics, carpenters, construction laborers, factory workers, and a few who were between jobs. The realm of chemistry and those who inhabited it were as distant to my everyday experience as one could imagine.

My preconceived image of a chemist was shaped by clichés and stereotypical portrayals: a figure garbed in a crisp white coat, the epitome of intellect and precision, with a pocket protector brimming with an assortment of pens—a symbol of their meticulous nature and expertise. Despite the simplicity and perhaps naivety of this visualization, it emboldened me with a sense of determination and a touch of whimsy. *I can do that*, I quietly reassured myself, buoyed by a mix of optimism and the desire to transcend my current boundaries and delve into the unknown mysteries of chemistry. This was more than just a job change; it was a leap into a completely different life path.

That inaugural morning at Borden Chemical, after completing my check-in with human resources, I was instructed to head over to building number 10 to officially start my day under the guidance of Dr. Goldstein. I walked in, filled with a blend of anticipation and apprehension, ready to immerse myself in the new world of chemical research. However, the reality of my first assignment was far removed from the clean, orderly tasks I had envisioned for a chemist. I was handed my first laboratory task: to take 100 grams of PVC resin in dried powder form, meticulously blend it with 0.5 grams of carbon black, and then process this mixture in a RO-TAP machine. This wasn't taking place in a brightly lit, state-of-the-art lab but rather in a dark, somewhat eerie cellar. The task was not only physically messy and unappealing but also monotonous and far from the intellectually stimulating work I had.

Building number 10 cellar imagined

So my first week passed in a blur of repetition and dirty work, handling mixtures and measuring screen sieves, far removed from the glamorized version of science work I had conjured in my mind. To add to the dissonance between expectation and reality, I wasn't even provided with the quintessential symbol of a chemist—the iconic white lab coat, let alone one adorned with the pens and tools of the trade. It became abundantly clear that my journey in this new career was starting from the very foundation, both metaphorically and quite literally, in the basement of the profession. This stark introduction served as a humbling beginning and a clear indication that there was much to learn and many steps to climb in the world of chemical research.

The transition into my new role felt increasingly like I had unwittingly stepped into an episode of the *Twilight Zone.* The stark contrast between my previous work environment and my current one was disorienting. I had left a promising career in electronics, where I worked in well-lit, clean spaces, for a position that had me relegated to a dimly lit, almost-gothic cellar, spending my days operating a grimy RO-TAP machine. Covered in carbon black from head to toe after each shift, I couldn't help but question my decision to switch careers. However, just when I thought my situation couldn't become more surreal, it did.

The following weeks saw me being introduced to new equipment: the spray dryer and the micro pulverizer, both of which, unsurprisingly, were also located in the depths of the same eerie cellar. The tasks associated with these machines involved converting a liquid PVC latex solution into a fluffy white powder through the drying process, which would then be fed into the raucous micro pulverizer for further processing.

This new assignment, while slightly more complex, was no less messy or tedious. Processing just one gallon of the latex solution through these behemoths took an exhaustive three hours, and the aftermath was chaotic. White PVC powder was scattered everywhere, coating the floor and ceiling and clouding the air. By the end of each day, I was a walking ghost, covered from head to toe in the pervasive powder, finding it in my hair, on my clothes, and up my nose and irritating my eyes.

The promise of engaging in meaningful chemical research seemed more distant with each passing day, and the physical discomfort coupled with the monotony of the tasks at hand left me desperate for a change. I had hoped for a challenging and rewarding career in chemistry, but the reality I faced was testing my resolve and making me question whether I had made the right career move. The need to find a way out of this underground purgatory and into the kind of work I had envisioned was becoming ever more urgent.

Three weeks had elapsed since I began my tenure at Borden Chemical, and each day had been a replica of the last—confined to the subterranean depths of the cellar with my daily existence oscillating between being shrouded in carbon black dust or cloaked in white PVC powder. The physical toll, combined with the mental monotony of the tasks, had reached a breaking point. It was evident that if I was to find any semblance of fulfillment and leverage my skills effectively, something had to change. Fueled by this realization, I mustered the courage to approach my group supervisor. My query was straightforward yet loaded with the weight of my dissatisfaction and hope for something more engaging: were there other job opportunities within the company that would offer more in the way of mental stimulation and less in terms of physical strain? His response came without hesitation, a beacon of unexpected optimism in the dim confines of my current job landscape. "Absolutely," he asserted with a certainty that took me by surprise. He elaborated that starting the following Monday, I would be reassigned to tackle the chemistry formulation issues that had been a persistent thorn in the company's side for over three decades.

The gravity of the task was not lost on me. This was not just a step away from the manual labor I had been mired in but a leap into a role of significant responsibility and intellectual challenge. "Does that sound mentally challenging enough, Eric?" he asked, his question cutting through the haze of my current disillusionment with a sharpness that rekindled a sense of purpose and ambition within me. This unexpected turn of events was exactly what I had been yearning for—a chance to truly make a difference and apply myself in a way that was both meaningful and intellectually rewarding.

I couldn't hide my initial shock and apprehension at the prospect. The leap from the manual, tedious work I had been doing to tackling complex chemical formulation problems seemed immense, especially for someone like me, who, despite my educational background, had zero practical experience in this specific aspect of chemistry. "It seems a bit extreme," I admitted, my voice laced with a mix of disbelief and caution, "especially for someone with no experience in chemical formulation."

However, my determination to rise to the challenge shone through. "But I'm willing to study and learn whatever is necessary," I assured him, ready to embrace the steep learning curve ahead.

He responded with a reassuring smile, one that seemed to acknowledge the vastness of the journey I was about to embark on. "Son, you have a lot to learn," he acknowledged, his tone both serious and encouraging. "So let's get started right now. I will teach you all I can for you to solve the unsolvable."

His words, rather than daunting, ignited a spark of excitement within me. This was the mentorship and the challenge I had been seeking. The path ahead would undoubtedly be arduous, filled with long hours of study, experimentation, and probably more failures than successes initially. But it was an opportunity to grow, to apply myself fully, and to potentially make a significant impact. The unexpected turn in my career at Borden Chemical was shaping up to be the intellectual adventure I had longed for.

The sensation of having overcommitted myself was palpable as I navigated through the weekend, contemplating the immense responsibilities I had taken on. The analogy of having sold my soul to the devil in exchange for a leap into the deep end of chemical formulations loomed large in my thoughts. So as Monday approached, I metaphorically fastened my seat belt, mentally preparing myself for what I anticipated would be a challenging, albeit educational, journey ahead.

Upon my arrival that Monday, I discovered that my previous tasks, those mundane and dirty responsibilities in the cellar, had been handed off to a college intern. The intern, who worked only part-time during the mornings, seemed undaunted by the gritty nature of the work. Observing their readiness to tackle the tasks I had so eagerly escaped, I was reminded of the varied motivations and stages we all navigate in our career paths. It was a humbling reminder that what may be a stepping stone for one can be a valuable learning opportunity for another.

Following this transition, my new routine was laid out before me. I was to spend every morning, from that day forward, in the conference room, engaging in intensive classroom instruction on PVC formulations. This marked a significant shift from the physical labor I had grown accustomed to into the realms of academic study and theoretical application. These sessions were designed to equip me with the foundational knowledge necessary to understand the intricate world of chemical formulations that I had so boldly chosen to dive into. After the morning's academic endeavors, my afternoons were allocated to practical application. I was to draft chemical formulation instructions, which would then be implemented in a small-scale one-gallon PVC mini reactor the following day. This hands-on approach allowed me to translate theoretical knowledge into tangible practice, a crucial step in the learning process.

Once the reactions were complete, my duties extended to testing the chemical and physical properties of the produced PVC. This step was crucial as it would determine the success of the formulation and guide any necessary adjustments. Based on the results of these tests, I would then refine the formulation, preparing for another iteration the following day. This new routine was a far cry from the monotonous and dirty work in the cellar. It was intellectually demanding, requiring constant learning, adaptation, and critical thinking. I was on a steep learning curve, but each day brought new understanding and skills, inching me closer to becoming adept in the complex and fascinating field of chemical formulations.

The classroom sessions were more intense than anticipated, requiring full mental engagement to grasp the extensive information presented. Despite the challenge, I was determined to prove myself and stay ahead. In the laboratory, I was surrounded by renowned chemists specialized in polyvinyl chloride (PVC) resins. These experts had revolutionized the industry with their contributions to PVC-based products such as pipes, siding, flooring, vinyl records, apparel, food packaging, foams, and various coatings. It was a privilege to learn from these industry leaders. They shared their vast knowledge and insights, significantly advancing my skills and understanding in this area. Borden Chemical's investment in my development was a chance not only to excel personally but also to make substantial contributions to the company's diverse product range.

The training sessions extended over the course of a year, providing a comprehensive foundation before I transitioned to independent work. As a research and development chemist focused on PVC reactor formulations, I was stepping into a role that required both innovation and adherence to established protocols. This was my opportunity to demonstrate the value I could bring to my new position within the company. The training had instilled in me a conventional approach, aligning my thought processes and actions with what was deemed acceptable by the management while also operating within a defined set of parameters. In the laboratory, my days were filled with methodical experimentation. Through a process of trial and error, I conducted formulation experiments repeatedly, each time tweaking variables with the hope of reaching the desired outcomes. This meticulous approach, while time-consuming, was essential for developing new and improved PVC products.

The process began with a conventional chemical reaction formula, VC-47BL, a well-established PVC pipe resin that had been a reliable component of Borden's offerings for years. This specific formula was recognized for its consistent performance and was extensively used by pipe manufacturers across the United States. Its successful extrusion process produced pipes at an optimal rate, resulting in a product that was both stable in quality and commercially viable.

The primary objective, however, was to enhance the resin's properties to allow for faster extrusion speeds, thereby increasing the volume of pipe produced within the same time frame. The principle was straightforward; the more efficiently we could manufacture the pipes, the greater the profit margins for the producers. This efficiency gain would, in turn, position Borden as a preferred supplier in the market for PVC resin because of the added value delivered to the end users. Thus, the challenge laid before us was not just a matter of tweaking a few ingredients; it also required a profound understanding of the resin's chemistry and a meticulous approach to experimentation. By modifying the chemical composition of the resin, we aimed to optimize its performance during the extrusion process. However, this had to be done without sacrificing the product's quality, as maintaining the structural integrity and functionality of the PVC pipes was paramount. The balance between increasing production speed and preserving product quality was delicate and required a series of carefully planned and executed adjustments to the chemical formulation.

The approach to refining the PVC resin involved making minor adjustments to its chemical makeup, a process that required precision and patience. We altered the concentrations of existing components or introduced new chemical elements into the mixture to influence the resin's properties. Following each modification, we conducted tests to evaluate the resin's suitability for the PVC pipe extrusion process, a critical step in validating the effectiveness of the changes. This method of incremental adjustments was meticulous and often slow. The nature of such experimental work meant that progress was typically gradual and not without its setbacks. Frequently, alterations to the formulation did not yield the improvements we hoped for, leading to outcomes that were less than satisfactory. In these instances, the phrase "back to the drawing board" became a familiar refrain among my colleagues and me as we confronted the reality of yet another failed experiment.

This recurring cycle of trial, error, and revision led to moments of frustration and reflection. I found myself constantly questioning our approach and wondering if there existed a more efficient, less cumbersome method to achieve our objectives. The challenge was not just in identifying the right changes to make but in doing so in a manner that was less random and more systematic to avoid the frequent restarts and to make our research process more productive and less time-consuming. Correlation-based experimentation often felt akin to navigating through darkness, particularly when the underlying mechanisms remained hidden within the proverbial "black box." This type of empirical approach, while sometimes effective, could be frustratingly indirect and opaque, offering little insight into the actual processes at play. The lack of understanding about the internal workings of these experiments was disconcerting. It turned what should have been a process of scientific inquiry into a game of chance, where outcomes were observed without a clear grasp of the causal relationships.

This period of reflection brought me to a significant personal realization. My innate desire for knowledge extended beyond mere surface-level understanding. I found that I was not content with merely observing effects and drawing correlations. Instead, I harbored a deep-seated need to penetrate the mysteries of the "black box" to unravel the intricate details of its inner workings. This need was driven by more than just professional curiosity; it was a fundamental aspect of my approach to problem-solving and learning. I realized that, for me, true understanding required delving into the underlying mechanisms and principles, dissecting processes to their core elements, and reconstructing them in a way that illuminated their true nature.

This epiphany underscored a broader philosophical stance: the importance of seeking comprehensive understanding and clarity rather than accepting the convenience of ambiguity or the ease of superficial explanations. It was a mindset that not only defined my approach to scientific inquiry but also shaped my worldview and professional ethos. It highlighted a commitment to thoroughness, a dedication to clarity, and a refusal to be satisfied with incomplete explanations.

In my position at Borden's, the methodology predominantly hinged on trial and error, a strategy that, while traditional, often left much to be desired in terms of deep scientific understanding. When probing into the specifics of PVC resin chemistry, responses from colleagues typically lacked depth, boiling down to a formulaic "mix reagent A, B, and C, and it works" approach. This was akin to navigating a complex landscape with blinders on; we were moving forward but without the benefit of full vision or understanding. This lack of transparency and understanding wasn't just a minor inconvenience—it represented a significant barrier to innovation and progress. Many of the resin formulations we worked with were inherited from predecessors or adopted from other companies. Unfortunately, with these acquisitions and hand-me-downs, the fundamental chemical principles often weren't communicated, got lost over time, or were deliberately kept confidential for proprietary reasons. This omission of essential information was, in my eyes, a major oversight—a travesty even.

The absence of a clear grasp on the underlying chemical mechanisms meant that our ability to critically analyze and adapt our processes was severely limited. We were making changes without a comprehensive understanding of the potential consequences, akin to altering the pieces of a machine without knowing their function. Real control over the manufacturing process—being able to predict outcomes and innovate with intention—requires a thorough understanding of all internal mechanisms. In other words, to truly master and evolve the process, one must first unravel and comprehend the mysteries of the black box.

This deep-seated fascination with demystifying black boxes inspired me to take initiative beyond the confines of my assigned projects at Borden's. Motivated by the desire for clarity and understanding that was lacking in my day-to-day work, I crafted three distinct electronic devices, each serving a crucial role in the laboratory's array of tools. These were not mere academic exercises; they were practical instruments designed to enhance our research capabilities: a particle size analyzer circuit, a timing circuit for a viscometer, and a BTU (British thermal unit) integrator for a miniature chemical reactor.

Unlike the opaque formulations I grappled with daily, these devices were creations of transparency and understanding. I built each from the ground up, which meant I possessed a comprehensive grasp of their operational mechanics. This deep understanding allowed me to continuously refine and improve them based on solid scientific principles and observations rather than relying on serendipity. This was a significant departure from the norm in my professional environment, where too often, processes were conducted without a complete understanding of the underlying principles.

This personal project underscored a broader philosophy that I carried with me: the belief that understanding the intricacies of the systems we work with leads to better outcomes, both in science and in life. Each of these "black boxes," whether literal electronic devices or metaphorical personal challenges, contains lessons and opportunities for improvement. By dissecting and mastering them, we can make informed decisions, foster innovation, and lead more productive and fulfilling lives. In essence, the journey to unravel and understand our personal and professional "black boxes" mirrors the process of self-improvement—continually striving to understand the components that make us who we are, thereby enabling us to live more insightful and impactful lives.

Similar to previous phases in my career, my tenure as a PVC research chemist at Borden's, although substantial, lasted just nine years—a relatively short period in the grand tapestry of a professional life. During this time, I gained invaluable experience and knowledge, but an internal voice whispered that my journey was not yet complete. There remained an uncharted path ahead, a calling to explore beyond the familiar confines of laboratory walls. I felt a burgeoning sense that there was more for me to discover, more for me to contribute to the world, though I hadn't yet pinpointed what that might be.

The next chapter of my life marked a significant departure from my previous roles. I decided to become a self-employed entrepreneur. This decision represented a profound shift not just in my career but also in my personal identity. For years, I had navigated the structured environments of academia and corporate research, always answering to supervisors and adhering to the visions of others. Now I faced the prospect of carving out my own path, of being my own boss. It was a daunting transition, fraught with uncertainty but also brimming with potential.

Becoming an entrepreneur meant stepping into a realm where the only limitations were those I set for myself. It was a world vastly different from the one I knew, characterized by new challenges and opportunities. The decision to venture into self-employment was not made lightly; it was a culmination of introspection and a desire for self-determination. I was driven by the aspiration to harness the skills and insights I had acquired over the years, applying them in new and innovative ways. This turning point was a test of my adaptability, creativity, and resilience. It was an opportunity to apply the principles of research and development I had honed as a chemist to the dynamic landscape of entrepreneurship. The transition from working for someone else to working for myself was transformative, teaching me lessons about independence, leadership, and the value of forging one's own destiny. It was time to see if the qualities that served me in scientific inquiry—curiosity, meticulousness, and a willingness to experiment—could also bring success in the unstructured world of business.

Retired at Sixty-Seven

Ah, at last, I've reached the venerable age of sixty-seven. To me, this milestone signifies more than just a number; it heralds the opportunity to finally recline in my easy chair and embrace retirement, just like many others my age. That's right—I'm ready to indulge in the leisurely life, relishing the Social Security benefits that I've diligently contributed to since I was fifteen, marking over fifty years of hard work. Now I can spend more time at home, tackling those long-neglected projects that I've been too busy to address and spending more time with family. Perhaps I'll even embark on travel adventures with my wife, exploring the corners of the globe that have always captivated my imagination but remained out of reach because of work commitments. With my health still robust and a small nest egg carefully set aside for this very phase of life, the prospect of retirement is tantalizing, but lingering questions remain. Can I really retire? Is it truly time to slow down and savor the rewards of a lifetime of labor?

To answer the pressing question of whether I should retire, it's crucial for me to take a comprehensive look at my current life situation and assess what my next steps should be. Is it truly feasible to switch from a work-oriented mindset to one of retirement as easily as flipping a light switch, or is there a transitional phase required to bridge the two? Perhaps I should closely observe my peers who have already embarked on their retirement journeys. By examining how they managed the transition and how they feel about their new lifestyle, I might gain valuable insights. After all, many people do retire around the age of sixty-five and appear to thoroughly enjoy it. Observing their experiences could help me decide if it's time for me to join their ranks and embrace the next chapter of my life with enthusiasm and confidence.

I face two significant hurdles when contemplating retirement at the age of sixty-seven. The first is that I simply don't want to retire, and the second is that I cannot afford to. My reluctance stems from a deep-seated passion for my work, which continues to fulfill and engage me daily. On the practical side, my expertise remains crucial for the day-to-day operations of my business, making my presence indispensable. Furthermore, I feel a personal and moral obligation to ensure the financial well-being of my staff, who depend on the stability and continuity of the business.

I firmly believe that maintaining good health—both mentally and physically—is essential in this context. Staying active in the workforce not only fulfills a professional role but also imposes a beneficial discipline on maintaining one's health to meet the demands of the job.

An inspiring example of this principle in action is my employee Bernice, who recently celebrated her ninetieth birthday. I first met Bernice in a nightclub where my band was playing. Despite being eighty-five at the time, she was the life of the party, dancing energetically with her friends and showing no signs of slowing down. Intrigued by her vitality, I approached her during a break to find out her secret. She shared that staying vigorously engaged in activities like dancing—or working—was her formula for maintaining high energy and longevity. Bernice explained that she had retired a decade earlier but needed to stay active to feel fulfilled, so she and her friends took up dancing regularly at local nightclubs. She also expressed a desire to return to work but found it difficult to get hired because of her age.

Seeing an opportunity for both of us, I offered her a position in my laboratory where she could set her own schedule. Bernice accepted and has been working an average of twenty hours a week ever since in both shipping and the lab. Over the past five years, she has proven to be one of my most diligent and dependable employees, embodying the ethos that age is just a number and demonstrating remarkable resilience and capability. I truly was blessed meeting Bernice; she taught me well about retirement and what it means to remain active.

On the other hand, there are many individuals who retire at sixty-five and some even earlier who initially have no apparent health issues but find themselves feeling lost and alienated in their new circumstances. I have observed a significant number of these individuals rapidly regress in health because of a combination of inactivity and the development of detrimental habits such as overeating, gambling, drug use, and excessive alcohol consumption. This decline may stem from having too much time on their hands and a lack of purpose or community to engage with. When people transition from a structured work life to an unstructured retirement, they often struggle to fill their days meaningfully. This sudden shift can lead to feelings of isolation and boredom, which, in turn, may drive them toward unhealthy behaviors as a means of filling the void. Thus, it becomes crucial to find new ways to stay active and connected, ensuring that retirement doesn't lead to a deterioration of both mental and physical health but rather to a fulfilling and vibrant chapter of life.

Personally, my straightforward philosophy regarding retirement centers on the notion that if you are healthy and active, you should strive to remain active at all costs to preserve your health. This might mean continuing to work, albeit perhaps in a more comfortable or less demanding capacity. I believe that feeling needed is a fundamental component of leading a full and happy life.

Staying engaged in some form of productive activity not only keeps the body and mind active but also provides a sense of purpose and belonging that is crucial for mental health. Work, in this context, does not necessarily mean remaining in a high-pressure job but could involve part-time work, consultancy, volunteer roles, or even pursuing passion projects that provide a sense of accomplishment and contribution.

The benefits of maintaining an active lifestyle into retirement are manifold. It helps stave off diseases associated with aging, maintains cognitive function, and can significantly boost emotional well-being. Therefore, the goal should not be to cease all forms of work abruptly but to transition into a phase of life where you can still feel productive, valued, and, most importantly, happy.

CHAPTER 5

Taking Care of Business

Self-Employed Entrepreneurial Journey

During my tenure as a PVC research and development chemist at Borden Chemical, an unexpected event marked a crucial moment in my professional journey. This change came in the form of a new colleague, a man named Andy, who was notably younger than me by about a decade. His arrival at the laboratory was not just a routine addition to the team; it was an event that preceded his established reputation. Andy had already made a name for himself in certain circles, which piqued the curiosity and anticipation of the entire staff.

One particular day, this sense of anticipation came to a head when the laboratory director convened a meeting for all employees. The purpose of this assembly was to announce a significant new hire. The director shared that a young man, merely in his early twenties, would be joining our ranks. This announcement might have been standard fare except for the fact that this new addition, Andy, came to us without any formal background in science. It was an unconventional choice, to say the least, as he was slated to assume the role of a chemist assistant within our PVC research and development department.

This news was met with a mixture of surprise and intrigue among the staff. Andy's appointment challenged conventional hiring norms within our field, particularly in a research environment that typically valued academic credentials and scientific experience above all. The director urged us to welcome Andy with open arms, signaling a new direction and an openness to diverse perspectives in our department. Little did I know at the time, Andy's arrival would not only transform the dynamics of our team but also profoundly influence my own career trajectory and outlook.

As I surveyed the room, it was evident from the puzzled expressions all around that I wasn't the only one taken aback by the lab director's announcement. The atmosphere was charged with a mix of curiosity and unease. This wasn't an ordinary meeting nor an ordinary introduction of a new team member. The lab director, who had been quite straightforward up until now, chose to unveil this piece of information with a noticeable weight in his tone, signaling its significance.

He revealed an unexpected twist; the new team member was not only an addition to our workforce but also held a personal connection with the upper echelons of our corporate structure. Specifically, he was a close friend of the president of Borden Corporate. This revelation shifted the dynamic dramatically. It was no longer just about integrating a new member into our team; it was about accommodating someone who had direct ties to the power center of the company.

The director's final remark, laden with a sense of urgency and gravity, underscored the situation's delicacy. "Please, for the sake of all of us, treat him special and accommodate whatever he needs," he said. This wasn't merely a request; it felt like an unspoken mandate, hinting at the broader implications and potential consequences of our interactions with this individual. The phrase "for the sake of all of us" suggested that our careers, the team's harmony, and perhaps even the company's future might hinge on how well we adhere to this directive.

This left us in a state of bewilderment and speculation. Why was a personal friend of the company's president being inserted into our ranks? What was the rationale behind sending him specifically to our department? Was this a test, a surveillance mission, or perhaps a chance for him to learn the ropes? The lack of clarity and the high stakes involved turned what could have been a routine induction into a source of intrigue and potential tension. The room, once abuzz with the typical sounds of a workday morning, fell into a contemplative silence as everyone processed the weight of the lab director's words and pondered the implications of this unexpected development.

The long-anticipated day had finally come when the young man, known to be a close acquaintance of the Borden Corporate president, was set to begin his role in the PVC research and development department. From the moment he stepped through the door of the laboratory, it was clear that he had become the center of attention, sparking widespread curiosity among the staff. The air was thick with speculation—was his true purpose to act as a corporate spy, monitoring and relaying our actions back to the higher-ups? This unsettling thought nudged everyone into a state of heightened caution and formality, as if walking on eggshells.

He introduced himself with a simple "I'm Andy," presenting a figure that was neither imposing nor remarkable: an average build, a fair skin tone, standing modestly at five feet six inches, and with a body weight that appeared to be around 140 pounds. Despite this, his calm and somewhat aloof demeanor only served to amplify the whispers of caution among us. The old warning "be careful of the quiet ones" reverberated silently through the group, urging a careful, measured interaction. However, as time passed, the tension that had initially gripped us began to dissipate. Andy's actions belied the fearsome rumors that had preceded him; he was notably friendly and approachable, showing no signs of the ominous overseer we had imagined. His aim seemed to be nothing more complex than settling into his new role and becoming part of our team. This experience reminded us of a common workplace phenomenon. Often, our fears and the narratives we construct around new or unknown elements are vastly out of proportion to reality. Andy, despite the powerful connections implied by his background, was simply another colleague looking to make his mark in our shared endeavors.

On his first day, Andy's integration into the PVC pipe resin research team was met with a mixture of anticipation and strategy. Under the leadership of Paul, a person known for his rigorous commitment to excellence and the company's objectives, the team was a well-oiled machine, dedicated to innovating and refining the quality of their product. Paul's reputation as a staunch advocate for the company's success was not just well-earned; it was a badge he wore with pride, setting a high bar for his team members. The decision to place Andy in this particular team was not incidental. It was a calculated move, possibly devised by the higher echelons of management, perhaps even the plant president himself. The underlying intention seemed clear. By aligning Andy with Paul, the company might be hoping to instill in Andy the same level of commitment and drive that Paul exemplified. This, in turn, could result in positive feedback reaching the ears of the corporate president, given Andy's close relationship with him.

Paul and his team were thus in a unique position. They were not just continuing with their groundbreaking work on PVC pipe resin; they were also under the indirect spotlight, tasked with the dual responsibilities of maintaining their high standards of research and development while also serving as a model for the new, notably connected team member. This added an extra layer of complexity to their roles, blending the pursuit of scientific advancement with the nuances of corporate politics and interpersonal dynamics.

The separation of Andy from my team by the laboratory director added an intriguing layer to our workplace dynamics. The rationale behind this decision was never explicitly explained, leading to much speculation. It's plausible that my openly differing viewpoints, particularly around the balance between personal needs and company loyalty, prompted this separation. In an environment where the prevailing culture leaned heavily toward prioritizing the company's interests, my more individualistic approach stood out. Despite this deliberate segregation, Andy and I naturally gravitated toward each other, forging a bond that transcended professional barriers. This friendship wasn't rooted in opportunistic motives; I was genuinely attracted to his adventurous nature and his open-minded approach to life and work. Andy's zest for new experiences and his fearless attitude toward innovation and experimentation struck a chord with me. He embodied a youthful spirit that seemed unburdened by the fear of failure, a stark contrast to the cautious, results-oriented atmosphere of our laboratory.

This unexpected friendship between Andy and me served as a reminder that personal connections can thrive even in the most structured or divisive of settings. It also highlighted the fact that diversity in thought and personality can bring a refreshing change to a conventional work environment, fostering a culture where new ideas are not just welcomed but celebrated. Andy's presence and our ensuing friendship underscored the value of embracing different perspectives and the potential for personal growth and innovation that comes with it.

As time unfolded, the initial excitement and curiosity that surrounded Andy's arrival began to wane. A year into his tenure, the repetition and lack of variety inherent in his position as a lab bench technician became increasingly burdensome for him. The tasks that once may have offered new insights and learning opportunities had transformed into a relentless cycle of redundancy, leaving Andy craving something more meaningful and stimulating from his professional life.

The laboratory director, aware of Andy's growing dissatisfaction and keen on maintaining a favorable relationship with the corporate leadership, attempted to address the issue by moving Andy across various departments. This strategy was aimed not only at providing Andy with new environments and challenges but also at safeguarding the director's own reputation and connection with the company's upper echelon. Yet this approach failed to address the root of Andy's disillusionment. The shifts between departments, while offering temporary changes in scenery, did not provide the substantive engaging work experiences Andy yearned for. His sense of purpose and engagement remained unfulfilled as the new roles were variations on the same theme rather than opportunities for genuine growth and learning.

Andy's continued discontent highlighted a deeper issue within the company's approach to employee satisfaction and development. Despite the changes in his work setting, the lack of real progress or variation in the nature of his tasks led to a persistent sense of stagnation. The situation underscored the importance of understanding and addressing employees' aspirations and the need for roles that offer not just a change of environment but real opportunities for personal and professional growth.

In the midst of Andy's and my own professional dissatisfaction, his unexpected proposition marked a significant turning point. His words "Let's get the hell out of this place and start a business together" resonated with a sense of rebellion and adventure, yet they also sparked a flood of conflicting emotions within me. The idea of stepping away from the monotony and frustrations of our current jobs to build something of our own was enticing. It promised a fresh start, autonomy, and the excitement of shaping our future. Why not? We're still in our twenties. However, this thrilling prospect was immediately countered by the stark realities of my personal life. With a family to support, including a child at home and another on the way, the stakes were incredibly high. The comfort and security provided by a steady paycheck were not just luxuries; they were necessities. The idea of venturing into the unpredictable world of entrepreneurship, with all its inherent risks and uncertainties, was daunting. The fear of jeopardizing my family's financial stability loomed large, making the decision far from straightforward.

In the face of such a life-altering choice, I knew that mere enthusiasm or the desire to escape our current circumstances would not be enough. What I needed was a solid, well-thought-out business plan, one that outlined a clear path to not only sustaining our families but also achieving financial growth and stability. This plan would need to account for the risks and lay out realistic strategies for overcoming the challenges of starting and growing a new business. Only with such a plan in place could I seriously consider the possibility of joining Andy in this bold, new endeavor. The decision was not just about leaving a job; it was about reshaping our lives and futures. Driven by a shared ambition to transform our professional lives and create a more fulfilling future, Andy and I embarked on a comprehensive brainstorming journey. Our objective was clear: to find a business idea that was not only viable but also resonant with our personal values and professional backgrounds. We sought a concept that would not only ensure the well-being of our families but also hold the potential for significant growth and contribution to society.

We meticulously evaluated various business models, weighing the pros and cons of entering the product market versus offering specialized services. The discussions ranged from exploring the feasibility of manufacturing innovative products to considering the establishment of a business that capitalized on our accumulated knowledge and skills. The aim was to identify a niche where we could apply our scientific acumen and experience in a manner that was both personally rewarding and economically viable. After extensive analysis and creative thinking, we found our eureka moment: the concept of starting a drinking water testing laboratory. This idea perfectly bridged our collective expertise in scientific research and our shared commitment to public health and safety. Recognizing the increasing public awareness about environmental issues and the importance of clean drinking water, we saw an opportunity to contribute positively to the community while establishing a sustainable business model.

The decision to focus on water testing was informed by our understanding of the market demand and the potential for making a meaningful impact. With our backgrounds in science and research, we were well-equipped to understand the technical nuances and regulatory requirements of the industry. We envisioned a laboratory that not only provided essential water quality testing services to individuals and businesses but also championed public health and environmental stewardship. By aligning our venture with societal needs and leveraging our professional backgrounds, we positioned ourselves to build a business that was not just profitable but also beneficial to the community at large. This alignment of personal, professional, and societal goals provided a solid foundation for our new entrepreneurial journey.

Building a Drinking Water Testing Business

The choice to establish a drinking water testing laboratory was deeply rooted in our belief in playing to our strengths while simultaneously identifying and addressing a gap in the market. This decision aligned with the business philosophy we adopted: "do what you do best, and do it better than your competition." Although we recognized our initial understanding of the specific nuances of drinking water testing as somewhat basic, our backgrounds in scientific research provided a strong foundation to build upon. We acknowledged our status as novices in the intricacies of water testing procedures and the precise equipment required, yet we saw this not as a deterrent but as an opportunity for growth and differentiation.

Our resolve to enter the drinking water testing market was fueled by the clear vision we had: to develop a laboratory that could deliver services more efficiently and cost-effectively than existing options. This vision was underpinned by our confidence in our ability to learn quickly, adapt, and apply our scientific skills to overcome any initial shortcomings. We were driven by the potential to offer significant value to our customers through faster turnaround times and lower pricing, all without compromising the accuracy and reliability of the results.

Moreover, our commitment to this venture was not just about filling a market need; it was also about contributing positively to public health and safety. By providing accessible and affordable drinking water testing, we aimed to empower individuals and communities to make informed decisions about their water quality, thus enhancing their well-being. In embracing the challenges that came with our limited initial understanding, we committed ourselves to rigorous study, training, and partnership with more experienced professionals in the field. This approach not only facilitated our own growth and expertise but also ensured that we could offer top-notch services to our clients. By focusing on our strengths, acknowledging our weaknesses, and committing to superior service and continuous improvement, we aimed to carve out a niche for our laboratory in the competitive landscape of water testing services.

Our foray into the drinking water testing business began with a rudimentary yet crucial step: gauging the market interest. Understanding the potential demand was vital before diving deeper into the venture. With this goal in mind and constrained by a limited budget, we took a lean approach to test the waters, so to speak.

COULD HAVE BEEN; SHOULD HAVE BEEN; HERE I AM

A modest investment of twenty-six dollars was allocated to place an advertisement in the local newspaper, a strategic move to reach a broad audience with minimal financial risk. The ad was straightforward, offering water testing services at a compelling price point of $10, and listed Andy's personal home phone number for contact, demonstrating his commitment and the personal touch we were willing to provide.

The response to the ad, though seemingly small, was incredibly insightful. Within just a few days, inquiries came from three varied sources: a real estate agent, a well-drilling company, and a homeowner. This diversity in our initial clientele hinted at the wide-ranging need and interest in water testing services across different sectors of the community. It suggested potential market segments we could target: real estate transactions requiring quality checks, well drillers needing regular testing for their clients, and individual homeowners concerned about their water safety.

Andy's role in personally collecting water samples from these first few inquiries was emblematic of our grassroots approach. Despite the glaring fact that we did not yet have a formal laboratory or established testing protocols, this hands-on experience was invaluable. It not only provided us with direct contact with potential clients but also gave us a real-world sense of the logistics and customer service aspects of the business. These early interactions were critical in shaping our understanding of the market and the practical challenges ahead. They underscored the importance of building our services from the ground up, focusing on customer needs and expectations, and highlighted the necessity for rapid development of our testing capabilities. This initial market test, modest as it was, served as a cornerstone step in our journey, providing both encouragement and clear direction for our new enterprise.

In response to the unexpected interest generated by our initial advertisement, we found ourselves needing to deliver on our promise despite the absence of a testing laboratory facility or a fully developed service plan. Committed to fulfilling the obligations to our first potential clients, we sought immediate, practical solutions to the challenges at hand.

Our initial concern was securing a space to conduct the necessary water tests. Fortunately, our current positions provided us with access to our research laboratory. We rationalized that the lab's resources could be utilized temporarily to analyze the three water samples we had collected. This decision was made under the assumption that our brief use of the lab for a small number of samples would be acceptable, given our familiarity with the space and its operations.

The second significant challenge we faced was deciding exactly which tests to perform on the water samples. Our professional expertise in PVC resin research, where the purity and quantity of plant process water are essential factors, served as a guiding principle. From this background, we understood the importance of certain water quality parameters such as pH, conductivity, and turbidity. These were not only critical in our previous research but also generally important indicators of drinking water quality. Thus, we decided to apply this knowledge as a starting point for our water testing services.

By leaning on our existing expertise and resources, we addressed the immediate challenges presented by our new venture. This approach allowed us to begin establishing our presence in the drinking water testing market while also providing a learning experience to refine our services and operational strategies moving forward.

Leveraging the initial success of our rudimentary water testing service, we proceeded to formalize our findings for each client by diligently typing out individual reports. This personalized approach, combined with our commitment to delivering results promptly, marked our early steps into professional service delivery. Completing these transactions not only validated our business concept but also provided us with the initial profits that signified our venture's potential viability.

To our surprise and delight, the positive feedback from our initial clients acted as a catalyst for our business's growth. Word of our efficient and reliable service spread quickly within the community, leading to an increasing number of referrals. The demand for our water testing services grew at an unexpected pace, with the weekly sample count rapidly escalating to between five and ten. This surge not only affirmed the market's need for our services but also underscored the effectiveness of our customer-focused approach. However, with this success came the realization that our makeshift arrangement—using Borden's research laboratory for our personal business—was neither a sustainable nor ethical solution for the long term. The increasing volume of water samples and the commercial nature of our activities necessitated a more formal and dedicated workspace. Thus, spurred by the burgeoning demand and the need to establish a legitimate and responsible operation, we initiated the search for a dedicated laboratory space.

This move marked a significant transition from an opportunistic side project to a serious, ethical, and sustainable business venture. We understood that securing a dedicated space would not only address the practical challenges of handling a growing number of samples but also solidify our commitment to providing professional water testing services. It was a crucial step toward legitimizing our business and laying the foundation for future growth and development. Andy's residence, characterized by its generous Victorian design and close proximity to our initial makeshift lab at Borden's, presented a convenient solution at the outset of our venture. I learned later that the house was owned by his close friend Roe, the president of the Borden cooperation. The attic, though not yet finished, offered just enough room to set up the basic equipment we needed to get our Water Works laboratory off the ground. This arrangement allowed us to transition from using Borden's facilities to establishing a more permanent, albeit humble, base for our operations. It symbolized the transition from an idea to a tangible enterprise, a crucial step in the evolution of our business. However, this initial setup, while practical from a business standpoint, soon began to strain Andy's personal life. The blending of professional and private spaces created an environment that was less than ideal for family living. Andy's wife, understandably concerned with the intrusion of business operations into their personal space, became increasingly uncomfortable with the arrangement. The presence of lab equipment, chemicals, and the constant flow of water samples in what was supposed to be their private residence created tension and unease.

The situation escalated to the point where Andy was faced with a significant dilemma. His wife's ultimatum—the lab had to go or she would—was a stark indication of the seriousness of the issue. The decision was not just about finding a new location for the lab; it was about balancing the demands of our burgeoning business with the well-being and happiness of his family. This unexpected domestic challenge underscored the often-overlooked personal sacrifices and decisions entrepreneurs face when starting a new business, especially when home and work boundaries blur. It became clear that for our business to continue growing and for Andy's family life to stay harmonious, finding a new, separate location for the now-named Water Works laboratory was imperative.

Andy's decision to move the laboratory to a trailer behind his house stemmed from a desire to maintain close proximity to his work while respecting his family's living space. This move, however, came with its own set of challenges, particularly the moral and ethical implications he faced because of the initial use of Borden's facilities. The guilt Andy experienced was not just a personal burden; it influenced the collective decision to come clean to the local authorities, a choice driven by a sense of responsibility and a desire for transparency. Andy's disclosure to the town council, while well-intentioned, led to unforeseen complications. The immediate backlash was not only a reflection of the strict zoning laws in place but also highlighted the often complex relationship between private ventures and public regulations. The council's stern response, demanding the removal of the laboratory trailer and threatening fines and legal action, underscored the legal constraints and bureaucratic challenges faced by private individuals and entrepreneurs when their activities intersect with public interests and safety concerns.

This turn of events serves as a reminder of the importance of due diligence and legal compliance in any venture, especially those that may impact the local community or environment. It also raises questions about the balance between innovation and regulation and the need for clear communication and understanding between private citizens and local authorities. Andy's situation is a stark example of how good intentions can lead to complex legal and ethical dilemmas. However, one lesson we learned was that it was easier to ask for forgiveness than permission from the town council, who let us off with no fines.

After the unfortunate incident with the town council, we found ourselves at a crossroads again. The need to relocate was clear, but the right location was yet to be found. Then, almost serendipitously, we came across an old airplane hangar that was being leased as commercial space. This unexpected discovery presented a unique opportunity; the hangar was not only spacious enough to accommodate our expanding operations, but it also aligned with the industrial and commercial zoning requirements, mitigating the legal issues we faced previously. This new location required adjustments on our part. The hangar's ample space allowed for a more organized and efficient setup, facilitating the expansion of our activities. However, this expansion also meant a greater commitment of time and resources. We found ourselves juggling our existing responsibilities at Borden's with the demands of our growing enterprise. Our days became a careful balancing act, dedicating early mornings and late evenings to analyzing water samples and preparing reports for our clients before transitioning to our day jobs.

This phase of our journey was marked by long hours and hard work, but it was also a time of growth and learning. The challenges we faced not only tested our resilience but also our ability to adapt and innovate under pressure. The hangar became more than just a new location; it symbolized a fresh start and a step forward in our venture, proving that even in the face of setbacks, determination and adaptability can lead to new opportunities.

Our routine at the airplane hangar became our new normal for the better part of a year. We had adapted to the rhythm of balancing our commitments to Borden's and our own burgeoning enterprise, working tirelessly to meet the demands of both. However, as with all journeys, change was on the horizon, presenting itself in the form of a new opportunity that promised to reshape our professional landscape. This opportunity arrived unexpectedly through one of our clients, a home inspection agency owned by Greg Smith, who had come to not only value our services but also recognize the potential for deeper collaboration. He proposed a partnership, suggesting that we join forces with him on a full-time basis. This was no small offer; it represented a significant shift from our current trajectory, moving us from the confines of our niche into a broader arena.

The proposal was enticing for several reasons. First and foremost, it offered the chance to expand our operations beyond the limited scope we had known. This wasn't just about growing in size; it was about enhancing our capabilities, reaching new clients, and making a more substantial impact within the industry. Furthermore, transitioning to a full-time partnership would provide a level of stability and focus that our current split between Borden's and the hangar did not allow.

This turning point was pivotal. The decision to embrace this partnership meant stepping into unknown territory, but it also held the promise of growth and the establishment of a more significant footprint in the industry. It was a chance to transition from a state of constant juggling to one of concentrated effort and potentially greater reward. This new path was fraught with risks, but the potential benefits made it a compelling proposition, signaling a new chapter in our entrepreneurial journey.

Greg's situation was not unique in the realm of home inspection businesses, but his particular circumstances underscored an urgent need that had become increasingly critical as his company grew. His expanding clientele, a testament to the quality of his service and reputation, brought with it a diverse range of needs and expectations, particularly from those clients who owned private wells. For these clients, water testing was not just a routine check but also an essential service, crucial for ensuring the safety and quality of their drinking water.

The industry's standard practices for water testing, however, were proving to be a significant bottleneck for Greg's operations. The norm of waiting up to three weeks for results was unacceptable for clients needing immediate information to make important decisions about their home purchase and health. Moreover, the high costs associated with these tests added an additional barrier, making it difficult for Greg to offer competitive prices while still ensuring the quality and reliability of the service.

Recognizing these challenges, Greg identified a clear set of criteria that any potential partner laboratory would need to meet to support his business effectively. This included the capacity to handle a large volume of samples, which was essential given the growing demand from his client base. Speed was another critical factor; a turnaround time of forty-eight hours would not only set his service apart from competitors but also meet the urgent needs of his clients more effectively. Lastly, maintaining affordability was essential to ensure that his water testing services remained accessible to a broader range of clients.

This set of needs formed the basis of Greg's critical demand for a new kind of partnership with a laboratory—one that could break the mold of existing home inspection services and provide a solution that was both fast and cost-effective without compromising on quality or reliability. Confronted with the pressing needs of his expanding business, Greg saw in us a solution to the challenges he faced. His offer was both generous and strategic, designed to address his immediate needs while providing us with a compelling incentive to join his team.

Greg proposed a one-year contract to Andy and me, offering a salary double what we were currently earning at Borden Chemical, along with full medical benefits. This represented a significant investment in our expertise. However, the offer came with significant conditions. The first was that we resign from Borden Chemical—a decision not to be taken lightly, considering the stability and history we had with the company. It meant stepping away from a known entity into a partnership that, while promising, was not without its risks. The second condition was the relocation of our water testing operations into Greg's facility. This move would mean leaving behind the airplane hangar that had become our operational base, adapting once again to a new environment and integrating our operations within the existing framework of Greg's business. This integration would not only be physical but also operational, requiring adjustments to workflows, communication, and perhaps even methodology. The third, and perhaps most significant, condition was the exclusivity clause. Committing to test water samples solely for Greg's company would mean putting all our eggs in one basket, so to speak. It would limit our client base and make us reliant on the continued success and expansion of Greg's business for our own growth and financial security. Following the conclusion of the contract, the option to renegotiate or part ways offered a safety net and an opportunity for reassessment. This clause acknowledged the uncertainties inherent in any new venture and provided both parties with a predefined moment to evaluate the partnership's success and potential future.

Accepting Greg's offer would mean embarking on a new chapter, filled with both opportunities and challenges. It represented a leap of faith into a partnership that promised to change the trajectory of our professional lives, requiring careful consideration of the risks and rewards involved. The conventional wisdom—the sort dispensed by the risk-averse and those well-versed in the art of maintaining the status quo—would likely have dictated a cautious retreat. After all, the language of prudence speaks in hushed tones of safety, urging us to cling to the known and the tangible. Yet there was another voice—a more impetuous counterpart, buoyed by the effervescence of youth and the intoxicating allure of what could be. It was this voice that whispered, "Why not?" with the temerity of someone who hasn't yet learned to fear the fall. It was a siren call to the adventurous and to those unburdened by the cynicism that often accompanies age and experience.

In the end, we did not linger long over the ledger of potential losses. The allure of the unknown, of what lay beyond the well-trodden path, was too compelling. With hearts ablaze with the spirit of "why not," we chose to step off the edge of our familiar world, embracing the exhilarating uncertainty of this new venture. We were all too aware that this decision could not be unmade, but in that moment, driven by a blend of naivety and boldness, we were ready to sail into uncharted waters, eager to discover what lay beyond the horizon of our current lives.

The choice that Andy and I made to join forces with Greg represented a pivotal turn in my career trajectory and financial landscape. Up to that point, my professional life had been characterized by modest income and a background position in the broader narrative of other people's projects. With this new venture, however, there emerged an opportunity to create something of my own and to step into a role where my decisions and actions could lead to something lasting and personal. Despite the lack of certainty about what the future held, an internal compass assured me this was the path I needed to follow.

With feelings oscillating between excitement and a tinge of sadness, we finalized Greg's one-year contract and handed in our two-week notices at Borden Chemical. Leaving was not without its complex emotions; it meant moving away from a familiar setting that had provided us with stability and camaraderie. We were not just leaving a job but parting ways with colleagues who had become significant in our lives, with whom we had shared innovative breakthroughs and daily challenges. As we said our farewells and stepped out of the Borden Chemical environment, we could not foresee that the company would shut down three years later. This unforeseen closure would thrust many of our former peers into the harsh reality of job hunting, career shifts, or the contemplation of premature retirement. This occasion marked the second time I had left a well-established company, and curiously, both companies dissolved into obscurity shortly after my departure. I hope their downfall wasn't due to my leaving or perhaps some other unseen force at play. This unexpected change underscored a fundamental truth: the impermanence of everything around us, including careers, belongings, relationships, and even life itself. All things must come to an end.

This realization led me to contemplate the essential difference between humans and other species: our deep-seated consciousness of our own existence. We know that someday, we will die—unlike any other animal on the earth. This consciousness doesn't paralyze us; instead, it propels us to seek meaning in our actions, to contribute to society's cumulative wisdom, and to nurture the next generation's ability to thrive. In doing so, we secure a piece of ourselves that endures, fueling the onward march of civilization. Meanwhile, animals, driven by instinct, dwell in the immediate, without a care for legacy or the transmission of knowledge across generations. This stark contrast underscores the uniquely human ability to leave a mark that extends far beyond our temporal lives, which is the intended purpose of these writings.

Andy and I took a leap of faith across the chasm, transitioning into careers that not only provided for our families but also brought personal fulfillment and growth over the years. What's particularly intriguing is the role of building number 10, the very Borden research facility we had left behind. Unbeknownst to us at the time, this building harbored unforeseen significance in our lives, wielding an almost mystical influence over our future trajectories. This may seem far-fetched, but let me delve into the curious, albeit comforting, series of events that unfolded between us and building number 10.

Despite the physical departure from the building, it seemed as though an invisible thread tethered us to it, guiding our paths in unexpected ways. Over the ensuing years, our careers took divergent paths, yet they were subtly intertwined with the legacy of building number 10. It was as if the building, with its myriad of laboratories and memory-soaked corridors, had embedded itself in our destinies, refusing to be just a backdrop of our past.

Forty-three years later, the connection became undeniably clear. It's as if building number 10 had been silently orchestrating a reunion, a confluence of past and present that neither Andy nor I could have anticipated. This bond, transcending mere brick and mortar, influenced decisions, sparked collaborations, and even steered us back to crossroads reminiscent of those within its walls. The unfolding of these events, orchestrated by the unseen hands of time and memory, reveals the profound impact places and experiences can have on our lives long after we've moved on from them.

Three years following our departure, the Borden company's facility in Massachusetts, including the storied building number 10, ceased operations and relocated to Louisiana, leaving behind a vacant shell where innovation once thrived. This unforeseen event opened up an unexpected opportunity; building number 10 was on the market, awaiting new ownership. Andy and I had often discussed the dream of owning a facility precisely like building number 10—a place already outfitted with lab benches and the necessary infrastructure to serve as a turnkey laboratory for ambitious projects and research. Constructed in 1961, the very year I embarked on my educational journey in first grade, building number 10 was originally designed to house cutting-edge research and development initiatives. Its historical significance and personal connection to my own life's timeline made it more than just a building; it represented a bridge between past aspirations and future possibilities. The building was clearly waiting for me.

Little did we know, the twists of fate were aligning to present us with a chance to transform this dream into reality. The closure of the PVC production plant and the subsequent availability of building number 10 set the stage for an unforeseen reunion with a place that had fostered our early careers and now beckoned us back, not just as former employees but as potential proprietors. The possibility of reclaiming a part of our past to fuel our future endeavors was an unexpected turn of events that held the promise of bringing our professional journey full circle.

Sometimes, the people you know can significantly impact your life. This was certainly true for Andy, whose connection with the president of Borden Chemical, Roe, proved to be incredibly beneficial. Their relationship was not just a casual acquaintance; it was built on a foundation of trust, mutual respect, and gratitude. Andy's connection with Roe dated back to a time before Roe's prestigious position as the president of Borden Chemical. Their relationship deepened when Andy took on the responsibility of looking after Roe's house. Living there, Andy ensured the property remained secure and well-maintained, protecting it from potential disasters like fires or burglaries. His role was to preserve the house in its pristine state, a frozen moment in time waiting for Roe's return. This house wasn't just a structure to Roe; it represented memories, hard work, and a slice of personal history he had to leave behind when he relocated to New York City to take up his new role.

But Andy's generosity extended beyond mere house-sitting. Years earlier, he had played a crucial role in an essential moment in

Roe's personal life, specifically involving Roe's son Mike. Andy and Mike were classmates and mutual friends in high school, a period during which Mike struggled significantly with his personal identity. Plagued by a severe drug addiction, Mike's life seemed to spiral out of control, teetering on the brink of disaster multiple times. However, Andy didn't turn his back on his friend. Instead, he stood by Mike, helping him navigate the treacherous path back to sobriety. Andy's unwavering support didn't go unnoticed. He didn't just provide friendship; he served as a mentor, a guide, and a sponsor, tirelessly working to ensure Mike stayed on the right path. This dedication ultimately led to Mike overcoming his addiction and finding a new sense of purpose as he approached graduation.

Roe was profoundly affected by Andy's selfless actions. Understanding the depth of despair his son had faced and recognizing Andy's vital role in Mike's recovery filled Roe with immense gratitude. He saw Andy's actions not just as a favor but as a lifesaving intervention for his only son. Moved by Andy's kindness and the dramatic positive impact he had on his family, Roe made it clear to Andy that his gratitude was boundless. He promised to support Andy in any way he could, a testament to the strong bond formed through years of friendship, trust, and shared experiences. This bond between Andy and Roe exemplifies the profound truth that sometimes, it's indeed who you know that can make all the difference.

Throughout their enduring friendship, Andy had only asked for Roe's assistance twice, each time with significant impact on his professional life. The first instance was a crucial moment in Andy's career trajectory. He expressed a desire to work at the Leominster Borden PVC Chemical plant, specifically targeting a position within the research and development department, a field that he was deeply passionate about. Understanding the importance of this request, Roe did not hesitate. With his influence and a simple yet effective gesture of support, Roe ensured Andy's placement in the coveted position. It was a testament to the strength of their relationship and Roe's recognition of Andy's potential and dedication. The second request came later after the Leominster PVC plant closing, and it was a testament to Andy's ambition and his trust in Roe's support. This time, Andy's aspirations were directed toward acquiring building number 10, a significant property within the Borden Chemical infrastructure. For Andy, obtaining this building was not a matter of prestige; it was a strategic move, aimed at expanding his research and development endeavors. He envisioned transforming building number 10 into an environmental water testing laboratory, a place where new ideas could flourish and lead to significant advancements in customer service.

Roe's response to this second request was vital. It was not just about granting a favor; it was about investing in innovation and showing faith in Andy's vision and capabilities. By assisting in the acquisition of building number 10, Roe was enabling a new chapter of growth and discovery within the new environmental testing company, fostering an environment where creativity and progress could thrive. These two occasions where Andy sought Roe's help were not merely transactions but milestones in their professional relationship and personal bond. They highlighted Andy's respect for Roe's judgment and Roe's unwavering support for Andy's professional growth. Each request and subsequent fulfillment underscored the depth of their mutual respect and the significant impact of their enduring alliance on both their lives and careers.

Because of Roe's generous assistance, Andy and I successfully secured the financing needed to purchase building number 10. This development felt surreal, a dream materializing into reality, marking a significant milestone in our careers and lives. The turn of events was poetic; here I was, returning to building number 10, but this time, the context was profoundly different. I was not just another employee clocking in for the day; I was returning as a 50 percent owner, a position that signified not only a change in status but also a profound personal achievement.

The building, which was once a mere workplace, had now become a symbol of our ambitions and efforts. It was set to house the drinking water testing laboratory, a project that resonated with me on multiple levels. This lab wasn't just another business venture; it was a return to origins, to the very place where the idea and initial operations had begun during the earlier Borden days. The historical significance of the building, combined with our personal connections to its past, added layers of meaning to our endeavor.

Our vision for building number 10 was clear. We aimed to transform it into a state-of-the-art facility, one that would not only pay homage to its historical roots but also push the boundaries of innovation in water testing. This lab was to become a beacon of quality and reliability, contributing significantly to public health and safety. Our commitment was to uphold the highest standards of testing and research, ensuring that the community and beyond had access to safe drinking water.

The journey from employees to owners of building number 10 symbolized more than just a change in our professional paths; it was a testament to our dedication, hard work, and the belief in our mission. Roe's support was instrumental in this transition, providing us not just with the means but also the morale boost to pursue this ambitious project. His faith in our capabilities was a constant source of encouragement, driving us to strive for excellence in our new roles.

As we embarked on this new chapter, we were acutely aware of the responsibilities that came with ownership. Yet there was an underlying excitement, a buzz of potential that filled the air of building number 10. We were ready to face the challenges ahead, inspired by the legacy of the place and motivated by the impact our work could have on the world. This was not just a business investment; it was a personal quest to make a difference, one test at a time. Shortly after acquiring the building, we initiated the process of transferring our testing equipment and office furniture into our new premises. It was during this phase that we discovered a lone item left behind lying on the lobby floor by the previous occupants, Borden Chemical. This item was a framed pencil drawing, an architect's preliminary vision of the building prior to its construction. This piece of architectural documentation had been prominently displayed in the front entry hall, ensuring that it was one of the first sights to greet all visitors.

The drawing served not merely as decoration but as a statement of intent and history, eloquently conveying the building's original purpose as a dedicated research and development laboratory. It was as if the drawing stood as a testament to the building's inception, a visual chronicle of its origins. The image seemed to declare to every entrant that they were stepping into a space specifically crafted for innovation and scientific inquiry. The presence of this architectural rendering in such a prominent location emphasized the building's identity and heritage, imbuing it with a sense of purpose and a reminder of its dedicated mission from the moment of its conception.

When Andy and I discovered the architectural drawing abandoned on the floor, we felt a strong impulse to restore it to its rightful place. Without hesitation, we rehung it in the entranceway, on the very wall where it had been displayed since 1961, reviving a piece of the building's history. Once we had the drawing properly hung and had adjusted the frame to be perfectly level, Andy pointed out an oddly peculiar detail that neither of us had noticed before.

In the drawing, on the front left side of the building, there were two vehicles depicted in the parking lot. One was illustrated as black and the other as blue. Both were portrayed as large-sized sedan automobiles parked side by side and facing the building. This detail might have seemed mundane at any other time, but what made it striking was the scene outside the building's front window at that very moment.

In our parking lot, there were precisely only two cars—both 1988 Lincoln Town Cars belonging to Andy and me, positioned side by side and facing the building, mirroring the image in the drawing. The similarity was uncanny; the 1988 Lincoln Town Car was known for its distinctive boxy, square body frame, a design that stood out against the more rounded car designs of later years. Our vehicles, one black and the other blue, were exact matches to those depicted in a drawing from 1961. And there we were in 1990, confronted with this bizarre echo from the past.

The coincidence was both mystical and eerie. How could it be that nearly three decades later, our own cars would so perfectly replicate the image immortalized in the building's original architectural rendering? It felt as though the building, or perhaps time itself, had somehow anticipated this moment. The peculiar synchronicity left us pondering the mysterious ways in which the past can sometimes mirror the future, making us question the very nature of coincidence and the intertwined threads of time and space. How, indeed, could the building have "known" this? The question lingered in the air, adding an enigmatic layer to our new workplace's atmosphere.

This was my second stint at building number 10. The mere thought left me both perplexed and inexplicably drawn; how could a mere inanimate structure exert such a magnetic pull on my being, luring me back into its silent, looming confines? There was an enigmatic charm, a whispered invitation that seemed to resonate from its aged walls, reaching out to me across the realms of logic and reason. Puzzlement deepened when I discovered an item—the sole occupant in the otherwise deserted expanse. An architectural drawing, nondescript at first glance, lay abandoned on the cold, hard floor. But upon closer inspection, a jolt of disbelief coursed through me. There, sketched with precise strokes on the parchment, were our vehicles. My heart raced as questions flooded my mind. How? Why? The drawing bridged the gap between personal and impersonal, intertwining my fate with that of the building in a mysterious symphony.

Compelled by an unseen force, my feet carried me with urgent haste down to the cellar. The air grew cooler with each step, the silence more profound. I found myself standing in the middle of an expansive floor area, the dim light casting long shadows that danced around me. Alone, with the weight of the moment pressing down, I could only voice the disbelief that echoed through the cavernous space, "I can't believe this is happening." The incident was more than an eerie coincidence; it was a puzzle wrapped in the enigmatic folds of time and space, with pieces that refused to fit in any conventional pattern. Each moment spent within the confines of building number 10 added layers to the mystery, compelling me to unearth the truth behind the inexplicable connection between this structure and the intertwined destinies it seemingly held in its grasp.

The following five years of conducting business in building number 10 proved to be not only exhilarating but also immensely profitable. The term "successful" seems too modest to encapsulate the essence of the laboratory business that Andy and I cofounded and operated. It was a journey that, from modest beginnings, soared to remarkable heights. Starting with an initial investment of merely $26, we defied expectations and conventional benchmarks. By the end of our twelfth year, the average annual income of our laboratory had surged to an astonishing $3.6 million, culminating in an impressive total in sales. Reflecting on this, it's clear that what we had was not merely a business but a phenomenal enterprise that thrived on innovation, dedication, and an unwavering commitment to excellence.

Our success was no stroke of luck; it was the result of relentless hard work, strategic planning, and an unyielding passion for our field. We were pioneers, venturing into uncharted territories, breaking new grounds, and setting standards that others in the industry could only aspire to. The business became a beacon of success, attracting attention not just locally but also from around the globe. We had cultivated a reputation that spoke of quality, reliability, and groundbreaking achievements. The growth of our business was not incremental but exponential, each year outperforming the last by significant margins. It felt as though there was no ceiling to our potential, no horizon too distant.

Yet, as is often the case, the greatest stories of triumph are not without their turning points. Despite the unprecedented growth and the accolades, my world was about to take a dramatic turn. What appeared to be an unassailable fortress of success and innovation was, unbeknownst to me, perched precariously on the edge of a cliff. It all came crashing down suddenly, without warning, like a house of cards caught in a gust of wind. This unforeseen calamity marked the beginning of a new chapter, one filled with challenges and uncertainties that I could never have anticipated.

Throughout the years, Andy and I were not just business partners; we were like family. Our partnership in the laboratory was perfectly balanced, with each of us holding an equal share of 50 percent, but our bond extended far beyond the confines of our business. We shared our lives with each other, discussing personal matters that ranged from family dynamics to challenges faced by our children and our relationships with our wives. Our trust went deep, as deep as it possibly could between two individuals not bound by blood. We were, in every sense, brothers from different families, sharing a connection that transcended typical business partnerships.

This profound trust and shared life experiences fostered a partnership that seemed unbreakable. It was more than just a business arrangement; it was a shared journey and a mutual commitment to each other's well-being and to the success of our laboratory. Our relationship was the bedrock upon which the business was built, solid and unwavering. It seemed as if our collaboration was guided by a shared destiny, with each success in the laboratory further cementing our bond and reinforcing our commitment to our shared vision. The path we were on seemed to only ascend, with no peaks in sight, only ever-increasing heights of achievement and innovation.

In this context, our laboratory wasn't just a place of work; it was a symbol of our shared dreams and efforts, a testament to our synergy and mutual respect. It was an embodiment of what can be achieved when two like-minded individuals join forces, both professionally and personally. We were patriotic to our shared cause, champions of our collective ambitions, and architects of what we believed to be an unshakable future. However, life, as it tends to do, had unexpected twists in store. With great success often comes unforeseen challenges and, sometimes, great sorrow. The very fabric of our partnership, which seemed indomitable, was about to be tested in ways I could never have imagined. What loomed on the horizon was beyond my wildest fears, a scenario so unthinkable it never crossed my mind in a million years. This unforeseen event would challenge the very core of our bond and the future of our thriving business.

One unremarkable morning, the dynamics of our office subtly shifted with the arrival of a new employee named Phil, who was appointed to our marketing department and assigned the office next to mine. From what I gathered, he was a recent graduate of the Harvard Business School, a detail that Andy had proudly shared, suggesting a high level of competence and ambition. Andy had brought him in to work alongside our existing marketing team with the aim of enhancing their sales strategies and overall performance.

However, Phil was notably reserved, a man of few words, which piqued my curiosity. Unlike other members of our staff who were open and collaborative, Phil maintained a distance, immersing himself in his work without much social interaction. This prompted me to inquire, with increasing frequency, about the nature of his role in our company. Each time, his response was the same, delivered with an unsettling consistency: "I work directly for Andy to continually improve the company."

This vague explanation raised a red flag for me. Until this point, Andy and I had shared an open-book policy regarding business decisions. Phil's presence and elusive role were the first instances where things didn't seem to align with our established trust and transparency. The situation nagged at me, leading me to confront Andy directly about Phil's exact duties and the reasoning behind his secretive employment.

Andy's response was a gut punch, completely unexpected and alien to the partnership we had nurtured over the years. He expressed a desire to dissolve our fifty-fifty partnership, leaving me with an ultimatum: either buy out his shares or watch as he placed the company into receivership and sold it off for its current value. The gravity of his words floored me. We stood there, in a moment that felt like an eternity, as I searched his face for signs of the familiar partner I thought I knew. "You've got to be kidding," I said, disbelief coloring my tone. "Tell me the real truth, and we can resolve whatever this is."

But the Andy I knew seemed absent in that moment; he avoided my gaze, looking down at the floor, and reiterated his decision with a finality that left no room for doubt: "This is what I want to do. There is no other reason."

The revelation was not just a shock; it was a betrayal that cut deep, challenging everything I thought I knew about our partnership and casting a long shadow over the future of our enterprise. It's an undeniable fact of life that everything must come to an end eventually, and the business partnership between Andy and myself was no exception to this rule. In an unexpected turn of events, Andy expressed his desire to part ways in our professional journey, stating his need to explore new horizons and opportunities without my involvement.

Although this revelation was initially hard to swallow, I've come to understand and respect his decision. As the world evolves, so, too, do the needs and ambitions of individuals. This often leads people to forge new paths and sever existing ties, all in the pursuit of personal growth and advancement. The experience has taught me a valuable lesson about the transient nature of relationships and the constant march of time. Indeed, while many aspects of life can be bought, replaced, or recovered, time is the one commodity that marches on, indifferent to our wishes or circumstances, forever eluding our grasp. This realization has imbued me with a newfound appreciation for the present moment and a resolve to make the most of the time that remains.

The termination of our laboratory partnership was a complex and emotionally taxing process. There were countless steps, negotiations, and difficult decisions that had to be meticulously handled to dismantle the shared components of our business. In the end, Andy decided to take over the entire laboratory business, resulting in him buying out my share. As part of the settlement, I received a substantial sum of money as a parting gift. With a heavy heart, I vacated building number 10, the place that had been a second home to me, filled with memories of experiments, discoveries, and long nights of research.

Leaving behind the world I knew, I retreated to the solace of my home, embarking on a much-needed vacation. This time away from the lab provided me with the opportunity to reflect on the series of events that led to the dissolution of our partnership and to contemplate my future path. It was a period of introspection, healing, and planning for the next chapter of my life, which was now wide-open with possibilities. Meanwhile, Andy took the reins of the laboratory and continued its operations. For the next two years, he managed the business, navigating through the ups and downs that come with running a scientific enterprise. However, despite his efforts and dedication, Andy eventually encountered significant challenges. He fell on hard times, facing unforeseen difficulties that tested his resolve and the stability of the laboratory. This turn of events underscored the unpredictable nature of business and the personal journeys we each must undertake.

The downturn of our once-thriving laboratory culminated in Andy filing for bankruptcy. The tangible remnants of our shared dreams and years of hard work and the laboratory assets were dismantled and sold off piecemeal to various buyers within the second-hand laboratory equipment market. It was disheartening to watch as the physical manifestations of our efforts were scattered to the winds, reducing our once cohesive enterprise to memories and financial statements.

Amid this fallout, the fate of building number 10, a significant asset and symbol of our former partnership, hung in balance. This property, entwined with countless memories and scientific endeavors, became the center of a financial dispute between Andy and me. Despite the dissolution of our business relationship, Andy still owed me a substantial sum of money for the property—a debt that was about to become even more complicated.

In a turn of events that felt almost like a bitter echo of the laboratory's bankruptcy, Andy filed for personal bankruptcy. My name was listed among the creditors, a stark reminder of the financial entanglements that lingered between us. However, the final judgment granted him relief from his debts, including what he owed me for building number 10, leaving me to receive zero dollars on the debt.

Easy come, easy go, I mused, attempting to find a semblance of humor in the grim situation. It was a stark lesson in the impermanence of success and the volatility of business ventures. I resolved to grin and bear the current circumstances, recognizing this ordeal as a harsh but valuable lesson. It was a reminder to approach future partnerships and financial agreements with greater caution and discernment. The experience, while painful, underscored the importance of due diligence and the need to prepare for all eventualities in business and in life.

The recent transition of building number 10 has stirred a blend of emotions within me. Reclaimed by the bank because of Andy's bankruptcy, this iconic structure found a new owner through an auction, falling into the hands of a local electrical contractor. When the news of its sale reached me, a profound sense of finality washed over me. The thought of never being able to revisit the interior of building number 10 sparked a feeling of loss, tinged with a hint of melancholy. This wasn't merely a building to me; it was a haven, a place that, not once but twice, served as my professional abode. Like a nurturing mother, it provided me with shelter, guarding me against the tumultuous storms of the external world. To some, it might seem an exaggeration to attribute such significance to a mere structure. Yet in my heart, I've always believed that building number 10 played an instrumental role in my journey over the past two decades. It was within its steadfast walls that I cultivated my career, faced and surmounted challenges, and carved a path of success.

Departing from its familiar confines felt akin to leaving behind a trusted friend, a constant in my life that I had come to rely on. The bond I formed with the building was not merely physical but also emotional and spiritual, intertwining with my personal and professional growth. The thought of it now housing different dreams, different ambitions, leaves me with a bittersweet sentiment. As I step forward into new chapters without the silent, comforting presence of building number 10, I carry with me the memories, lessons, and the undeniable impact it had on my life, reminding me of where I've been and how far I've come.

Embarking on a new business venture is always a journey filled with anticipation and potential. My latest endeavor brought me into collaboration with a new partner and investor, Terry Barter. Our paths crossed in an unexpected setting—the auction proceedings of my previous laboratory which I had run with my colleague Andy. It was amid this backdrop of transition and change that a groundbreaking idea began to take shape in my mind. I envisioned the creation of a drinking water testing laboratory, a concept that seemed uncharted in the realm of retail and public health. The venue? A bustling, popular mall in my hometown, a place frequented by a diverse array of individuals, each a potential beneficiary of our service. The rationale was simple yet compelling. If malls could cater to people's nutritional needs through food courts, why not cater to their health and well-being by offering a service to test the purity of their drinking water? After all, clean water is as fundamental to health as good food.

Considering the unique intersection of convenience, necessity, and public health, the mall seemed the ideal locale for such an innovative service, offering exposure to the everyday man and woman who might otherwise remain unaware of the importance of water purity in their lives.

With the concept fully formed, I approached Terry, presenting him with this novel idea. I laid out the vision, the potential impact, and the financial aspects, hoping to ignite in him the same passion and belief in the project that I felt. To my relief and excitement, Terry saw the promise in the venture. He agreed to invest and join me as a partner, bringing with him a wealth of knowledge and resources. Together, we embarked on this pioneering journey, establishing what would become the first drinking water testing laboratory within a US mall. This venture wasn't just about starting a new business; it was about introducing a new concept to the public, merging retail convenience with essential health services and, ultimately, fostering a safer, healthier community.

Through this partnership, Terry and I are not just aiming to provide a service but to educate and empower individuals about the significance of water quality in their lives, making it as integral and accessible as their daily meals. This innovative approach to public health represents a leap forward in making essential services available to the broader public, right in the heart of their community.

Terry and I embarked on this ambitious journey with a clear vision and unwavering determination. Within six short months from the initial groundbreaking, the doors to our innovative laboratory swung open, welcoming the public into a new era of health awareness and convenience.

Remarkably, the business flourished from the outset, surpassing even our most optimistic forecasts. It was evident from the community's response that we had tapped into an essential, previously unmet need for accessible water testing services.

Fast-forward seven years, our presence in the mall had become a cornerstone of the community's health and well-being. The business had grown exponentially, a testament to the public's increasing awareness and our unwavering commitment to service quality. However, with growth came new challenges and considerations. Our laboratory, once spacious and cutting-edge, began to feel the constraints of its initial confines.

One day, unexpectedly, my old partner made an appearance at the laboratory that Terry and I had established as our own. His arrival wasn't unaccompanied; he carried a gift, extending it toward me as a token of reconciliation, an olive branch for the unresolved issues lingering from our past engagements. Despite the rocky history, I harbored no resentment toward Andy. After all, he had significantly contributed to my journey toward success. The present he bestowed upon me was not just a mere gesture of peace; it was a profound and unsettling surprise. In his hands, he held the architectural drawing of building number 10, a notable relic from our past ventures, the only piece salvaged from the wreckage of a bankruptcy. As he placed the intricate drawing into my grasp, he uttered, "Eric, this belongs to you and you alone—cherish it." Without awaiting a response, he turned on his heel and departed, leaving a trail of silence and a chapter of our lives closed behind him. I would not lay eyes on him again for many years, the memory of that day lingering like a silent echo in the halls of our laboratory.

In my grasp, bestowed upon me by Andy, was a tangible echo from the past—a historical artifact of days long gone, an era irrevocably lost to time. Holding the architectural drawings of building number 10, I felt a wave of emotions washing over me. Gratitude for the gesture was intertwined with a sadness, a reflection of what once was and could have been. In that moment, I stood at a crossroads, uncertain and contemplative about the next steps to take with this symbol from my past.

The options before me were varied and significant in their own ways. I could choose to display the drawing prominently in our new laboratory, a testament to the journey from there to here, symbolizing both a foundation and a lesson. Alternatively, placing it within the personal sanctuary of my home could serve as a daily reminder of my evolution and the undulating path of life and career. Or perhaps,

I should consider preserving it, tucked away safely as a relic to be revisited on a future day when time has dulled the sharp edges of the past. However, the sight of the architectural drawing was daunting, a mirror reflecting a parallel universe where the present was vastly different. It served as a stark reminder of a divergent path, one filled with what-ifs and might-have-beens, a past that nearly paved the way for a future now forever altered.

In the end, I chose to safeguard the drawing, storing it away from the light of day. It seemed prudent to let it rest, allowing both it and me the space to breathe and adapt, waiting for a time when its presence would inspire rather than weigh heavily on my heart. Thus, I decided to tuck it away, a chapter to be revisited when the time felt right, turning my focus instead to the vibrant and promising endeavors of our current laboratory. The future, with its infinite possibilities and undiscovered frontiers, beckoned with a bright, unwavering light, urging me forward on a path filled with new challenges and achievements.

The demand for the new laboratory services had expanded beyond our original scope, leading to a pressing need for more comprehensive testing capabilities and additional space to accommodate our growing team and technological requirements. Terry and I stood at a crossroads, faced with a decision that would shape the future of our venture. Should we extend our footprint within the familiar confines of the mall, securing additional units to house our expanding operations, or should we venture out, seeking a larger, stand-alone facility that could not only meet our current needs but also provide the space for future expansion and innovation?

The option to rent more space in the mall presented a certain appeal, maintaining our established presence and continuing to leverage the foot traffic and convenience that had contributed to our success. However, the alternative—moving to a larger independent facility—offered the tantalizing prospect of a customized space designed specifically for our advanced testing needs, allowing for greater operational efficiency, expanded services, and the ability to adapt and grow unhindered by physical constraints. As we deliberated, Terry and I weighed the immediate benefits against the long-term vision we held for our business. Our commitment to providing accessible, top-quality water testing services remained at the forefront of our decision-making process, guiding us toward the path that would best serve our community, our employees, and the future of our thriving enterprise.

Suddenly, a call emerged from the depths of my ever-expanding past, a surprising reminder of days gone by. My cousin Dave, along with his wife, Ann, reached out to me one unassuming evening, delivering news that struck me like a bolt of lightning. They informed me that building number 10, a structure steeped in memories and potential, was on the brink of a new chapter as it was being auctioned off the following day. The revelation was both shocking and serendipitous, as the building's previous occupants, an electric engineering firm, had fallen into bankruptcy, leaving the property firmly in the clutches of the bank. This institution, seeking to liquidate the asset, had organized an auction open exclusively to qualified bidders.

The news set my heart racing for I was in dire need of a new laboratory to nurture my burgeoning projects and experiments. Building number 10, with its familiar contours and latent possibilities, presented the perfect sanctuary for my scientific endeavors. However, amid the rising tide of opportunity, a significant obstacle loomed on the horizon; I needed to secure my position as a qualified bidder to participate in the auction. The challenge was daunting, but the prospect of occupying building number 10 for the third time into a cradle of innovation and discovery was too enticing to ignore. I knew I had to navigate the bureaucratic hurdles and legal intricacies to claim my stake in this unexpected opportunity.

The details that my cousins relayed to me next were crucial yet daunting. To secure a place among the bidders for building number 10, one required not just an interest or a dream but a tangible commitment: twenty thousand dollars in cash for the initial bidding fee. Beyond that, the winner would need the financial prowess to settle the remaining balance within a mere thirty days post-auction. The terms were clear, but the timing was far from favorable.

Here lay the crux of my predicament; the auction was scheduled for an early start at eight the following morning. This timing clashed inconveniently with the operational hours of local banking institutions, which swung open their doors to the day's business at nine. This one-hour discrepancy left me in a financial limbo, effectively penniless at the crucial moment of the auction's initial fee requirement.

The race against time intensified the urgency of my situation. With the banks out of reach until after the auction commenced, I was faced with the daunting task of sourcing the necessary funds in less than twenty-four hours. The situation demanded not only rapid action but also creative financial solutions as I had to circumvent conventional banking hours to gather the hefty sum required. The looming deadline set the stage for a frantic scramble, underscoring the necessity of ingenuity, resourcefulness, and perhaps a touch of luck to bridge the gap between opportunity and capability at the dawn of the auction.

Despite the daunting setback of not possessing the twenty thousand dollar bidder's fee required for participation, our resolve remained unshaken. Undeterred, we made our presence felt at the auction, directly addressing the auctioneer with our predicament. We explained our financial bind, unable to provide the initial fee before the banks' opening at 9:00 a.m. To our surprise, the auction landscape was less competitive than anticipated with only one other individual, a proprietor of the land adjacent to building number 10, standing as our rival in this financial duel.

Fortuitously, our unique situation led to an unexpected turn of events. The auctioneer, faced with the prospect of a lackluster auction because of insufficient bidder participation, made the unprecedented decision to delay the event until 10:00 a.m. This grace period provided us with the crucial window needed to access the necessary funds, a twist of fate that felt nothing short of miraculous.

As the auction recommenced, the atmosphere was charged with tension and possibility. The initial bid, set at fifty thousand dollars, quickly soared to an imposing three hundred thousand as we exchanged bids with our lone competitor. During a momentary lull in the bidding war, I locked eyes with my adversary, asserting my determination to secure the building with a bid of up to half a million dollars if pushed. His response was unexpected; after a brief, contemplative pause, he extended a smile of concession, effectively withdrawing from the competition with words of acknowledgment: "Congratulations, this building could only be yours."

Winning the bid felt surreal, a mix of triumph and disbelief washing over me. The acquisition of building number 10 for the third time in my life was more than a mere business transaction; it felt predestined, a recurring chapter in my life's journey that bore the unmistakable mark of destiny. The building, steeped in personal history and memories, was once again mine to transform, serving as a testament to persistence, timing, and a touch of mystical fate. What happened next, we could have never predicted.

In the aftermath of our unexpected auction victory, the building still harbored remnants of its past. The electrical engineering company, once the heartbeat of building number 10, clung to existence within its walls, occupying a modest corner. Kenny, the beleaguered owner of the company, emerged from the dim corridors that had witnessed the rise and fall of his dreams. He approached Terry and me with a sense of urgency, his demeanor reflecting a mix of desperation and hope.

Kenny unveiled a proposition that took us by surprise. Despite the recent downfall that led his company into bankruptcy, he was determined to revive his business from the ashes. His request was straightforward yet bold; he wished to rent half of the building, hoping to secure a lifeline for his struggling enterprise. His offer sparked a series of negotiations, as we delved into discussions to strike a fair balance between our interests and his precarious situation.

Remarkably, through these negotiations, we arrived at a mutually agreeable lease agreement. The terms were beyond favorable; the rent Kenny could afford not only seemed reasonable but was also unexpectedly generous. Astonishingly, the income from leasing half the building to Kenny would comfortably cover our mortgage payments and the property taxes for the next three years. This unforeseen windfall meant that our initial twenty thousand dollar down payment was the only immediate financial burden we faced. Moreover, the deal became sweeter when we learned that the mortgage company, the very entity that had listed the building for auction, offered us a mortgage devoid of any closing costs or fees. The confluence of these favorable circumstances felt like a surreal stroke of luck, as if we had indeed hit a lottery beyond our wildest dreams.

The evolving saga of building number 10 and my intertwined destiny with it carried a peculiar, almost gothic, allure, reminiscent of a narrative that could have been penned by the legendary Edgar Allan Poe. Yet the tale was far from its conclusion. The building, which had once been a symbol of professional aspirations and subsequent downfall, was now a beacon of redemption and newfound possibilities. This journey, marked by serendipitous turns and unexpected alliances, continued to unfold with more twists and layers than one could have anticipated, proving that reality can sometimes rival the most intricate of fictional plots.

The morning following our triumphant victory at the auction, I found myself standing once again within the familiar confines of building number 10, this time clutching the building's original 1961 architectural drawing—a relic that had once defined its very essence. With a sense of ceremonial reverence, I positioned the aged drawing back in its rightful place in the entrance hallway where the original frame hangers still hung. It was a strategic location, ensuring that the drawing would capture the attention of anyone who stepped through the doors, acting as a silent guardian welcoming them into the building's embrace.

As I affixed the drawing back on the wall, I felt a deep connection to the edifice that had been a cornerstone of my career. "This belongs to you," I whispered to the venerable walls. "Display it with pride." It was a moment of reconciliation, of returning something of profound significance to its original owner—a symbol of respect and continuity. Feeling a pull toward the building's roots and my own beginnings, I descended for the third time back into the cellar, the very place where my career had ignited. In the dim expansive space, I pulled a chair to the center of the floor, creating an island of reflection in the midst of vast emptiness. There, surrounded by the echoes of the past, I addressed the silent walls, seeking guidance, "By your mystical influence, I am here for the third time. What lies before me now?"

The response was not in words but in the ambient life of the building itself—the rhythmic clanking of heating and water pipes and the steady hum of power transformers concealed within the depths of the cellar. This symphony of mechanical sounds, so familiar and strangely comforting, was the building's way of acknowledging my presence, welcoming me back as it had done twice before.

As I ascended from the cellar, a surge of emotion washed over me. It was a profound realization that no matter the turns my life had taken, building number 10 had remained a constant, a place where my past, present, and future converged. In its steadfast presence, I found a sense of home, a reassurance that no matter how far I ventured, I could always return to this sanctuary. Building number 10 was more than just a structure; it was a repository of memories, dreams, and the undying spirit of resilience.

In the days following the acquisition of building number 10, an unexpected and heart-wrenching turn of events unfolded, casting a shadow over the joy my cousins Dave and Ann had brought into my life. They, who had been instrumental in reconnecting me with a piece of my past and setting the stage for future triumphs, now faced their darkest hour. Ann, the embodiment of kindness, generosity, and compassion, was diagnosed with cancer. Despite a fierce and spirited battle against the merciless disease, her fight was tragically short-lived, leaving a void in the hearts of all who knew her. The depth of sorrow and grief that enveloped us was profound. Ann was not just family; she was a beacon of light and love in our lives. The news of her passing sent ripples of despair, particularly through Dave, who had lost not just a wife but a soulmate. In the midst of this turmoil, I faced the delicate task of supporting my cousin Dave, who stood shattered by the loss.

The eve of Ann's funeral brought its own unsettling experiences. Disturbed by a vivid nightmare, I awoke in a panic, my cries piercing the quiet night. My wife, Lori, stirred by the commotion, sought to soothe my rattled nerves. In my dream, the familiar yet ominous surroundings of building number 10 morphed into a scene of foreboding. Drawn inexplicably to the cellar, I encountered an unsettling sight—two black arms extending from the shadows, a silent scream etched into the cold air. This cryptic vision, whose meaning eluded me, seemed an ill omen, leaving me unnerved and searching for answers.

The solemnity of the next day, as we gathered around Ann's graveside, was profound. The atmosphere, laden with sorrow, served as a silent testament to our final goodbye. As the priest began his prayers, I was enveloped by an eerie sense of familiarity. The tranquil yet mournful scene was suddenly disrupted. A pallbearer's misstep caused a moment of sheer panic as Ann's casket nearly slipped from his grasp, threatening to fall through the safety straps. Acting on reflex, echoes of my nightmare spilled out, "No! Somebody help!"

As I lunged forward, reaching to grasp the handle at the end of Ann's casket, I noticed that the arms extending from my black London Fog overcoat were identical to those in the nightmare I had the previous night. It seemed that, by some twist of fate, I was exactly where I needed to be at the right moment to help and possibly avert a dire situation. This prompted a swirling thought: was this intervention a message from building number 10 or merely a random stroke of luck? The answer remains elusive, but it's intriguing how this building has seemed to act as a guardian angel over the past forty-five years.

As I reflect upon this, I've just celebrated my seventieth birthday, yet I continue my daily pilgrimage to work at building number 10. There's a peculiar sense of attachment; the building seems to have a magnetic hold, intertwining with my life in ways I can't fully understand or explain. It's as though building number 10 has become a silent witness to my life's journey, its walls echoing the chapters of my past and perhaps holding the key to my presence there. The mystery remains, but the connection is undeniable, a constant in my life that, despite everything, never seems to wane.

This series of events, marked by profound sadness and eerie premonitions, left us all reflecting on the fragility of life and the mysterious connections between our dreams and reality. In the wake of such turmoil, I was reminded of the strength found in family, the bonds that tie us to our past, and the unspoken warnings that sometimes visit us in our darkest hours. The loss of Ann, a tragedy that deeply affected each of us, brought us closer, forging our resolve to support one another through life's most challenging moments.

I later found out from my cousin Dave that Ann had been the first to discover that building number 10 was going up for auction. She immediately recognized the significance of this moment, knowing my long-standing fascination and connection with the building. With a sense of urgency, she suggested to Dave that he should quickly inform me about the auction before the opportunity to bid on this meaningful property slipped away. Ann's intuition and swift action were reflective of her understanding and support for my interests. This revelation added another layer of significance to building number 10 in my heart, intertwining Ann's memory with the building even more deeply. Her proactive approach not only demonstrated her thoughtful nature but also her belief in the importance of preserving connections to the past. In this way, Ann played a pivotal role in a critical moment of my life, further cementing her influence and the sentimental value of building number 10 in my personal history.

In loving memory of my dear cousin Ann Liberty, I express my deepest gratitude for all the contributions you have made to our world. Your presence alone has significantly improved the quality of life for those around you, leaving an indelible mark on our hearts and in our lives. The epitaph etched upon your headstone encapsulates the very essence of your being: "When help is needed, be the one who gives it." These words are not just a testament to your character, but they also serve as a guiding principle for all who knew you. You were truly a great child of God, an embodiment of kindness and compassion. Your spirit continues to inspire us, and your absence is profoundly felt by everyone whose life you touched. We all miss you dearly, Ann. Your legacy of love and selflessness will forever remain with us, urging us to be better, to do better, and to help one another just as you did.

It had been approximately three years since Terry and I had acquired building number 10 when we were met with the shocking news of Kenny's sudden demise. Kenny, who had been the proprietor of the electrical company housed within the building for those years, left behind a legacy tinged with both innovation and tragedy.

Following his unexpected passing, the company he had built from the ground up ceased operations, and its remaining assets were earmarked for auction to the highest bidder.

The history of building number 10 is complex and marked by a series of tumultuous events. Kenny and his wife initially came into possession of the property through an auction. This opportunity arose after the bankruptcy of Andy's laboratory, which previously occupied the space. It was Kenny's wife who was the driving force behind the extensive renovations and the establishment of their electrical contracting business within the building's walls. She handled the intricacies of daily operations and was pivotal in the company's initial phases. However, the pressures of business ownership and the demands of rebuilding a company from the ground up took a heavy toll on her. Within a short period, the immense stress led to a tragic outcome; Kenny's wife ended her life, leaving a void in both the company and Kenny's heart. This event sent shock waves through their lives and the electrical business, leading to a downward spiral. The company, once full of promise and potential, found itself in dire straits, grappling with insurmountable challenges.

The unfortunate series of events culminated in the company's bankruptcy, an outcome that forced the relinquishment of building number 10. This is how Terry and I came to acquire the building—through circumstances that were both unexpected and somber. Kenny, a figure once central to the vibrancy and operation of the building, had become a memory, his dreams and aspirations for the company dissolved.

Kenny's departure and the dissolution of his electrical company signified a significant change in the building's narrative. What was once a bustling hub of electrical contracting was now quiet, leaving Terry and me to ponder the next chapter. The building, now completely under our ownership, stood as a silent witness to the highs and lows of entrepreneurial dreams, a reminder of the unpredictable twists and turns of business and life.

My narrative would be incomplete without the acknowledgment of a cherished companion, who was the very heart of building number 10 from the very day Terry and I became its caretakers. This individual is Norman Martin, whose bronze likeness now graces the maintenance room door, etched with the dates that mark the span of his life. Norman harbored a profound affection for the building, nurturing it with a dedication akin to a father's unwavering care for his child. Over the years, he nurtured a hope to continue his labors well into his twilight years.

Norman was then seventy-eight years old, a testament to the enduring spirit and resilience he exhibited. However, the twilight of his years was shadowed by the onset of an incurable lung cancer, a malady that foreshadowed an inevitable parting. With his departure, a palpable void permeated our world, yet it was swiftly bridged by the flood of memories, reflecting the depth of his personal friendships and his unwavering commitment to his duties, commitments he ensured were always met with diligence and care.

I vividly recall a moment that encapsulates his spirit, just two days before he passed. We were replacing a balance transformer in one of the hallway lights of building number 10. Norman had noticed a subtle dimness pervading the space and, true to his nature, insisted on rectifying it immediately. That same day, with the characteristic thoroughness that defined his life, he made sure his wife's car was fully fueled, attending to every detail, ensuring everything was in its right place before his departure.

To have known Norman was an honor of the highest order, a sentiment shared by all who were fortunate enough to cross his path. His memory, etched not just on a plaque but in our hearts, continues to inspire and guide us. Norman, you are deeply missed, but your legacy of dedication, care, and love lives on within the walls of building number 10 and within the hearts of all who knew you.

Going Forward: What to Expect for Completing My Career Journey

Throughout my life, I have ventured into a diverse array of professions, embracing roles as varied as a "fix it" man, a rock star, a medical doctor, an electronics engineer, a photographer, a professional gymnast, a research chemist, and a business entrepreneur.

Each of these experiences has enriched me with unique skills and perspectives, turning my career path into a rich tapestry of adventures and learning. From the hands-on problem-solving of a "fix it" man to the disciplined creativity of a rock star, the meticulous precision required in the medical field, the analytical thinking of an engineer, the artistic eye of a photographer, the physical prowess of a gymnast, the scientific inquiry of a chemist, to the strategic foresight of an entrepreneur, I have explored the vast landscapes of professional life.

Now as I stand at this crossroads, pondering "What next?" I find myself reflecting on the lessons learned and the passions ignited by each past venture. The question isn't merely about choosing the next job title but about seeking a path that aligns with the deeper currents of my interests and aspirations. As I contemplate the future, I consider not only what profession might come next but also how it will contribute to my ongoing journey of personal and professional growth. How can I synthesize the diverse skills and experiences I've acquired into a cohesive and fulfilling career trajectory? The answer to this question will guide my next steps as I continue to weave the intricate mosaic of my professional life.

A Profession Is Like Trying on Pants for Fit

From a tender age, my journey through the working world was a diverse and enriching experience, offering me a glimpse into various professions before I even reached adulthood. My initial foray into the job market began with a role at the local newspaper, the *Fitchburg Sentinel*, where my primary task involved inserting advertisement flyers into the daily publications. This job, which I pursued three times a week after school, was more than just a means to earn a modest income; it was my first real exposure to the workforce. Standing in line, hopeful among a crowd of over twenty boys, I eagerly awaited the chance to be selected as an inserter for the evening. Although the pay was minimal, this role ignited in me a curiosity about the print industry. The pressroom, with its relentless pace, was a place of both fascination and intimidation, filled with dedicated workers navigating the cacophony and hazards of the machinery. Despite the evident satisfaction some found in this environment, I was uncertain if a future amid the heat, grime, and noise was what I desired.

My journey didn't stop there; it led me next into the realm of the food industry. After school, I took on a position at a catering business, working as a dishwasher. This stint, however, was short-lived. The experience, while valuable, made clear that the fast-paced, behind-the-scenes world of catering was not where my passion lay.

In search of a new path, I ventured into the retail sector, landing a job at a local RadioShack outlet. This position represented my first step into what could be considered a professional career. At RadioShack, I was introduced to the complexities of sales, customer service, and electronic gadgets, marking a significant departure from my previous roles. Yet despite the potential for career growth, I felt that this path was not the right fit for me either.

My exploration of professions took another turn when I became a service manager at a Dodge dealership. This role was a step up in responsibility, requiring me to oversee the mechanics' team and address client issues regarding their vehicles. It was a challenging position that tested my management skills and problem-solving abilities. Unfortunately, my performance did not meet the dealership's expectations, leading to a reassignment to the task of washing and cleaning used vehicles. This demotion was a clear signal that it was time to move on and seek new opportunities.

Each of these positions, though not always a perfect fit, contributed to my growth and understanding of the working world. They taught me about the diversity of labor, the importance of finding one's passion, and the reality that not every job is meant to be a lifelong career. As I moved from one job to the next, I gathered a collection of experiences and lessons that would shape my approach to future endeavors, guiding me toward finding a profession that truly resonated with my interests and abilities.

Embarking on the quest to find the right profession often resembles the process of trying on a pair of pants, a quest for the perfect fit that aligns with one's aspirations and capabilities. In my personal journey, I experimented with a myriad of roles, only to discover that some fell short of my expectations, akin to a pair of trousers too snug or lacking in length. Others were overwhelming, much like pants so voluminous and long that I seemed lost within their folds. The pivotal lesson I gleaned from these experiences is the importance of persistence in the pursuit of the ideal match. It's about the willingness to explore a diverse array of options, to engage in trial and error, until you find that one career path that feels tailor-made for you.

Once you stumble upon a profession that feels as though it was crafted to suit your unique blend of skills, interests, and ambitions, it's crucial to invest yourself fully in it. Embrace it with enthusiasm and dedication, striving to excel and grow within that chosen field. However, it's equally important to recognize when you've reached a point of growth that suggests it's time to seek new challenges and to ascend to greater heights. This realization is not an admission of failure but an acknowledgment of personal development and the natural progression of one's career journey.

Remember, the landscape of life and work is ever-changing, marked by transitions and transformations. Nothing, especially in the realm of professions, is immune to the passage of time and the evolution of individual aspirations. The understanding that nothing lasts forever serves as both a reminder and a motivator to continually seek opportunities for advancement and fulfillment. In embracing this mindset, we open ourselves to the endless possibilities that lie ahead, ready to navigate the shifts and turns with resilience and an open heart.

In the upcoming chapter, I will share the valuable lessons I have accumulated over the past seventy years—insights that have shaped my journey and will hopefully fortify my path ahead. These lessons constitute a personal encyclopedia, with volumes that extend across the decades of my life. Each lesson arrived just when needed, equipping me with strategies to tackle future challenges and presenting potential solutions. Once applied, these lessons are etched into my memory, ready to be passed on to others or revisited as circumstances require. This chapter is not just a reflection on past experiences but also a guide filled with wisdom that can serve as a road map for navigating the complexities of life.

CHAPTER 6

Lessons I've Learned

Pathways and Doors

The concept of pathways in life often features metaphorical doors, which may appear at the beginning, throughout, or at the culmination of these paths. A prevalent notion is that one frequently encounters numerous closed doors before finally reaching one that is open and inviting. To me, a door represents a threshold, serving either as a barrier or as a gateway that one may pass through when sufficiently prepared. Doors in our lives may indeed be necessary, functioning to synchronize the timing of the various paths we take. These doors often remain closed if we have not yet reached the requisite level of maturity or readiness, thereby safeguarding us from potential failure or harm. They only open when we are sufficiently prepared, ensuring our safe transition.

Consider, for example, a young child of four years who aspires to drive a car like their parents. It is not feasible for them to simply get behind the wheel and navigate the roads. They must first mature and acquire the necessary driving skills. Even if they try to circumvent these safety measures, there will be numerous doors that remain firmly closed for their protection, thus ensuring they only embark on this pathway when truly ready.

Experiencing frustration when you've met all necessary criteria and are well-prepared for a particular task, only to find that the opportunity remains stubbornly elusive, is indeed perplexing and disheartening. This situation prompts an important question: what does it truly take to unlock these elusive doors? I am convinced that the secret ingredient is timing. To illustrate, think of the analogy of a lock and key. While numerous keys might fit into a lock, only the right key, with its precise combination of cuts, can turn the mechanism and open it. In a similar vein, when it comes to seizing new opportunities or opening "path doors," the right timing is absolutely crucial. No matter how many times you attempt to open these doors, if the timing is not spot-on, they will remain closed.

This concept became very personal to me in my own journey to becoming an author. Despite numerous attempts throughout my life, my dream didn't materialize until much later. Becoming an author is not just about possessing knowledge on a particular subject; it's also about being able to translate those unique ideas from your mind onto paper in a way that others find valuable and insightful. My field of expertise was in science, specifically focusing on private drinking water quality. Early in my career, my attempts to write were based on common knowledge and lacked the unique insights that could set my work apart. It took over forty years of practice and deep engagement in my field before I was truly ready to write about it. When that moment arrived, everything clicked—my insights had matured and my perspective had deepened significantly. The words flowed effortlessly, as if channeled from some divine source, culminating in my first book *Wellwaterology*. At that point, the timing was perfect, and the door to becoming a published author flung wide-open, marking a pivotal moment in my career.

Timing is a fundamental element in many aspects of life, significantly influencing outcomes and experiences. Consider the intricacies of a musical composition—without precise timing, the melody would descend into chaos, losing its rhythm and harmony. Similarly, timing is crucial for athletes, particularly gymnasts, whose performances rely on meticulously synchronized movements. A routine performed out of sync not only looks uncoordinated but can also jeopardize an athlete's career, underscoring the significance of timing in achieving excellence.

Our lives unfold within a finite span, during which certain milestones ideally occur at predetermined intervals. For instance, a child's first steps and first words are anticipated to follow a natural progression in early development. Accelerating these events is not typically feasible without consequences nor is delaying them without potential long-term impacts. What happens if these milestones are significantly postponed? Does missing the initial window for an opportunity mean it is lost forever, or can such chances resurface at a later time?

This raises the profound question of free will's role in seizing opportunities. While some doors may close, seemingly never to reopen, others might reappear, albeit in different guises. Opportunities, therefore, are not perpetually lost but can reoccur, often requiring patience and readiness to be fully realized. It's a dance of timing and choice, where the universe might provide multiple chances, yet it's our personal decisions that ultimately determine their capture or loss.

There Is a God

Take God out, what's left is the Devil.

—Rev. Howard Underwood

I was baptized as an infant in the Episcopal Church, a serene place of worship nestled within walking distance from our family home, serving as a spiritual cornerstone for the local community. This ceremony was steeped in tradition, a momentous occasion that brought together family and friends to witness and celebrate this significant milestone in my life. It was during this sacred event that I was blessed with two additional guardians—my godfather and godmother. These roles are essential, designed with the profound responsibility of fostering me as their own should anything happen to my biological parents. While tradition often sees godparents being close relatives, in my case, they were my uncle Louis and aunt Fay. This couple, whom I held in high regard, became figures of admiration and affection throughout my childhood. Their presence in my life added a layer of love and guidance, reinforcing the familial bonds that were celebrated on that day of my baptism.

Throughout my childhood and well into our adolescent years, my mother steadfastly maintained the tradition of taking us to church every Sunday. This weekly ritual remained unchanged even when we relocated from our original community to a new neighborhood across town. Adapting to this change, my mother quickly found a new church in our new district, ensuring that our spiritual education and connections would continue uninterrupted.

I particularly looked forward to attending Sunday school each week, where I was captivated by the biblical stories recounted by the minister during the services. These narratives, spanning from creation to the prophets from the life of Jesus to the acts of the apostles, unfolded like a vast and intricate tapestry of faith and history before me. As a child, the allure of these stories was in their drama and moral lessons rather than their deeper theological implications. At that young age, the ancient world of the Bible seemed an intriguing but distant reality, far removed from the contemporary world I inhabited.

While I was fascinated by the events and characters of those ancient times, I must admit that their true meanings often eluded me. The complexities of faith, the nuances of the moral lessons, and the depth of the spiritual messages were layers I would only come to appreciate more fully as I grew older. Back then, I understood these stories as distant echoes from a time long past, not fully grasping how they connected to my own life. It was a world vastly different from mine, yet through these Sunday school sessions, I began to understand that the values and lessons they imparted were timeless, intended to guide us regardless of how much the world around us may change.

As I transitioned out of my teenage years and stepped into the realm of young adulthood, a notable shift occurred in my life—my regular attendance at church gradually ceased, becoming a part of my past rather than a staple of my present. This change marked a significant physical and emotional separation from the church and, by extension, from the faith that had been a cornerstone of my identity for so long. The absence of this spiritual anchor left me feeling adrift, haunted by a sense of loss for something that had once been integral to my sense of self and community.

The reasons for this drift were manifold and complex, ranging from the demands and distractions of young adult life to a burgeoning quest for personal identity that often questioned previously held beliefs. As I navigated new responsibilities, relationships, and realities, the familiar structure and community of the church fell to the wayside. Yet this distance from my faith was not without its inner turmoil. There were moments when this separation felt like a tangible loss, a void where once there had been certainty and support.

In the midst of this spiritual hiatus, I often pondered whether my path would eventually lead me back to the church or if this chapter of my life was closed for good. The question of rejoining the church or continuing without its direct influence became a recurring theme in my reflections. Despite the uncertainty of my religious future, the values and lessons I had absorbed during my years of attendance lingered, continuing to shape my thoughts and actions in subtle ways.

This period of my life was marked by exploration and questioning, a journey that was as much about rediscovering myself as it was about understanding the role of faith in my adult life. Whether I would find my way back to the church or carve out a new path remained an open question, but the impact of my upbringing in the faith continued to resonate within me, influencing the person I was becoming.

Upon starting my career at Borden Chemical Company, I had the pleasure of being introduced to Richard Sontag, the supervisor of the analytical department. Over the years, our professional relationship blossomed into a genuine friendship, anchored by shared interests that went beyond the confines of our workplace. Richard was not only a colleague but also a talented musician who dedicated his free time to performing in two distinct bands. One was a family-based wedding band while the other played a more spiritual repertoire as part of a church service band every Monday night known as the prayer group meeting.

Richard's passion for music and his involvement in these bands piqued my interest, especially when he extended an invitation for me to join the Monday night prayer group sessions with my guitar. Intrigued by the opportunity to blend my musical skills with a communal spiritual experience, I accepted his invitation to give it a try. This decision opened a new chapter in my life, offering me a chance to explore my musical talents in a nurturing and spiritually enriching environment. The experience promised not only to strengthen our friendship but also to provide a unique avenue for personal growth and expression within the context of a faith community.

My involvement with the church group initially lasted about one year. As time went by, my schedule grew increasingly busy, making it difficult to dedicate time to the activities of the church. Consequently, I decided to put my church involvement on hold. It wasn't until approximately forty years later that I reconnected with my faith and joined a new church congregation. This new chapter allowed me to engage with a community that shared my values and provided a sense of belonging and spiritual growth.

I met a wonderful young woman named Lori, who was fifteen years younger than me and swiftly became the love of my life. We initially connected when she joined my company as a general office worker. Over time, our relationship blossomed, and after two years of dating, we exchanged vows in the church where her father, Howard Underwood, presided as pastor. This charming church, nestled in the small town of Winchendon, Massachusetts, became the setting for many of our cherished memories. Howard, along with his wife, Jane—a woman with an innate talent for the piano and superb administrative abilities—led the services. The congregation might have been modest, numbering fewer than twenty parishioners at times, but the intimate setting fostered a profound sense of community. Our shared faith and the tight-knit bonds among the congregation members created a powerful connection that deeply enriched our lives. This sense of unity and spirit made us feel as if we were part of a much larger vibrant community.

After we were married, Lori and I became regular members of the congregation, attending the church on a consistent basis. For me, the church had a captivating format, rich with musical performances and congregation participation, followed by the articulate teaching of the scriptures masterfully orchestrated by Pastor Underwood. This format rekindled memories of my earlier church experiences, yet the superior structure and delivery of the services here made them even more impactful. The combination of lively music, engaging participation, and clear, insightful sermons brought a refreshing depth to our weekly worship, enhancing my spiritual journey and connecting me more deeply to the community.

I genuinely believe that, for me, God has brought my life full circle, with a brief intermission allowing me to find meaning and purpose once again. I have found a spiritual home in Pastor Underwood's church, where the community and teachings resonate deeply with my soul. I have made a solemn vow to remain a part of this congregation, immersing myself in its activities and growth, until the day I meet my Maker. This commitment stems not only from a sense of belonging but also from a profound appreciation for the journey that has led me here and the guidance I've received along the way.

The Black Box in Your Life

Is your life shrouded in mystery, akin to a black box? This realization has dawned upon me. My life, too, is an enigma. I've come to understand that the capability for comprehension is a universal attribute, available to everyone, rather than an innate mechanism that automatically activates. We possess the extraordinary potential to unravel the mysteries of the unknown and to delve into depths yet unexplored. However, more often than not, we opt for only surface-level understanding, content with a cursory glance at the outer shell of the proverbial black box. We leave the intricate exploration of its depths for another time or, perhaps, delegate the task of decoding its profound meanings to others. This choice, whether conscious or not, dictates the extent of our understanding and engagement with the world around us and, indeed, with the very essence of our lives.

How much do we truly need to understand about the complexities within our personal "black box"? The question beckons us to consider whether we should decode only the essentials needed to navigate our daily existence or whether we should delve deeply into the core of our being, harnessing every facet it has to offer. Perhaps there exists a balanced path—a middle way—that enriches our lives without overwhelming us with excessive minutiae. This dilemma mirrors the broader inquiry concerning the extent of our awareness regarding the inner workings of our bodies. Should our knowledge be limited to recognizing basic needs, such as the necessity of sleep when fatigued or eating when hungry? Alternatively, is there merit in possessing a comprehensive understanding of the biochemical processes that sustain us every moment or being acutely aware of how our nervous system interacts with environmental stimuli?

The value of in-depth knowledge about our physiological functions may vary. For some, a detailed understanding could enhance life's quality or performance in demanding tasks while for others, it might serve as an unnecessary distraction from everyday pleasures and responsibilities. Ultimately, the appropriateness of such knowledge might depend heavily on individual circumstances and aspirations. Those who engage in activities requiring peak physical or mental performance may benefit from a deeper insight into their body's mechanisms. In contrast, for individuals whose lives are more sedentary or routine, a cursory understanding might suffice. The decision on how much to learn and apply about our inner workings could well depend on the balance each person seeks between achieving their goals and maintaining a sense of simplicity and contentment in life.

For me, the exploration of my personal "black box" necessitates a deliberate and timely approach, engaging with its complexities only as circumstances demand. This methodological exploration is particularly relevant when I aim to modify my physical or mental capacities in any significant manner. Before any transformation can occur, a comprehensive understanding of the relevant capability is essential.

This process begins with an in-depth investigation into how a particular condition or state came to be, followed by the application of strategies designed to effect the desired change.

Take for instance, the goal of losing ten pounds to reduce belly fat—my initial step involves a thorough analysis to identify the root cause of the weight gain. Was it a result of excessive carbohydrate intake over a brief period, or could there be an underlying medical issue warranting further examination? Understanding the cause is crucial for determining the most effective course of action, which might include dietary adjustments, increased physical activity, or seeking medical intervention if necessary. This approach ensures that any efforts to alter my state are informed, targeted, and likely to be more effective. By incrementally acquiring knowledge and applying it judiciously, I can make informed decisions that positively impact my well-being. This strategy not only facilitates specific changes, such as weight loss, but also enhances my overall understanding of my body and mind, empowering me to maintain or improve my health and capabilities over time.

Navigating through life's myriad decisions is akin to deciphering a complex black box, where each choice we make is a journey down a path filled with uncertainties. It's essential, therefore, to approach these crossroads with a blend of intelligence and common sense, utilizing a decision-making protocol that optimizes our chances of success while minimizing the risk of adverse outcomes. Such a strategy doesn't merely rely on arbitrary selection but incorporates a systematic approach to making choices that are more likely to lead to desirable results. Personally, I also place a significant emphasis on intuition, allowing my gut feelings to serve as an initial litmus test for the viability of a potential path before subjecting it to further scrutiny. This approach was particularly pivotal when I found myself at a career crossroads, torn between the fields of medicine and chemistry. Both disciplines held a profound allure for me, and I was confident in my ability to excel in either. However, the true test came when I assessed them through my intuitive decision-making system, focusing on the level of commitment each path demanded. The prospect of becoming a doctor, with the immense responsibility of caring for hundreds of patients whose lives might hinge on my decisions at any given moment, was somewhat daunting. This role required an unparalleled level of attentiveness and dedication that, upon reflection, did not resonate with my personal aspirations. In contrast, the field of chemistry, while devoid of the immediate patient care demands, presented an intellectually stimulating challenge. It required a deep concentration and the application of my skills to specialized areas, such as the PVC formulations I had encountered at Borden Chemical. This path felt inherently right, resonating with my intuitive sense of direction and ultimately guiding my initial decision.

While it's conceivable that the right combination of influences could have swayed me toward a career in medicine, such persuasive elements were conspicuously absent. Thus, guided by my intuition and a systematic evaluation of both commitment levels and personal affinity, I embarked on the chemistry path. This choice, shaped by a thoughtful blend of gut feeling and rational analysis, exemplifies the nuanced process of navigating life's complex decision-making landscape.

The ancient maxim "Know thyself" is a piece of wisdom that I have encountered repeatedly and have come to recognize as the pivotal key to unlocking the enigmatic black box that governs our individual existences. This black box, unique to each person, encompasses an intricate tapestry of characteristics ranging from physical appearances to the microscopic intricacies of our intercellular makeup and extends to the vast complexities of our personalities. There is no universal blueprint for understanding the contents of this black box, as the diversity inherent in human nature defies simple categorization or analysis.

Embarking on a journey of deep self-exploration and introspection enables us to peel back the layers of our own unique onion. By earnestly engaging with our inner selves, we begin to unravel the nuances of our likes and dislikes, our moral compass, ethical frameworks, spiritual beliefs, and the breadth of our capabilities and talents. This introspective process is not a mere act of self-indulgence but a crucial exercise in self-awareness that lays bare the essence of our being.

The revelation of our true selves through this exploration serves as a key to deciphering the perplexities of the black box that each of us carries. With this key, we gain access to a more profound understanding of who we are at our core, which, in turn, illuminates our paths with a clearer vision. This clarity is instrumental in guiding our choices and decisions, allowing us to navigate the myriad pathways of life with confidence and purpose. The mysteries of the black box, once daunting in their opacity, become less inscrutable as we learn to understand ourselves better, making the journey of life not only more navigable but also more meaningful.

Charting My Own Path: The Journey of Self-Growth

Throughout my life, I have consistently experienced a profound sense of unity and purpose in everything I undertake. For instance, when faced with the challenge of transporting a twelve-foot board, I intuitively knew that finding its center and lifting from there was essential to avoid it dragging along the ground. This principle of balance and self-reliance extends beyond physical tasks to my interactions with family and friends. Although they are always within reach, I often hesitate to ask for their assistance because of concerns about timing and the desire for personal fulfillment.

Handling tasks independently not only provides a deep sense of satisfaction but also allows me to fully own the outcomes of my efforts. There is a unique pleasure in celebrating successes that I've achieved through my own endeavors—sharing these moments can sometimes dilute the joy. Conversely, when projects do not go as planned, managing them solo shields me from the discomfort of external blame. This approach has shaped my personal and professional life, reinforcing a preference for self-sufficiency and the rewarding feeling that comes from tackling challenges on my own terms.

From a young age, I perceived myself as the center of my universe, with everything around me serving as my vast playground. I was surrounded by all the resources I needed, and I harbored a deep belief that whatever I desired—whether good fortune or good health—would eventually be mine simply by wishing for it. However, a word of caution is warranted; be careful what you wish for as the universe can just as readily deliver misfortune and poor health.

This perspective might suggest a self-centered childhood, focusing solely on my own needs. Indeed, many of my peers were taught the virtue of prioritizing others before themselves. As a child with limited resources, this posed a dilemma. With no money, possessions, or profound wisdom, what could I possibly offer? My existence seemed meager, and demand for my contributions was virtually nonexistent.

Reflecting on this, I now see the value in sharing personal achievements with others. We are not isolated; every thought, energy, and physical entity is interconnected. Our lives are shaped by our environments, and it is paramount that we contribute our successes back to the community, enabling others to build upon them in the future. The notion that a gravestone marks only birth and death dates overlooks the essential truth; it is the dash between these dates—the life lived—that truly matters. This dash represents the unique journey of each individual, as distinctive as each snowflake.

Throughout my life, I've often felt alone yet always in control of my decisions, especially when navigating critical paths. Whether I succeeded or learned a lesson, the satisfaction was mine alone, making me completely responsible for my actions. Although others have accompanied me at times, our paths inevitably diverged. The stark reality is that all relationships, whether through personal choice or the inevitable course of nature, will end someday. This may seem harsh, but in my youth, I believed in the eternal nature of ideas, friendships, love, and existence itself. However, experience taught me that these, too, fade, leaving only memories behind us.

We are the sole navigators of our lives, metaphorically picking up and dropping off passengers along the way, ultimately reaching our final destination alone. My father often said that we are born with our mother beside us and pass through life engaging in various relationships, only to die alone. As I grew older, this perspective resonated more deeply with me. From birth until our last breath, we are entirely responsible for navigating the events of our life, crafting our unique journey marked by that all-defining dash.

ERIC KOSLOWSKI

Hey, Buffalo Bill, What Did You Kill?

The phrase "Thou shalt not kill," a well-known edict from the Sixth Commandment, holds various interpretations for different individuals. Traditionally, this commandment prohibits direct and intentional killing, deeming it a gravely sinful act. Commonly understood as a prohibition against murder, this raises the question: does this directive apply solely to human beings, or does it extend to other forms of life such as animals, birds, fish, plants, insects, and microbes? The application of this commandment to nonhuman life-forms is not universally agreed upon and varies significantly based on cultural, religious, and personal beliefs. From a conservative standpoint, one might argue for erring on the side of caution: to avoid killing any living being that exists freely.

My personal beliefs on this matter were instilled in me during my childhood. From an early age, I was taught to discern right from wrong, and I understood that causing harm, especially to the extent of taking a life, was something I could never condone. This deep-seated conviction was profoundly reinforced by an incident when I was about eight years old—an experience that has stayed with me to this day.

On an early spring morning, I visited my schoolmate Peter at his home. Eager for a bit of adventure to satiate our young curious minds, we decided to play outside, engaging in typical boyhood antics. I distinctly recall us in his driveway, tossing small pebbles at a tin can to see who could topple it first. What unfolded next was both unexpected and unintentional. As we were engrossed in our game, a quartet of small sparrow birds fluttered close to the target. During the excitement, my next pebble veered off course and struck one of the sparrows, causing it to tumble over, unconscious. We rushed to the bird, hoping it would awaken and fly away, but fate had other plans. The tiny sparrow lay lifeless, a victim of my unintended action. Overwhelmed by guilt, I broke down in tears on Peter's shoulder, devastated by the irreversible harm I had caused. Peter tried to offer solace, insisting it was an accident and that I hadn't meant for this to happen. While his words were meant to comfort, the harsh reality lingered—I had ended a life, and the weight of this truth was profoundly unsettling.

To this day, perhaps influenced by that distressing incident, I find myself incapable of harming an animal for any reason, whether for sustenance or perceived human necessity. This deep-seated aversion extends to everyday situations. I frequently find myself stopping in the middle of the road to spare the life of a small rodent, be it a chipmunk, rabbit, or a squirrel. My actions often exasperate my wife, but there's a compelling force within me that drives me to go to great lengths to avoid ending an animal's life. This instinctual need to preserve life has profoundly shaped my behavior, making it impossible for me to play the role of a predator. In a metaphorical sense, this "Buffalo Bill" simply can't kill.

Relationships

In a lifetime, one can encounter a myriad of relationships—those with parents, siblings, relatives, friends, colleagues, pets, and many others. Among these, there are special relationships that I find particularly compelling: those that appear destined to last a lifetime but can, without warning, vanish in an instant right before our eyes. Each of these relationships is unique and sometimes unforgettable, leaving a lasting impression on our hearts and minds.

These fleeting connections often serve as invaluable teaching tools, guiding us in our journey to finding a soulmate. They teach us about love, loss, resilience, and the importance of cherishing each moment. The relationship I'm referring to is the profound and often complex love for another person. This type of love can be transformative, shaping our lives and choices in profound ways, even when the relationship itself does not endure. Such experiences, while sometimes painful, enrich our understanding of human connections and help us appreciate the depth and variety of love.

Falling in love with another person often seems like an act graced with magical powers. I'm not entirely sure what forces are at play, but I do believe there's a special something—a mysterious spark—that ignites when love appears. Is it mere coincidence, a serendipitous alignment of life's events between two people, or is it orchestrated by some higher power, akin to how chemical elements combine to form a stable compound? The mechanisms of love remain a profound mystery, layered with complexity and wonder.

Growing up, love always seemed like a challenging concept for me to grasp. It was elusive, unpredictable, and I struggled to understand its rhythms—how it could suddenly manifest in my life or why it would remain hidden for extended periods. The unpredictable nature of love made it a puzzling yet endlessly fascinating subject. Each experience of love, whether fleeting or enduring, taught me more about its depths and the contours of human relationships. As I matured, these experiences helped shape my understanding of love's potential power to transform and enrich our lives even in its most transient forms.

It all began for me seven years old in the first grade. The style at the time for young girls was to wear two small bells dangling from ribbons attached to their hair perched on top of their heads. There was a girl seated in front of me whose back of the head I found myself staring at day after day, sparking an interest in her for reasons I couldn't quite fathom. Was it the tinkling bells in her hair, the way her hair fell, her face, her size, or the way she carried herself with a certain poise? Whatever it was, I knew I was too afraid to approach her, yet somehow, she knew I admired her.

When Valentine's Day rolled around, she wrote me a beautiful card expressing her interest in me as well. It was exhilarating—I now had my first girlfriend, but I was left wondering, *Now what do I do?* This small gesture of affection was monumental for me, marking the beginning of my journey into understanding relationships and interactions. The mystery of those early feelings and the joy of receiving that card taught me the profound impact of acknowledging someone's feelings and the importance of expressing our own even in the simplest forms. This early experience laid the groundwork for how I would approach relationships in the future, always with a sense of wonder and a desire to connect deeply with others.

This marked the beginning of my romantic journey, and if I had known then just how many winding paths lay ahead, I might have paid more attention to the choices I made. Each relationship, each interaction, was like stepping onto a new trail whose twists and turns were unknown. With hindsight, I see how every decision influenced the course of my heart's travels, teaching me invaluable lessons about love, compromise, and personal growth. If I had understood the complexities of these paths early on, I might have approached my decisions with greater care and thoughtfulness, potentially steering my journey in different directions. Yet each choice, whether seemingly minor or major, was integral in shaping not just my romantic life but my understanding of human connections.

My romantic journey truly began at the tender age of thirteen, when I was in the sixth grade. As I transitioned into junior high school the following year, I found myself navigating the tumultuous waters of puberty—a pivotal period marked by the onset of secondary sex characteristics. This developmental phase, often awkward for many, brought about significant changes. My voice began to deepen, my body started to grow rapidly, and acne appeared, adding to the self-consciousness typical of this stage. Additionally, this was the time when I started to experience a newfound attraction to the opposite sex, adding an exciting yet confusing dimension to my adolescent life. Each of these changes signaled the end of my childhood and the beginning of a new uncharted chapter in my personal growth and romantic explorations.

Then unexpectedly, Billy arrived on the scene. He was the new kid in the neighborhood and seemed to arrive just as we were all grappling with the complexities of adolescence. With an air of confidence, Billy offered to guide us through the maze of understanding girls, claiming to possess insider knowledge and secrets that he was eager to share. Our little group, consisting of four friends—Chip, George, John S., and John W.—often gathered around the block to hang out, but it was clear that not everyone was prepared or interested in Billy's revelations about girls. In fact, among our group, I was the only one who was genuinely intrigued and willing to listen. Billy's arrival sparked a mix of skepticism and curiosity, but for me, it marked the beginning of an enlightening chapter, as I was eager to learn and navigate the new social dynamics that his insights promised.

Billy was an interesting figure, with a charm that was difficult to ignore. By most accounts, he was quite handsome, and his shiny set of braces only added to his distinctive appearance. However, what truly set Billy apart was his uncanny resemblance to a celebrity. He bore a striking similarity to Paul McCartney of the legendary rock group the Beatles—only a younger version. This resemblance did not go unnoticed, especially by the girls in our neighborhood. They were utterly smitten with him, often trailing behind him, each hoping to be considered his girlfriend.

The attention Billy garnered from his McCartney-alike looks was nothing short of magnetic, drawing admirers with the ease of a pop star. Witnessing his effortless allure, I found myself standing before the mirror, scrutinizing my own reflection. In a mix of envy and aspiration, I wished to see a glimpse of someone famous staring back at me, yet all I saw was myself—just me, without the glamorous echo of celebrity. This moment of self-reflection sparked a deeper understanding of my own identity and the realization that perhaps, in time, I could find my own unique qualities that might draw others to me, just as Billy's resemblance to McCartney drew his admirers.

What I came to understand later was that Billy didn't entirely relish his resemblance to a rock star. He found that looking like Paul McCartney set certain expectations on him, particularly when he met new people, especially girls. They often anticipated the charisma and charm associated with the famed musician, and this expectation weighed heavily on him. In an attempt to deflect these pressures, Billy would often quip with a smile, "I don't look like Paul. It's Paul who looks like me." This playful reversal was his way of managing the lofty expectations placed upon him and lightening the burden of his celebrity-like image.

Ironically, what Billy saw as a burden, the rest of us viewed with a mix of envy and admiration. To our young minds, his looks were a golden ticket to popularity and admiration, particularly from the opposite sex. We couldn't help but imagine the excitement of navigating social interactions with the ease that his appearance seemed to afford him. His situation highlighted a curious aspect of adolescence; the grass always seems greener on the other side. While we longed for his magnetic pull on others, Billy yearned for a sense of normalcy that eluded him because of his starlike appearance.

Billy was unaware that his supposed secrets about girls weren't the most valuable lessons he was imparting. Through him, I stumbled upon a far more intriguing subject—the phenomena of attraction. What really draws one person to another? Faced with this enigmatic "black box" of attraction, I was determined to decode it, aiming to surpass even Billy in popularity.

Realizing the complexity of attraction, I knew it wouldn't be a straightforward task. Unsure of where to start, I decided to turn my attention to observing the relationships around me. I began asking others simple questions like "What made you attracted to him or her?" The responses varied, but many highlighted good looks or a great personality as key factors. While the importance of physical appearance was straightforward, the concept of a "great personality" intrigued me further.

What exactly constitutes a great personality? Is it kindness, humor, intelligence, confidence, or a combination of these traits? I pondered these questions, realizing that understanding the nuances of personality could be crucial in unraveling the secrets of attraction. This exploration was not just about becoming more popular—it was about understanding deeper human connections and what genuinely draws people together beyond superficial attributes.

Let's face it, not all of us are destined to resemble a famous rock star, and ultimately, beauty really is in the eye of the beholder, isn't it? While we can't change our genetic blueprint, there are certainly ways to enhance what we've been given. Proper nutrition and regular exercise can dramatically improve one's appearance, not to mention overall health. Additionally, experimenting with new hairstyles, wearing clothes that fit well and express personal style, and even exploring cosmetic techniques can make a significant difference in how we present ourselves to the world.

But at the end of the day, we are limited to our physical genetic characteristics, and that's not necessarily a bad thing. Imagine how dull life would be if we all looked identical, like robots produced on an assembly line. The diversity in human appearance is something to be celebrated, not lamented. I find it fascinating to observe the unique features and qualities each person possesses; these differences are what catch the eye initially and make someone stand out in a crowd. Personality, however, plays a critical role after that initial physical attraction. It's the personality that sustains and deepens connections, transforming superficial interactions into meaningful relationships. So while our looks might draw others to us, it's our unique traits, behaviors, and ways of engaging with the world that truly define our attractiveness in the long run.

As a young teenager, I realized it was time for me to carve out my own identity and craft a distinct personality to navigate the intricate social landscape of adolescence. I was determined to be the fresh, charismatic figure in the neighborhood. While some of my peers gravitated toward sports, my interests lay elsewhere—I was fascinated by the complexities of relationships with girls, which seemed like an essential pursuit for any teenage boy. Surprisingly, many boys my age seemed more enthralled with sports like football and basketball than with forging romantic connections. At the time, I couldn't quite grasp their indifference, but it worked in my favor, reducing the competition and leaving more opportunities open for me.

I was fortunate to have a natural advantage: blond hair, blue eyes, and a toned physique, thanks to years of gymnastics training. These attributes certainly helped in gaining attention, but I knew that looks alone wouldn't be enough. The real challenge lay in developing a compelling personality. How could I become someone who was not only visually appealing but also genuinely engaging and charismatic? This question prompted me to explore various aspects of my character and interests, aiming to become a well-rounded individual who could connect with others on multiple levels. The journey to discover and refine my personality was about to begin.

There was no question that my personality required significant refinement. I often reflected on Billy, a classmate who epitomized confidence and popularity in our school. His ability to navigate various social groups with ease and his consistent presence at the center of attention were traits I admired deeply. Billy's appeal wasn't just superficial; his compassion and intellect set him apart. He possessed the charisma of a rock star, coupled with a well-rounded and engaging personality.

In contrast, I found myself frequently battling feelings of awkwardness and uncertainty, especially around girls my age. This self-awareness sparked a determination within me to embark on a journey of personal development. I knew I needed to transform these insecurities into strengths and forge a personality that was both authentic and appealing. This quest was not just about superficial change; it involved deep introspection and learning to embrace and project my unique qualities. It was about finding a balance between improving myself and remaining true to who I was at the core.

Reflecting on those years, I can discern certain personality traits that were absent in my youth but which I only developed as an adult. I grappled with the challenge of cultivating a unique identity that my peers would accept. There is a subtle yet critical distinction between uniqueness and strangeness—one that requires careful awareness. Possessing a unique personality often means embodying rare qualities that are highly sought after, providing a distinct advantage in social settings. On the other hand, a personality deemed strange can be viewed as undesirable by the majority. My own experience placed me in a delicate position, straddling the fine line between uniqueness and strangeness, navigating the complex dynamics of acceptance and individuality.

Confidence plays a crucial role in the delicate balance between uniqueness and strangeness. It often determines whether an action or expression stands out positively or veers into awkwardness. People who perform any emotional or physical action with confidence generally achieve greater success than those who exhibit hesitation or self-doubt. Consider gymnastics, for instance. A floor routine typically involves a sequence of specific body movements that, when fluidly linked, form a complete exercise segment. These movements must be meticulously coordinated to ensure a seamless flow, starting with an initial sprint that leads into a roundoff, followed by two back handsprings, and culminating in a backflip with a full twist.

Executing this sequence safely requires a deep focus on mechanics and an unwavering confidence, which can only be gained through rigorous training. Indeed, consistent practice not only helps in perfecting the moves but also in building the gymnast's confidence. With each successful repetition during training sessions, a gymnast's confidence grows, gradually leading to mastery of the routine. This development underscores the idea that proper training does indeed build confidence, enhancing both the execution and the perception of their skills.

By adopting a training approach similar to that used in gymnastics, one can effectively address and overcome emotional and physical awkwardness, cultivating a sense of unique self-confidence in the process. Confidence isn't just about receiving support from friends and relatives; it's built through dedicated practice and mastery of skills.

To enhance one's abilities, it's crucial to practice both strengths and weaknesses. Focusing on what you do well and refining these skills will naturally lead to improvement. For example, if the goal is broader social acceptance, a more comprehensive set of skills must be developed. This includes honing interpersonal skills such as active listening, clear and articulate speech, and enhancing overall knowledge in both specific and general fields. Learning more about your area of expertise, increasing your general knowledge, and becoming more aware of your surroundings are all beneficial. Additionally, studying history and other relevant subjects can provide deeper insights into various situations, enriching your understanding and interactions. These practices not only improve social skills but also contribute to a well-rounded persona, boosting confidence in a variety of settings. By systematically addressing and improving these areas, one can truly excel and stand out, turning what might once have been awkwardness into a distinguished and confident individuality.

From a young age, I recognized that with increased knowledge, life not only became easier but also more fulfilling, and my capacity to assist others expanded. This understanding underscored the importance of personal development; I realized that by making myself mentally and physically strong, I could become a source of strength for others. If you are well-grounded and robust, you have more to offer to those around you; but if you are struggling with your weaknesses, your ability to contribute effectively to others may be limited.

I always believed in the value of self-improvement—not just for personal gain but also for the broader impact it could have. Strengthening oneself involves a holistic approach that includes nurturing one's intellectual capacities through continuous learning and keeping oneself physically healthy and capable. Such strength becomes a reservoir from which others can draw. Whether it's providing advice, offering emotional support, or demonstrating resilience in the face of challenges, the benefits of personal strength are manifold and extend beyond the individual to influence the community at large. Thus, the pursuit of knowledge and personal growth is not merely a self-centered endeavor but a communal one, where the dividends of your strength are shared with and bolster the people around you.

Throughout my life, every relationship I've encountered has enriched my existence in numerous ways. Positive connections have brought joy and companionship while even the negative ones have been instrumental in teaching me valuable lessons. Essentially, every interaction—regardless of its nature—has contributed to my personal growth.

These relationships have served as both mirrors and windows: mirrors that reflect my own behaviors and values and windows that offer insights into different perspectives and life strategies. Even challenging relationships have taught me resilience, empathy, and the importance of setting boundaries—skills that are crucial in navigating personal and professional spaces. Thus, all relationships, past and present, constitute a repository of experiences from which I can draw wisdom. They inform my decisions and strategies, not just in personal matters but also in broader aspects of life such as career choices and social interactions. By reflecting on these experiences and applying their lessons, I am better equipped to handle current challenges and make decisions that will lead to a fulfilling future. My advice: be strong, knowledgeable, confident, sincere, compassionate, and kind, and the world will take notice.

Hobbies

When I researched the definition of a *hobby*, I was intrigued by its fascinating etymology. The term *hobby* dates back to the thirteenth century when it was used to refer to a small horse or pony. Over time, the meaning evolved to include the toy replica of a horse known as a hobbyhorse. The leap from this object to the contemporary meaning of *hobby* is particularly interesting. It is believed that the transition occurred because riding a hobbyhorse was a common leisure activity, particularly among children, symbolizing an activity pursued purely for enjoyment. This is how the term came to denote a "favorite pastime"—an activity that one engages in for pleasure rather than for financial gain and which is usually practiced with some regularity. Examples of hobbies include diverse activities such as collecting stamps, cultivating roses, or indulging in books. Each of these pursuits represents a personal choice to spend free time in a way that brings joy and satisfaction.

When I interview a new applicant for a position at my laboratory, right after the formal introductions, the first question I pose is "So tell me about your hobbies?" This question is crucial as it reveals much about a person's interests and intellect. The hobbies an applicant chooses can provide deep insights into their personality and way of thinking. I find the responses vary widely and include reading, painting, traveling, playing chess, gardening, collecting antiques, engaging in electronic games, and many others—all of which I consider to be enriching hobbies.

However, one response that I find disheartening is "I don't really have any hobbies. I can never find the time." To this, I usually reply, "Gee, that's too bad. You must lead a really busy life." It's important to note that I generally do not consider these candidates further. Why? I believe that a lack of hobbies indicates a lack of curiosity about the world. Engaging in hobbies often reflects an individual's ability to pursue personal growth and learning beyond professional and daily demands. It suggests a capacity for self-motivation and passion that can be very beneficial in a dynamic research environment. Thus, understanding an applicant's hobbies helps me gauge their potential for creativity and innovation in the laboratory.

When an applicant responds, "I have so many hobbies," and begins to enumerate them, it instantly puts a smile on my face, and the interview positively progresses from there. This enthusiasm about their diverse interests significantly increases their chances of being hired. Many people have questioned why I place such emphasis on whether a person has hobbies. My answer is straightforward: I find people with hobbies fascinating. Hobbies reflect a person's curiosity, energy, and engagement with the world beyond their professional obligations. They often indicate a well-rounded character, capable of passion and dedication—qualities that are highly valuable in any professional setting. Moreover, hobbies can foster creative thinking and problem-solving skills, which are crucial in a dynamic work environment like a laboratory. In essence, a candidate's hobbies give me a glimpse into how they balance their life, manage stress, and maintain personal growth, all of which are important for thriving in long-term roles.

Throughout my life, hobbies have played a significant role at every stage. As a child, my hobbies revolved around my toys—building blocks, Erector Sets, painting by numbers—and collecting items such as baseball cards and Matchbox cars, to name just a few. These activities not only entertained me but also began to shape my skills in organization and attention to detail.

As I transitioned into my teenage years, my hobbies evolved and became more sophisticated. I delved into model airplane construction, chess, chemistry sets, and building electronic devices. I also started playing musical instruments and exploring social hobbies like dating. Each of these pursuits helped refine my analytical skills, boosted my creativity, and improved my social interactions.

Entering adulthood, my hobbies escalated both in intensity and cost. They ranged from constructing a house to indulging in sports cars, motorcycles, and even full-size airplanes. Travel and reading across various subjects also became significant parts of my life, enriching my knowledge and broadening my perspectives. These adult hobbies required more significant investments of time and resources but provided richer experiences and deeper satisfaction.

What's fascinating is the dynamic nature of hobbies—they are not static but evolve as we do, adapting to our changing interests and circumstances. This progression of hobbies reflects our personal growth and shifting priorities over time. They continue to be a source of joy and a means to engage deeply with the world, illustrating how our passions shape and define the course of our lives.

Hobbies indeed have a way of coming and going, and sometimes they are shelved for a future "next time." I have several hobby projects that have been ongoing for years, which I engage with at my leisure. Will they get finished today? Perhaps not, but their enduring interest assures me that one day, I will see them to completion. It's akin to assembling a ten-thousand-piece puzzle—a few pieces added every day. Once the puzzle is complete, what do you do with it? Often, nothing because the joy was in the journey, not just the culmination.

That's what's great about hobbies; they are timeless and can be paused or continued whenever needed. They adapt to our life's pace and allow us to return to them whenever we find the time or inspiration. This flexibility is what makes hobbies a constant source of personal fulfillment and relaxation.

My advice to anyone without a hobby is to find one. It could be one of the most rewarding endeavors you undertake for yourself. Whether it's painting, writing, gardening, or learning a new instrument, the process of engaging deeply with something you love is beneficial not just for passing time but also for enhancing creativity, reducing stress, and improving overall well-being. Find something that intrigues you, and let it grow with you over time.

Our Inner Self

In this context, "pathways" metaphorically represent the various opportunities and directions our lives can take. These are not literal roads but rather the series of choices, circumstances, and events that lead us through different phases and aspects of our existence. These pathways are akin to invisible forces that attract us toward certain experiences or decisions, potentially shaping our skills, beliefs, and overall character—what is referred to here as our "inner self."

The "inner self" symbolizes the entirety of our being or sometimes referred to as our ego. It's constructed from our experiences, spirit, decisions, actions, reactions, and wisdom. Just as a physical house can be built up or broken down, our inner self can be fortified or damaged by the pathways we choose to follow. Positive pathways, such as education and healthy relationships, contribute to the construction and strengthening of our inner self. In contrast, negative pathways, like illness or harmful behaviors, can cause damage to our inner self possibly regressing us.

The notion here is that each person has their own unique set of pathways, predetermined and tailored to them, much like DNA is inherited from one's parents. These pathways vary in timing and relevance and can reemerge or change as life progresses. This perspective suggests that our journey through life is a personal and unique experience shaped by a mix of fate, personal choice, and circumstance.

In my journey through life, I have traversed various pathways, each leading to destinations that were either permanent or transient. The permanent pathways culminated in what I consider my home, signifying a definitive conclusion to those particular journeys, never to be embarked upon again. These paths represent final decisions, unalterable commitments that have shaped the bedrock of my existence. On the other hand, the transient pathways represent incomplete journeys that did not lead me home but paused, hanging in limbo, suspended in time, awaiting the right moment for continuation or conclusion, potentially leading to my doorstep in the future. These are the paths of possibilities and of decisions deferred and opportunities yet to be seized. Beyond these, there exists another category of pathways, ones that demand careful navigation: the pathways leading to habits, both good and bad. These routes are life-altering for they shape not just temporary experiences but also long-term character and destiny. The habits formed from these pathways can anchor us in stability or lead us astray. In the subsequent discussion, I aim to delve deeper into these critical paths, examining how they influence our lives and how we might steer them toward positive outcomes.

I consider myself extremely lucky to have navigated away from the grip of potentially life-limiting vices such as alcoholism, smoking, drug use, compulsive gambling, and unchecked weight gain, among others. These habits, insidious in their nature, have a way of embedding themselves into the fabric of daily life, subtly eroding one's sense of self and potential. Whenever I found myself entangled with these behaviors, they invariably disrupted my routine and diminished my capacity to live fully, acting as barriers that kept me from realizing my full potential.

However, it's important to acknowledge that my journey wasn't devoid of missteps. There were periods when I found myself succumbing to the allure of negative habits, particularly smoking and drinking. The need for an effective escape strategy became apparent, especially as I realized that conventional methods for breaking bad habits were often flawed. These traditional approaches, such as merely attempting to replace one harmful habit with another less detrimental one or gradually reducing consumption, frequently proved ineffective or most commonly just ignore that the habit exits all together. The truth is stark yet simple; abstaining from initiating a harmful habit is the only surefire way to avoid the necessity of quitting it. But what recourse is available when a habit has already taken root, stubbornly clinging to your lifestyle?

Over time, as I accumulated an assortment of habits—both beneficial and harmful—I recognized the pressing need to develop a strategy not just for managing but also for fundamentally changing or eliminating these entrenched patterns of behavior. In the forthcoming section, I intend to delve into the insights I've garnered regarding habit modification. I'll share the transformative approach that enabled me to decisively break away from detrimental habits, effectively relegating them to the past. This narrative is not just about the cessation of negative behaviors but about the journey toward self-improvement and reclaiming control over one's life.

Controlling and Eliminating Unwanted Habits through Distraction Techniques

Indeed, we are inherently creatures of habit, shaping and molded by our own repetitive behaviors that may subtly dictate our lives. Most of our habitual behaviors are advantageous, serving as reliable autopilots for our daily routines and even our sleep cycles. For instance, simple acts such as waking up to a programmed alarm or executing a sequence of actions before leaving home are rooted in habit. Similarly, driving to a destination involves utilizing skills that have become second nature through repetition, requiring minimal conscious thought. However, it's important to acknowledge that not all habits are beneficial; some, like excessive alcohol consumption, drug abuse, gambling, or succumbing to anger, can be detrimental over time. Whether positive or negative, these habits develop for myriad reasons and can persist for varying durations, potentially lasting a lifetime. Ultimately, the power to change, maintain, or eliminate these habits lies within us.

Habits serve as shortcuts, eliminating the need to continuously rethink actions by establishing entrenched patterns of thought that dictate our behavior for specific tasks. I refer to habits as entrenched methods of operation, immutable unless the underlying behavior is altered. Engaging in a habit, if faced with a slight behavioral modification, may temporarily disrupt the automatic pattern, reverting eventually to the original habit, albeit with slightly diminished recall, impacting the habit minimally. Conversely, if alterations to habitual behavior occur frequently and intensely, they can dismantle the established automatic responses, ending the habit completely. For instance, if by habit, you typically initiate walking with your right leg followed by the left, this sequence becomes a deep-seated pattern reinforced each time you begin walking. Choosing to start walking with your left leg instead initially disrupts the pattern, but without consistent attention, your old habit typically prevails, reverting to right-leg initiation. However, by consciously and consistently beginning with the left leg, the habitual pattern will gradually erode, leading to a permanent alteration of the habit.

The phonograph, or record player, provides an apt metaphor for the formation, execution, modification, and eventual cessation of habits. But first, what is a habit? Think of a habit as a song recorded on a vinyl record, played whenever a specific trigger occurs. A phonograph, known since the 1940s and later referred to as a record player or turntable, employs mechanical analog techniques to record and playback sound. Sound vibrations are translated into physical deviations within a spiral groove etched into a vinyl disc. Upon playback, a stylus traces this groove, vibrating to reproduce the original sounds. Similarly, a new behavior pattern, once learned and deemed beneficial, must be repeatedly enacted to ensure its retention, much like deepening a groove on a vinyl record. A "trigger" in this context is akin to selecting a song to play; each time this trigger is encountered, the corresponding habit "plays out" or is enacted. The more frequently a habit is performed, the more ingrained it becomes in our automatic behaviors.

Habits significantly impact our lives, both positively and negatively, which underscores the importance of managing them effectively. I suggest employing a cause-and-effect approach, analyzing what initially instigates the habit and understanding its impact on our lives. By finding this understanding, one can begin to manage them.

The initial step in habit management is to catalog all recognizable habits. Common essential habits include everyday activities like eating, talking, socializing, driving, working, and sleeping. Conversely, there are detrimental habits we could forgo, such as excessive drinking, overeating, smoking, gambling, maintaining a poor diet, and using offensive language. After listing these habits, we can assess each one, ranking them according to their impact, which helps determine the importance of the habit and whether it can be modified or eliminated to foster a better lifestyle.

For instance, dietary habits often change throughout one's life to align with varying activity levels. During the growth phases of youth, there's a tendency to consume large quantities of high-energy sugary foods like candy and chocolate, catering to high metabolic demands. However, this comes with the downside of potential long-term health issues, such as obesity and diabetes. The decision is always yours: the immediate gratification from a sugar rush or facing potential long-term health issues like pancreatic failure leading to diabetes. Let's see what can be done to change them.

By closely monitoring the effects habits have on our lives, we can use the "phonograph player" method as a metaphor for our ability to modify, replace, or eliminate habits. This involves recognizing the trigger (like putting on a record) and the habitual action (playing the song) and deciding whether this habit is worth keeping, altering, or stopping altogether.

The "phonograph player scratch" method offers a straightforward yet effective strategy to alter, substitute, or discard a habit by understanding four key principles relating habits to songs:

- Habits function like phonograph records, playing specific "songs" or actions in response to particular triggers.
- As long as the "song" remains clear and uninterrupted, the corresponding habitual behavior will continue to manifest.
- By evading the trigger or disrupting the clarity of the "song" (habitual response), we can phase out the habit.
- The power to manage and revise any habit lies within our own capabilities.

To illustrate the process of habit control, we'll simulate the formation, modification, and elimination of a habit, specifically cigarette smoking. Although we will not engage in actual smoking, we'll use a simulated case study—my own experience—to understand how someone may start smoking, develop a deep addiction, and ultimately quit successfully.

Smoking is a complex habit, incorporating social, emotional, physical, and chemical components, making it a multifaceted addiction that can disrupt normal life and lead to severe health issues like emphysema or lung cancer. It's a habit that many acquire with relative ease but find extremely difficult to abandon. My personal journey with smoking spanned a decade, during which I initially failed to recognize its harmful effects. Eventually, through a systematic approach, I managed to break free from this detrimental habit permanently.

Cigarette smoking often begins as a social habit, influenced by peer pressure from friends or family members who smoke and invite you to join their "private smoking club." Lighting up a cigarette can swiftly integrate you into this social circle, creating a powerful sense of belonging and acceptance. This social aspect plays a significant role since humans are inherently social creatures, often adopting behaviors to fit into a group, avoiding the discomfort of being an outsider.

Emotionally, the habit can be reinforced by the need to alleviate stress or anxiety, providing a temporary escape from reality and offering a momentary diversion. The physical ritualistic nature of smoking—finding a cigarette, lighting it, inhaling, and finally extinguishing it—serves to cement the habit further each time the trigger is encountered.

On a chemical level, the addiction is driven by nicotine, a substance that, once absorbed into the bloodstream, creates a dependency. Nicotine induces pleasant feelings in the brain, leading to temporary satisfaction. However, as this feeling wanes, the craving intensifies, compelling the smoker to reach for another cigarette. This cycle increases nicotine tolerance, meaning higher quantities are required for the same pleasurable effect. Attempting to quit smoking triggers both mental and physical withdrawal symptoms, making the cessation process challenging.

To begin developing a smoking habit, one typically finds a social group, often comprising close friends, who facilitate entry into the world of smoking. Emotionally, the individual then justifies the act of smoking, integrating it into their daily routine. Each cigarette smoked reinforces the physical aspect of the habit, solidifying the ritual. Concurrently, the chemical aspect kicks in as nicotine levels in the brain increase, deepening the addiction.

This process can be likened to creating a "smoking habit song track" on a phonograph record. With each cigarette, the grooves of this habit track become more defined, embedding the behavior more deeply. Triggers, such as falling nicotine levels in the brain, play this "smoking song," compelling the individual to smoke again to alleviate cravings. This habit loop persists until the song can no longer play—when the habit is broken.

Distorting or erasing the "song playback" to eliminate the smoking habit involves several strategies. These can include avoiding the social triggers that prompt smoking, replacing the habit with healthier alternatives, and dealing with the emotional reasons behind smoking. Additionally, understanding the physical and chemical aspects of nicotine addiction is crucial. By employing these tactics, the clarity of the "smoking song" diminishes, eventually becoming inaudible, thus breaking the cycle of addiction.

Logical reasoning presents a straightforward method for quitting the smoking habit. Typically, when we "hear" the smoking song triggered by a nicotine craving, our instinct is to smoke a cigarette. Since this song originates in our brains, the key is to reduce its clarity and volume until it becomes inaudible and meaningless. This can be achieved through the "track scratching" technique, a process akin to physically scratching a record to disrupt its music.

The track scratching technique involves substituting the urge to smoke with a different physical activity, such as walking, running, or dancing. This acts as a distraction, effectively "scratching" the habit's track and distorting the smoking song played by our brains. The interference from the distraction diminishes the song's clarity and volume, thus reducing the urge to satisfy the nicotine craving. By consistently applying these distractions whenever the smoking urge begins, the habit's soundtrack becomes increasingly unrecognizable until the habitual behavior ceases. For example, my own smoking habit started at twelve, influenced by my cousin Larry and his friend Steve. It became a deeply ingrained part of my routine, continuing for eighteen years. However, the turning point came unexpectedly during a routine drive: a mishap with a lit cigarette and a closed window resulted in burnt clothing and a moment of clarity about the dangers and absurdity of the habit. This incident spurred the realization that I needed to eliminate the habit to protect not only my wardrobe but also my health.

I decided to employ the "phonograph player scratch" method to rid myself of the pernicious smoking habit, requiring a strategy to muddle the entrenched smoking cue. Living adjacent to a low-speed railway with an extensive track provided the perfect backdrop for my diversion tactic. Each time the urge to smoke surfaced, instead of giving in, I headed out to the adjacent track for a run. Initially, because of the detrimental effects of smoking on my respiratory health, my running capability was limited to merely two hundred yards. Nevertheless, I persisted with this new routine for about two weeks, each day pushing a bit farther until I was able to run a full mile. Although the nicotine cravings persisted, they gradually weakened as the associated "habit song" started losing its clarity and influence over me. By the fourth week, the transformation was palpable; the trigger incited by low nicotine levels vanished, silencing the "smoking song" that once dominated my actions, effectively liberating me from the clutches of the smoking habit.

This triumph underlines the potency of the distraction method in habit elimination. With dedication and patience, this approach proved invaluable in dismantling the habitual cycle, setting me free from the addiction. Moreover, this method of distraction holds promise not only for quitting smoking but also for addressing other compulsive behaviors such as overeating, excessive drinking, drug use, gambling, and obsessive-compulsive behaviors. It's worth trying. You have nothing to lose but maybe a pesky bad habit.

Don't Always Look for Absolutes or Certainty, Instead Look for All the Possibilities

From my childhood, I was ingrained with the belief that nothing is worth undertaking unless it is executed perfectly. This notion, deeply rooted in a philosophy of absolute precision and accuracy, shaped my early perspectives on success and failure. However, as I matured, I began to question the rigidity of this mindset. The more I observed and experienced the world, the more I pondered the nature of truths we take for granted—like the simple equation of 1 plus 1 equaling 2. This led me to wonder: are all absolutes or certainties truly as fixed and immutable as they seem? The exploration of this question has revealed to me the fluidity of knowledge and understanding. It has taught me that adaptability, creativity, and the willingness to view problems from multiple angles are just as valuable as the pursuit of perfection. Life's complexities often defy binary solutions, suggesting that there's merit in embracing a more flexible approach to learning, problem-solving, and decision-making. This shift in perspective has not only enriched my understanding but has also opened doors to new ways of thinking and solving problems that a rigid adherence to "right" and "wrong" could never have allowed.

Embark on a journey less traveled by many and embrace the unique lessons that others may either shun or never have the opportunity to experience. This concept finds a vivid illustration in the realm of musical exploration. Consider the conventional path many musicians take, mastering instruments like the piano, percussion, and certain woodwind and brass instruments. These instruments are known for their defined and limited range of notes. A piano, for instance, traditionally offers eighty-eight distinct notes, each key locked into producing a specific pitch. This limitation bounds the musician to a finite sonic landscape, with each press of a key yielding the same note, time and again.

Contrast this with the world of string instruments, such as the violin or guitar, which not only can mirror the eighty-eight notes of a piano but also explore the myriad tones that reside between. The act of pressing, plucking, and bending a string opens up a universe of sound possibilities. Different techniques applied to the same note can yield a variety of tones, and the musician can slide between notes to discover new sounds. This fluidity allows for an expansive and limitless array of musical expressions, making string instruments a canvas for creativity and innovation.

I draw a parallel between this musical exploration and my approach to life. Rather than treading the well-worn paths that lead to predictable destinations, I seek out the spaces in between—the roads less traveled. This mindset reveals a spectrum of possibilities, transforming life itself into a rich tapestry of experiences. Just as a musician might explore the spaces between notes to create a unique piece of music, I explore the less obvious choices in life's journey. This approach has taught me that the most rewarding experiences often lie beyond the familiar and the conventional in the pursuit of the uncharted and the new. By embracing this philosophy, one can discover a world of endless potential and unforeseen adventures, each step an opportunity to learn, grow, and create something truly unique.

Only You Know You Best

During the tumultuous period of my second divorce, I encountered a significant challenge with my legal representation that pushed me to a pivotal moment of self-reliance and empowerment. With each court appearance, it became increasingly clear that my lawyer was inadequately prepared, often overlooking crucial details that not only escalated my financial losses but also tarnished my reputation. The frustration culminated during a crucial hearing when, yet again, my attorney failed to mention a vital aspect of our case, thereby weakening our position substantially.

Confronting him about this lapse, I expected excuses or perhaps a strategy to recover; instead, his response, though simple, struck a profound chord within me. He apologized and said, "You know your case better than anyone else. Don't ever forget that." This statement, intended or not, ignited a realization about the importance of personal agency and the limitations of relying solely on others for representation. Taking his words more as a directive than consolation, I made a decisive move that would alter the course of my proceedings. I terminated his services immediately, a decision that was both liberating and daunting. Fueled by a newfound resolve, I embarked on a journey to represent myself. I acquired a comprehensive book on the Massachusetts Probate Court protocols and dedicated myself to mastering the legal intricacies of my case.

Over the next two years, this self-taught legal journey was far from easy. It required immense dedication, countless hours of study, and the navigation of complex legal procedures. Yet this process was incredibly empowering. Representing myself not only allowed me to articulate my situation with genuine passion and precision but also gave me direct control over the narrative of my case. This experience taught me an invaluable lesson about the power of self-advocacy and the importance of understanding the intricacies of one's own challenges. It underscored the idea that while experts can provide guidance and support, the deepest understanding of one's situation often lies within oneself. This journey of self-representation was not just about winning a legal battle; it was a transformative period that reinforced my belief in my abilities and the significance of taking charge of one's destiny.

The profound adage "Only you know you best" underscores a fundamental truth about self-awareness and personal responsibility. In the vast expanse of the universe, it's a rare and precious insight to acknowledge that no one is more invested in your well-being than you are yourself, with the divine exception of God. While it's true that familial bonds, such as those with a mother, father, or close relatives, can foster deep-seated care and concern for your welfare, the reality remains that you are the constant guardian of your own life. Every hour of every day, all year round, it is you who is on vigilant duty, nurturing and safeguarding your well-being. This ceaseless companionship with oneself naturally leads to an unparalleled depth of self-knowledge. After all, spending every moment in your own company affords you a unique perspective on your thoughts, feelings, and reactions that no external observer could fully grasp. Recognizing this truth illuminates the understanding that, when it comes to truly knowing what's best for you, the most reliable expert is invariably yourself.

Given this perspective, placing your trust in others, especially in matters of great significance, becomes a nuanced consideration. The caveat here is not to diminish the value of external support but to highlight the importance of discernment. Particularly when the intentions or the level of commitment of those offering assistance might not align with your best interests, skepticism is not just warranted but wise. This realization steers us toward a compelling conclusion; it is essential to exhaust all avenues of self-reliance and personal initiative before seeking external intervention. This isn't to advocate for isolationism or to undervalue the benefits of collaboration and support from others. Instead, it emphasizes the primacy of self-dependence and encourages a thoughtful evaluation of when and how to incorporate external assistance. By adopting this approach, one not only affirms their own capabilities but also ensures that any help enlisted is truly complementary to their personal efforts and well-being.

When an individual surrenders to despair or abandons their self-belief, they relinquish the most formidable protector they could ever possess: their own self. This phenomenon, which I have observed in numerous forms and intensities, invariably sets off a downward spiral that can profoundly erode one's self-esteem. The consequences of giving up on oneself are not merely psychological; they manifest in tangible, often devastating ways, leading to a debilitating state where one's reliance on external support becomes not just a temporary crutch but a long-term dependency. This shift from self-sufficiency to dependence is marked by a gradual loss of autonomy where the individual increasingly looks outside for validation, direction, and sustenance, neglecting the immense reservoir of strength and capability within. Yet amid this bleak scenario, there lies a beacon of hope. The remedy, though it may seem daunting at first, is rooted in simplicity and profound self-empowerment. It involves a deliberate shift toward self-reliance and taking initiative. The act of doing something for oneself, no matter how small or insignificant it may seem, is a powerful antidote to the paralysis of despair. It's about reclaiming one's agency, one step at a time, and recognizing the inherent ability to influence one's own life path.

This process of reengagement with one's self doesn't just halt the decline of self-esteem; it actively rebuilds it, fostering a renewed sense of competence and self-worth. By prioritizing self-dependence and actively seeking to address one's own needs, an individual can gradually restore their faith in themselves. This transformation is not instantaneous nor is it always linear, but each act of self-sufficiency is a stone laid on the path out of dependency leading toward a renewed state of self-assurance and independence.

The journey back to self-reliance is both a challenge and an opportunity. It requires courage to face the vulnerabilities and strength to overcome them. Yet the rewards are immeasurable, offering not just a return to a state of equilibrium but the possibility of discovering a more resilient, empowered version of oneself. In embracing the practice of self-dependence, one not only escapes the shackles of external reliance but also opens the door to a life of greater fulfillment, autonomy, and self-discovery.

Who Are These Inner Voices and What Are They Telling Us?

Have you ever found yourself engaged in a solo dialogue, conversing with no one but yourself? If so, you're not alone; I find myself doing the same quite frequently. This phenomenon might prompt some to wonder if it's a sign of mental instability or if, conversely, it represents a completely natural aspect of human cognition. According to experts, the concept of an inner voice, also known as "internal dialogue," "the voice inside your head," or "inner monologue," is a well-documented cognitive process. This internal dialogue is the result of specific neurological functions that enable you to "hear" your thoughts internally without the need for verbal expression or sound production.

This inner voice is not just an abstract concept but has a biological basis. It's processed in a similar manner to how we perceive external voices, with the auditory components of the brain playing a crucial role. Studies have demonstrated that when we engage in inner speech or even silent reading, there's notable activity in the temporal cortex, an area of the brain associated with processing sounds. What's more, this internal discourse also involves the frontal motor cortex and Broca's area, regions linked to speech production and language comprehension (Amit et al. 2017; Perrone-Bertolotti et al. 2012).

The involvement of these brain regions highlights the complexity and naturalness of internal dialogues. The activation of the frontal motor cortex and Broca's area, in particular, underscores the brain's preparation for speech even when no actual speech occurs.

This suggests that talking to oneself, far from being a sign of mental distress, is actually a sign of the brain's intricate and dynamic processing capabilities.

My inner voices serve as my sanctuary of personal and private discourse, a realm where my deepest thoughts and musings are kept away from external ears. Often, when posed with the curious inquiry, "What are you thinking about?" I default to a reflexive "Nothing." This response, though automatic, feels superficial upon reflection. After all, to not be engaged in thought would suggest a state akin to nonexistence. Recognizing the inadequacy of such a reply, I instead opt for a more guarded stance, politely asserting, "It's none of your business." This is not out of rudeness but from an understanding that the dialogues within my mind are sacred, meant for me alone until I choose to give them voice.

The journey from thought to spoken word is not without its pitfalls. There have been numerous instances where I've found myself verbalizing thoughts that were meant to remain internal. These slips, often accompanied by a mix of regret and self-reproach, lead me to question, "Why did I just say that?" It's a reminder of the delicate balance between our inner and outer worlds. Our internal dialogues, rich with reflections, plans, and fantasies, are not always meant for external consumption. They are part of a complex cognitive process that allows us to explore ideas, emotions, and responses in the privacy of our own minds.

This process of internal dialogue is not just a matter of keeping certain thoughts private; it's also about the freedom to explore ideas without judgment or consequence. It's where we can be our most authentic selves, pondering over decisions, rehearsing conversations, or even engaging in self-admonishment for spoken gaffes. The transition from thought to speech involves a conscious choice, a moment where we decide which parts of our inner world we are willing to share and which parts remain under lock and key.

In essence, these inner voices are more than just mental chatter; they are the guardians of our innermost thoughts, emotions, and beliefs. They represent a space where we can freely navigate the complexities of our psyche, making sense of our experiences and the world around us. So while the occasional slip of the tongue may bring a moment of embarrassment, it also serves as a reminder of the rich inner life that informs our every word and action. Having an inner monologue is a testament to the human brain's remarkable ability to simulate conversation, prepare for future interactions, and process thoughts and emotions internally. So the next time you catch yourself engaging in a conversation with your inner voice, remember that it's a normal, natural part of human cognition, deeply rooted in our neurological framework.

Distractions

Distractions represent one of life's most formidable challenges, consistently hindering our ability to maintain focus and productivity. At its core, a distraction can be understood as anything that diverts our attention away from our immediate tasks or goals, leading us to temporarily lose sight of what we are engaged in. Various factors can serve as distractions, ranging from ambient noise, which can subtly erode our concentration, to more direct interruptions like active conversations, an overwhelming influx of information, the wandering nature of daydreaming, and notably, the pervasive influence of cell phones. These distractions do not merely interrupt our flow of thought; they can significantly disrupt our cognitive processes. This disruption often results in lost time that cannot be reclaimed, effectively halting our forward momentum and, in some cases, causing us to regress back to our starting point.

There exists a perspective that posits a certain level of distraction could be beneficial, offering a mental reprieve during times of heightened stress or tension. However, I contend that such moments of elevated tension demand not a retreat into distraction but rather an increased focus and deeper understanding. The argument for distraction as a form of relief overlooks the crucial opportunity for growth and resolution that comes from confronting and working through challenging situations. Instead of yielding to distractions, embracing a disciplined approach to maintaining concentration, especially under pressure, can lead to more meaningful progress and personal development. By recognizing the detrimental impact of distractions and adopting strategies to minimize their influence, we can better navigate the complexities of our lives and achieve the focus necessary for success.

The distinction between a genuine distraction and a deliberate pause in thinking is subtle yet significant, reflecting the nuances of our cognitive processes and individual attention spans. Every person possesses a unique capacity for concentration that varies not only from one individual to another but also from moment to moment within the same individual. This variability becomes particularly evident in situations that demand high levels of mental engagement, such as engaging with technically advanced material that requires intense concentration to fully grasp its intricacies.

Consider, for example, the act of reading a book laden with complex concepts and sophisticated terminology. Such an endeavor demands not only a deep focus but also a sustained engagement with the material, challenging the reader to maintain an elevated level of comprehension over extended periods. It is in these moments of heightened cognitive demand that the analogy of the brain functioning like a muscle becomes especially apt. Just as muscles perform optimally under usual conditions but may experience fatigue or cramps when subjected to intense or prolonged exertion, the brain, too, can reach a point of cognitive overload. This overload manifests not as a physical cramp but as a diminished capacity for processing information, making it increasingly difficult to absorb and retain complex ideas.

When faced with such cognitive fatigue, a pause in thinking—a deliberate, temporary disengagement from the mentally taxing task at hand—can serve as a crucial strategy for mental rejuvenation. Unlike distractions, which inadvertently draw our attention away from our focal activities, these intentional breaks are a form of self-regulated cognitive rest. They allow the mind to relax, reset, and recover from the strains of intensive thought, thereby restoring its capacity for high-level comprehension and problem-solving. This period of rest is not merely a cessation of activity but an essential component of the cognitive process, offering the brain the necessary respite to replenish its energy and enhance its functionality.

Understanding and respecting the difference between unwanted distractions and necessary mental breaks is critical for optimizing cognitive performance. By recognizing the signals our minds send us when they require a pause and distinguishing these from the lure of unproductive distractions, we can more effectively manage our mental resources. This approach not only aids in sustaining concentration over longer periods but also contributes to a more profound and nuanced understanding of complex materials, ultimately enriching our learning and comprehension experiences.

In conclusion, distractions are precisely what their name implies—an unwelcome interruption of our cognitive processes, which, if not managed properly, can severely undermine our ability to maintain high levels of thought and focus. Throughout my life, I have come to the realization that my capacity to handle distractions is notably limited. Even something as seemingly innocuous as the ambient noise present in a room can disrupt my concentration, effectively placing my mind into a standby mode until such disturbances are eliminated. This sensitivity to distraction extends to the point where I have chosen not to own a cell phone, a decision driven by my desire to avoid the constant interruptions it represents. The thought of being accessible to the outside world at any moment, subject to interruptions at their convenience rather than my own, is a prospect I find untenable.

My journey has taught me that my tolerance for distractions diminishes further as I age, necessitating a more deliberate effort to insulate my mind from external noises and interruptions. This endeavor to create a distraction-free environment is not a retreat from the world but a strategic approach to preserving my mental clarity and focus. By carefully curating my surroundings and minimizing potential sources of disruption, I am better able to maintain my course in life, dedicating my energies and attention to the tasks and pursuits that truly matter. This process of minimizing distractions is not merely a personal preference but a critical strategy for enhancing productivity and fostering a deeper, more sustained engagement with my work and interests. It underscores the importance of understanding and respecting one's own cognitive needs and boundaries, and it represents a commitment to cultivating an environment conducive to growth, creativity, and focused thought.

Storytelling to Yourself

Have you ever caught yourself weaving stories in your mind, stories that are not only untrue but also utterly implausible? Many of us have fallen victim to this behavior at one point or another. But one might wonder, is indulging in such flights of fancy truly beneficial for our mental health, and what drives us to create these narratives in the first place? Often, this tendency could be seen as a form of daydreaming, a mental escape providing relief from the harsh realities we may face. These imaginary tales can become so vivid and persistent that they start to feel like an alternate reality, a false truth that we begin to accept as real.

The adage "A lie told often enough becomes the truth" seems particularly relevant here. Through repetition, these fabrications can take root in our minds. Over time, I've observed that some individuals prefer to dwell in these constructed fantasies, where life appears simple and filled with pleasure, rather than confront the real and often challenging truths of their existence. However, it's crucial to recognize that living in a fantasy provides no genuine solutions—after all, one cannot resolve issues that don't actually exist in the tangible world, where real problems can be confronted and resolved.

Is there a method to halt this internal storytelling? Indeed, there is, and it's simpler than one might think. By acknowledging our tendencies to escape into fantasy, we can take the first steps toward grounding ourselves in reality. This involves mindfulness, the practice of staying present in the moment, and confronting our thoughts and emotions as they are, not as we might wish them to be. By doing so, we can start to discern the line between helpful daydreaming and harmful escapism, steering our minds toward healthier narratives that support our well-being and personal growth.

COULD HAVE BEEN; SHOULD HAVE BEEN; HERE I AM

What I have learned about the phenomenon of storytelling to oneself is quite enlightening. It boils down to the realization that these mental narratives are merely fabrications. They are not tangible. They hold no truth unless we choose to breathe life into them and convert them into our new reality. My approach to handling such instances is twofold and requires immediate action. Firstly, as soon as I perceive the storyline crystallizing in my thoughts—gaining structure and beginning to command my attention—I swiftly recognize that this is merely a tale I'm narrating to myself. This realization is crucial; it is the first step toward reclaiming control over my thoughts. The moment I discern that a narrative is forming and encroaching upon my consciousness, I acknowledge its presence. This acknowledgment acts as a mental signal, a red flag indicating that I'm veering away from reality. Secondly, with no delay, I actively remind myself, *This is not real. It's just a story.* I repeat this mantra with conviction, not merely as a whisper in the back of my mind but as a clear, assertive statement. This repetition is not a passive act; it's a deliberate, forceful intervention designed to disrupt the emerging narrative. I continue this practice, repeating the phrase like a protective incantation, until the imaginary tale starts to lose its grip and gradually fades into nothingness.

At this juncture, a remarkable transformation occurs. My mind, like a wayward traveler finding its way back, resets itself. A sign of relief is suddenly felt. It's as though a switch has been flipped, reconnecting me with the present with what is real and tangible. This instantaneous shift ushers my consciousness back from the realms of fiction to the solid ground of reality. Through this process, I've learned not only to recognize the onset of self-generated stories but also to effectively dispel them, reinforcing my connection to the actual world and my lived experiences.

Storytelling, like many behaviors intrinsic to human nature, is often habitual. This habit of mind can significantly influence our thoughts and actions if left unchecked. When I notice the tendrils of an unproductive narrative beginning to weave through my consciousness, I deliberately redirect my focus to a different, familiar subject. This could range from a simple mathematical operation, such as calculating 2 plus 2, to solving a complex trigonometry equation. The key lies in supplanting the habitual storytelling with more constructive thought processes, effectively relegating these unwelcome narratives back to the recesses of the mind from which they emerged. Over time, this practice of thought redirection can become a habit in itself, significantly reducing the frequency of involuntary storytelling.

For instance, I engage in jogging fourteen to twenty-one miles weekly, which serves as a prime example of this method in action. During these runs, my mind is actively engaged in coordinating my physical movements while simultaneously achieving a state of mental clarity and alertness. This state provides a fertile ground for creative and efficient problem-solving. Notably, I choose to run without the distraction of music, allowing my thoughts to flow freely and unencumbered. This approach facilitates a more profound engagement with my thought processes, enhancing my ability to address issues more effectively than if I were confined to a stationary location.

Nevertheless, this mental openness can sometimes become a double-edged sword. Without vigilance, imaginative scenarios, such as fantasies of revenge or unrealistic self-conceptions, can intrude and take root in my thoughts. If these storylines are not immediately recognized as mere stories, they can proliferate, ultimately affecting my mood and the quality of my run. However, through consistent practice and self-awareness, I have trained myself to identify and dismiss these narrative intrusions as soon as they appear, utilizing a technique of shifting my thoughts away from storytelling. This approach has proved invaluable, enabling me to maintain focus and derive greater satisfaction from my running experience. As the narrative starts to unfold in my thoughts, I gently remind myself by repeating, *This is only a story. It's not factual*, and proceed with my activities, undeterred.

There Are No Excuses in Life, Only Your Choices

Life is far from being a mere dress rehearsal for some grand final Broadway performance, yet many of us behave as though it is, perpetually postponing today's opportunities for tomorrow's convenience.

COULD HAVE BEEN; SHOULD HAVE BEEN; HERE I AM

This habit of deferring actions does more than merely procrastinate; it actively carves notches out of our finite lifespan, each delay subtly eroding the time we have left. The danger of this mindset lies in its cumulative effect—should we continue to remove enough chips, we might find that "tomorrow" becomes a horizon forever out of reach and that the aspirations we held dear may never come to fruition. This narrative is not unique but a common thread weaving through the tapestry of many lives.

But what drives us to squander time, this most precious of resources? Despite the universality of this tendency, it manifests differently in everyone. Some may fear failure, leading them to avoid taking the necessary steps toward their goals. Others might find themselves caught in the comfort of routine, hesitant to disrupt the familiar for the sake of progress. Then there are those, the very young who simply underestimate the value of the present moment, always looking to a future that seems infinitely flexible and forgiving. This widespread proclivity to delay, to treat life as something less urgent than it is, underscores a profound misunderstanding of time's nature. Time, unlike money or material possessions, cannot be earned back once spent. Each moment is a nonrenewable resource, and how we choose to spend it can define the essence of our lives.

Recognizing this truth compels us to confront why we allow fear, comfort, or oversight to dictate our actions.

Understanding that life is not a rehearsal but the live show itself can be a powerful motivator to embrace each day with purpose and intention. It challenges us to examine our priorities, to question the rationale behind our procrastination, and to make more conscious decisions about how we spend our time. After all, the realization that our days are numbered and that every moment counts should inspire, not fear, a fervent desire to live fully, making the most of the time we are given.

One way to maximize our existence on this fleeting journey through life hinges on the personal decisions we make at every crossroads. Each of us wields the power of free will, allowing us to chart our path forward—or choose inaction—fully aware that for all beings, this journey inevitably concludes with the passage of time.

The inescapable truth of our mortality should serve as a compelling catalyst, urging us to employ our moments judiciously rather than squander them. Yet embracing this philosophy in practice often eludes us.

Reflecting on my own life, I acknowledge countless instances where I've let precious minutes, hours, days, and even years slip through my fingers, contributing neither to my personal growth nor to the well-being of those who rely on me. This acknowledgment isn't about harboring regret but about recognizing the imperative to live more intentionally. By facing this truth head-on, we can begin to recalibrate our daily choices, steering them toward actions that not only enrich our lives but also positively impact those around us. It's a call to action—a reminder that while we cannot reclaim lost time, we are fully capable of making the most of the present, transforming our remaining days into a testament to a life well lived.

The realization dawns with striking clarity; we are fundamentally different from the mechanical constructs we have created, machines that operate with unwavering precision, tirelessly repeating the same tasks as directed without deviation. In stark contrast, we, as human beings, embody a rich tapestry of capabilities and imperfections. While we may engage in repetitive tasks, we do so while infusing them with our unique variations, often falling short of perfection. This distinction highlights our intrinsic human nature—our actions, though sometimes consistent, are never devoid of our personal touch, our errors, and our learning curves.

Moreover, while machines follow instructions with unerring fidelity, devoid of choice or preference, we stand apart in our ability to critically assess and either accept or reject the directives given to us.

Our capacity for autonomous decision-making sets us profoundly apart from any machine. A machine's "choices," if they can be called that, are preprogrammed responses dictated by the parameters we set. In contrast, our choices are fueled by a complex blend of reasoning, emotion, experience, and sometimes defiance.

This fundamental difference underscores the essence of human agency—the freedom to choose, to disagree, and to chart our own course is inherently ours, a trait no machine can truly possess. It speaks to the heart of what it means to be human, not just the ability to perform tasks, but to do so with creativity, fallibility, and the power of choice. Recognizing and embracing our imperfect, variable nature not only distinguishes us from the mechanical but also celebrates the unpredictable beauty of human existence. I have never heard wiser words than "Go forward and choose wisely your paths in life."

Don't Make a Permanent Decision over a Temporary Situation

Many of us are familiar with the phenomenon of knee-jerk reactions, where either we ourselves or someone else makes a swift and decisive action in response to a temporary situation, solidifying it into a permanent resolution. This tendency is particularly evident within our legal framework. Often, in the aftermath of an unprecedented and unfortunate event, legislators rush to enact new laws aimed at preventing its recurrence. However, this approach to problem-solving is fraught with two significant issues. First, the incident that triggered the legislative response might be an outlier, unlikely to happen again, rendering the law unnecessary. Secondly, even if the situation were to arise once more, there's no guarantee that the new regulation would effectively deter it. This hasty decision-making process overlooks the importance of thorough analysis and deliberation, potentially leading to laws that are either ineffective or, worse, inadvertently restrictive. It underscores the need for a more measured and thoughtful approach to lawmaking, one that balances the urgency of immediate action with the foresight of long-term implications. So how should we respond to a temporary situation?

In facing temporary challenges, the most effective initial approach is often to withhold immediate action, leaving you a way out. Embracing patience and understanding rather than resorting to a reflexive reliance on predetermined solutions is essential. This approach ensures that responses are guided by thoughtful consideration rather than automatic processes, allowing the true nature of the problem to be illuminated over time. Such patience emphasizes the importance of concentrating all efforts on the issue at hand, trusting that a solution will emerge in due course, not necessarily instantly but within a reasonable time frame.

This principle is readily illustrated by considering how we handle unexpected issues with our vehicles. For instance, if a vehicle suddenly begins making an unfamiliar clunking noise, the appropriate response is not to immediately consider replacing the car. Instead, a more sensible approach involves taking the time to investigate the source of the noise and addressing it directly. This methodical process of identification and resolution mirrors the advisable strategy for confronting personal challenges. When faced with unforeseen difficulties, hastily surrendering or reacting without a full understanding of the situation often leads to unsatisfactory outcomes. Conversely, maintaining an open-mindedness toward potential solutions can significantly increase the likelihood of uncovering an effective remedy.

My philosophy on this matter, which has served me well for many years, revolves around the understanding that no decision is truly final. This mindset allows for the flexibility to revise or reverse decisions as new information becomes available or as situations evolve. Such an approach fosters adaptability, freeing one from the misconception that every decision is irreversible and set in stone. This philosophy not only encourages a more dynamic and responsive attitude toward life's challenges but also cultivates a willingness to embrace change and uncertainty with confidence and resilience.

Where Is Your Life, Ahead or Behind You?

During my journey to becoming a pilot, I was consistently guided by a mantra from my instructors: to fly the airplane from the front, not from the back. This advice, while seemingly cryptic at first, unfolded profound wisdom, emphasizing the importance of taking proactive control rather than being a passive participant in the flight. They urged me to master the art of piloting with foresight and assertiveness, ensuring that I was always the one directing the aircraft's course rather than being dictated by it. This principle, I realized, extends far beyond the cockpit, resonating deeply with the essence of leading a fulfilling life.

Life, much like piloting, presents us with numerous pathways illuminated by the universe, each beckoning us toward potential destinies. It becomes our responsibility to not only discern these paths but to also engage with them actively, making deliberate adjustments to remain aligned with our goals and values. This proactive approach positions us at the helm of our existence, steering us toward our aspirations with intentionality and resolve. Conversely, failing to adopt this mindset can lead us to become mere passengers in our own lives, constantly reacting to circumstances rather than shaping them. This reactive stance often leaves us vulnerable, trailing behind the very existence we ought to command and inadvertently becoming victims to situations that could have been navigated with foresight. By embracing the wisdom of piloting from the front, we empower ourselves to stay ahead, ensuring that our life's journey is one of purpose, direction, and self-determination.

How, then, can the rich tapestry of our past experiences become a guiding force, enabling us to live our lives from the front, steering with purpose rather than being steered by circumstances? This intriguing question invites us to delve into the depths of our personal history, extracting lessons and insights that can illuminate our path forward. By consciously reflecting on our past—analyzing successes and setbacks alike—we equip ourselves with a compass of wisdom, guiding our decisions and actions in the present and future. Our past experiences, with their diverse outcomes, serve as invaluable data points, offering clarity on what works, what doesn't, and why. This reflective process transforms our history into a proactive tool, empowering us to anticipate challenges, seize opportunities, and navigate life with a sense of direction and intent. Thus, by harnessing the lessons of our past, we can pilot our lives with confidence, ensuring that we live each moment from the front, actively shaping our destiny with informed purpose.

Have you ever heard the expression that people sometimes use when attempting to jolt someone back to reality? It goes "Wake up and stop living in the past." This phrase is often employed to encourage someone to confront the present and let go of bygone events that can no longer be altered. It's a reminder that dwelling on past mistakes or glories can prevent us from making the most of our current situation and opportunities. By advising someone to "wake up," it metaphorically suggests that they are asleep, not fully aware of or engaging with the realities around them. "Stop living in the past" further emphasizes the need to focus on the here and now, to take active steps toward personal growth, and to embrace the possibilities that lie ahead. This expression is not just a call to action; it's a nudge toward self-awareness and the pursuit of progress, urging individuals to release their grip on what once was to make room for what could be.

An absolute truth that I have come to learn, time and again, is embedded in the simple philosophy that the past is immutable. Despite my numerous attempts to alter what has already transpired, I have never succeeded. Deep down, I understand that such a feat would necessitate the use of a time machine, which, as we all know, remains a figment of science fiction and not a reality of our current world. This realization begs the question: why do we persistently revisit the past with the hope of altering our current circumstances? Perhaps it is a fundamental aspect of human nature to struggle with accepting our past mistakes and living with their consequences. Instead of acknowledging our errors and learning from them, we often find ourselves wishing for another chance, a way to rewind and rectify our missteps. This inclination might stem from our innate desire for perfection and the refusal to accept failure or regret. It reveals our deep-seated belief that, given another opportunity, we can erase the repercussions of decisions that have long since passed. Yet this yearning to change the past speaks volumes about our resilience and our constant pursuit of self-improvement even in the face of the immutable nature of time.

I propose a nuanced approach to revisiting the past: venture back solely for the purpose of learning, not with the intent to alter what has transpired. The events that have unfolded in our lives should be perceived as chapters permanently etched into the personal history book of our existence, which continuously accumulates experiences as we progress through life. As this compendium expands, it transforms into an invaluable resource, offering insights into actions best avoided in the present. Imagine this process as a methodical guide to elimination, methodically weeding out previous misjudgments and guiding us toward more promising paths for our future. Envision the past as an ever-growing repository of wisdom, each lesson a deposit that enriches this intellectual vault. It's a resource that stands ready to be tapped into on a "rainy day," a treasure trove of learned experiences that, when reflected upon, can enlighten and guide our present decisions. In this light, the past is not a shadow to be escaped but a mentor whose teachings are integral to our growth and evolution. By adopting this mindset, we can harness our history to foster a future that is informed by the wisdom of our experiences, turning setbacks into stepping stones toward greater understanding and living our lives in front of us.

Practice Your Calling

Throughout the span of my life, I've encountered numerous powerful forces that have significantly influenced my journey. These forces, both seen and unseen, have exerted their influence in myriad ways, propelling me down diverse paths and, at times, safeguarding me from potential threats lurking in my surroundings. Yet among these myriad forces, there exists one particularly unique force distinguished solely by its profound resonance with my inner self—the force of my calling. The essence of this calling is so potent and compelling that it feels akin to a seal imprinted upon my forehead, a declaration to the world of my destined role. This calling is not merely a whisper in the heart; it is a thunderous directive that guides one's steps, relentless and unyielding. As I reflect on the tapestry of my years, the clarity with which I can discern my callings is striking. It is a narrative of transformation and realization, a journey of becoming and embodying the roles to which I was unmistakably summoned. These callings have not just shaped my choices; they have molded my identity, guiding me toward fulfilling the purposes that resonate most deeply with my essence.

Navigating through life, I often found myself at the crossroads of multiple callings, each beckoning with equal allure, leaving me perplexed whether to pursue one at the expense of the others or to embrace them all at once. This indecision wasn't merely a matter of choice; it stemmed from the intricate nature of callings themselves. Unlike straightforward career paths, callings felt more like distant echoes of potential futures, not concrete realities of the present but possibilities that could one day materialize. It was this elusive quality that made choosing not just difficult but complex, transforming what seemed like a straightforward decision into a profound journey of self-discovery.

Over time, I've come to realize that having faith in oneself is essential in navigating this journey. Such faith doesn't just help in choosing a path; it empowers us to carve out a niche where our unique calling can flourish. I now understand that these callings are not just whimsical desires but are deeply ingrained in who we are and who we aspire to be, guiding us toward fulfilling our true potential.

Once I became conscious of my life's calling, my immediate reaction was to delve into its essence. I sought to understand the breadth and depth of this calling—what exactly it entailed, what it demanded of me, and the timing it prescribed for me to fully embrace it.

Among the diverse callings that life presented, one stood out with unmistakable clarity: my destiny to be a guitarist in a rock band. This passion had coursed through my veins since the tender age of ten, instilling in me an unshakable conviction that my path inevitably led to the stage where I was destined to perform before an audience. This vision materialized repeatedly throughout my life—initially during my adolescence, followed by a brief hiatus, and then resurfacing with renewed vigor in my adult years over a span of three decades.

Embarking on this journey was nothing short of extraordinary. I found myself part of a compact yet refined production, where playing the guitar was not just an act of performance but a profound journey of personal mastery. With each show, I honed my skills, achieving levels of proficiency I had once deemed unattainable. Being on stage felt overwhelmingly natural and imbued me with a sense of purpose that was both exhilarating and addictive. Each performance was a step higher on an endless staircase of musical mastery, a pursuit that became a compelling obsession. The exhilaration of live performance, the connection with the audience, and the relentless drive to refine my artistry transformed my life into a thrilling odyssey of self-discovery and fulfillment.

This calling was immensely time-consuming, challenging me to transcend the norms and expectations of an average guitarist. To carve out a niche for myself and achieve a level of notoriety as a guitarist, it was imperative that I differentiated myself in a manner that would leave audiences in awe, much like a magician conjuring an object from the ether, eliciting gasps of "That was incredible. How did he do that?" The road map to such astonishment was as clear as the constellation-studded sky on a summer night: relentless, dedicated practice. It was through this unyielding discipline that I aspired to reach unparalleled heights of musical skills.

However, this journey taught me a vital lesson about the essence of mastering any craft: the indispensable investment of time. The kind of awe-inspiring performance I aimed for wasn't born overnight. It emerged from countless hours of practice, each note played and each chord strummed contributing to the refinement of my skills. This repetitive practice wasn't merely about playing the same pieces over and over; it was a deeply devoted exploration of the instrument, a quest to uncover its secrets and potential. The dedication required to this process was profound, testing my patience and resolve, yet it was the only pathway to achieving the extraordinary. It was a testament to the fact that true mastery in any field is a labor of love, requiring not just talent but a relentless commitment to growth and excellence.

Referring to the pursuit of one's calling as mere "practice" scarcely does it justice. Callings have a unique way of emerging at specific junctures in an individual's life, often cloaked in mystery initially, yet they promise to be steadfast companions until life's end once they make their presence known. The moment a calling springs to life—like my own journey through various stages as a musician—presents a critical decision point: either to defer its pursuit for a seemingly more opportune moment or to embrace it wholeheartedly, dedicating oneself to mastering its every subtlety and demand.

Throughout my life, I have stood at this crossroads time and again, faced with the callings of electronics, music, aviation, chemistry, biology, medicine, entrepreneurship, and now, that of an author compelled to share my myriad stories. Each calling, irrespective of its nature, has demanded of me a profound commitment to practice, imbued with intense and focused mindfulness at every stage of its unfolding. The encounter with a calling is undeniable, a clarion call to dedicate a segment of one's life to its exploration and mastery. The alternative—ignoring the call—carries with it a weight of regret too burdensome to bear, a stark reminder that the journey of engaging deeply with one's callings is not just about achieving proficiency but about honoring the essence of who we are and the contributions we are destined to make.

The exploration of callings is a profound journey of self-discovery that, upon reflection, unveils astonishing insights about one's identity and purpose. As the tapestry of my life gradually unfolded, so did the emergence of various callings, each bringing with it a crucial puzzle piece destined to complete the intricate mosaic that represents my life. These pieces, meticulously placed on a metaphorical puzzle board, awaited the arrival of their counterparts to reveal a cohesive picture. Yet the completion of this puzzle prompts a pivotal question: does it signify the culmination of one's life journey, or does it herald a phase of deconstruction, a regression back to a formative state of innocence and potential?

In my contemplation, the completed puzzle embodies the unique essence of an individual—a crystallization of their identity and their role within the greater tapestry of existence. The disassembly of this puzzle rather than a process of loss or diminishment becomes an act of generous contribution to the universe. Each piece, once a part of a personal narrative, is released back into the cosmos, imbued with the capacity to enrich the lives of others just as it enriched one's own. This cyclical exchange underscores the interconnectedness of all life, suggesting that our callings and the lessons they impart extend far beyond our personal boundaries, resonating through the fabric of the universe to inspire, challenge, and nurture the collective soul.

When the Time Is Right, You'll Know

The temptation to make hasty decisions can divert us from our true paths, potentially leading to future regret. As a child, I was captivated by the first shiny object I saw, longing to possess it. As I matured, my desires grew; I still yearned for shiny objects, but they had to be larger to satisfy my subconscious cravings. Yet even with age, our impulse to want does not seem to wane; perhaps it's a part of our survival instinct, the continuous chase from one desire to another. This pattern was interrupted by the experience with my mother. At eighty-one, her health was rapidly deteriorating, with no hope of recovery. She chose to reject food and medical help, her only wish being to leave this world. Despite my efforts to persuade her toward a path of healing, she remained resolute. On her last day, she lay still, in a silence that seemed to bring her peace. All her belongings, including her once beloved pet cat, Puff, became meaningless to her. It was evident she had released her attachment to the material world and was prepared to embark on her final journey. She knew her ultimate path to choose. Her passing taught me a profound lesson about life; it will inevitably end one day, and all the shiny objects we've gathered along the way will have to be relinquished back to the universe for others to acquire. That, too, is the law of the universe.

My father always advised me, "Never stay where you are not welcome," implying that disregarding this guidance leads to feelings of awkwardness, confusion, and despair. Throughout my life, I've frequently faced these emotions and eventually learned to extricate myself from such unwelcome circumstances. His advice proved invaluable in social situations that felt misaligned. Trying to diagnose and rectify the issue is futile when the root problem is a lack of welcome. By exiting such scenarios, I avoided mutual embarrassment and potential long-lasting discomfort. In instances of unwelcome interactions, taking time apart allows intense emotions to subside. With the passage of time, a more objective view may emerge, potentially transforming a once-unpleasant encounter into a positive one. Be patient, you'll know when the time is right.

The Power of Walking Away

It's undeniable that we often retreat and lose ourselves in places where we feel sheltered from the external world's oddities. Perhaps this tendency is what simplifies the process of walking away. I've always been cautious about discerning what's genuinely beneficial and safe for me to engage with. To address this, I developed a method: initially withdrawing from the proposition to observe the ensuing reactions. If the proposal were tainted with deceit, I wouldn't be beckoned back. On the contrary, if the deal were sincere and mutually advantageous, the other party would exert every effort to maintain my involvement. This approach, although straightforward, has consistently proven its effectiveness, likely sparing me from potential calamities.

Mick Jagger, the iconic lead singer of the Rolling Stones, famously penned the lyrics, "You can't always get what you want." However, with all due respect to Mick, I have a different perspective. I believe that you can indeed always get what you want, sometimes, by choosing to walk away. This idea might seem counterintuitive—walking away from something you desire could appear irrational to some. Typically, people exert maximum effort to seize the first opportunity that presents itself, driven by the fear of missing out. Yet I argue that such urgency isn't always necessary.

Opportunities to fulfill our desires are plentiful though they may not all manifest simultaneously. Here's an illustrative example. Imagine you're in the market for a new white Ford Mustang, which there are many of in existence. You find yourself at a dealership, but the only Mustang available is red, and it comes with an enticingly low price tag, valid only if you purchase that day. Faced with this scenario, what's your move? Do you compromise your preferences and purchase the red Mustang, potentially regretting your decision later? Or do you walk away and pass on this immediate yet imperfect opportunity, choosing to wait for what you really want? The choice should be straightforward: "No on the red one, I'll wait for a white one." If the red Mustang isn't precisely what you envisioned, why settle? By walking away, you stay true to your original desire, allowing space for the right opportunity to come along. Be patient, it will. This approach of holding out for what you truly want rather than accepting a near miss is liberating and effective.

Embracing this method teaches patience and reaffirms the belief in getting not just anything but exactly what you want. It challenges the conventional rush for immediate gratification, promoting a deeper understanding of personal goals and how best to achieve them. This strategy often proves itself over time, almost as if it were a law of the universe. By not settling, you open yourself up to future opportunities that will meet your needs more completely. So in the quest for your white Mustang or any heartfelt desire, remember that sometimes, the best way to get what you want is by not taking what you can get immediately. It's a powerful reminder that great things come to those who wait patiently.

Inch by Inch, It's a Cinch

Have you ever found yourself standing at the threshold of a project, one that you absolutely needed to complete, yet felt utterly overwhelmed by its sheer complexity? This sense of bewilderment isn't uncommon, especially when the task at hand is layered with intricate details and nuanced requirements that make it seem like an insurmountable mountain from the outset. It's a daunting place to be, knowing that there's a deadline looming, understanding the importance of the project's successful completion, yet feeling paralyzed by the uncertainty of where to even begin. This overwhelming sensation can stem from a variety of factors, including a lack of clear direction, the perception that the project's demands exceed your current skill set, or simply the fear of failing to meet expectations. The challenge then becomes not just the completion of the project itself but also overcoming the initial inertia caused by its complexities and navigating your way through the fog of uncertainty to find a starting point that will lead you to success.

Before a situation spirals beyond control, it's beneficial to pause and recall a straightforward yet powerful adage: "Inch by inch, it's a cinch." These six simple words carry profound wisdom, offering a strategy to dismantle what appears to be a complex and overwhelming challenge into manageable bite-size tasks. This phrase serves as a reminder that progress, no matter how incremental, is still progress. It encourages a methodical approach, advocating for tackling tasks one small step at a time rather than succumbing to the paralysis that often accompanies the prospect of a daunting undertaking.

This philosophy is not just about making tasks seem less intimidating; it's also about altering our mindset toward problem-solving. By breaking down a large project into its component parts, we not only make the task more approachable but also facilitate a clearer understanding of the work involved. This segmentation allows for a more organized approach, where each "inch" gained is a step closer to the final goal, making what seemed like an insurmountable obstacle a series of achievable objectives.

Moreover, adopting the "inch by inch" mentality can significantly reduce stress and anxiety, providing a sense of control and accomplishment as each segment is completed. It turns the focus from the overwhelming whole to the achievable parts, fostering a sense of achievement and momentum with each step forward. In essence, this simple phrase encapsulates a powerful strategy for tackling complex situations, transforming them from daunting tasks into a series of manageable actions that, when combined, lead to the successful completion of the project.

One strategy I consistently employ to tackle large and daunting tasks involves breaking them down into smaller, more manageable components. This method allows me to concentrate on making incremental changes without feeling overwhelmed. The next step in my approach is to reassemble these modified components, effectively piecing them back into their original configuration. This reassembly process is crucial as it enables me to evaluate my progress and ensure that each component fits seamlessly within the larger task.

To illustrate this approach, consider the ambitious project of building a house from the ground up—a monumental endeavor by any measure. The question then becomes, where does one even begin? My starting point would always be conceptualization, determining the architectural style of the house I aim to build, whether it be a ranch, colonial, or duplex. This initial decision shapes the entire project, guiding subsequent actions and decisions. With a clear vision in mind, the next logical step is to translate this concept into a tangible plan. This involves drafting a detailed two-dimensional blueprint, laying out the structure's layout and dimensions on paper. Such a diagram serves as a road map, outlining every phase of the construction process.

Following the blueprint, construction begins methodically, one component at a time. This phased approach includes laying the foundation, erecting walls and roof framing, and installing essential systems such as electrical wiring and plumbing. Each phase builds upon the previous one, gradually bringing the conceptualized house to life in time intervals. This methodical step-by-step process not only makes a seemingly insurmountable task achievable but also allows for adjustments and improvements along the way, ensuring the final structure is sound, functional, and aligned with the initial vision.

Reflecting on my childhood, I vividly recall numerous instances when I sought the assistance of adults for tasks that seemed beyond my capabilities to start, let alone complete. What stood out to me during these interactions was the methodical approach these adults took in responding to my requests. Initially, they would pose a fundamental question: what do you want? This query often highlighted a significant hurdle for me. Given my youthful inexperience, I frequently found myself unable to articulate precisely what I desired. This lack of clarity was, perhaps, the primary obstacle, preventing me from progressing with my tasks.

The adults, recognizing my dilemma, would then transition to suggesting potential solutions to my vague request, asking, "Is this what you want?" It was almost miraculous how, in 99 percent of the cases, they managed to decipher my nebulous desires and pinpoint exactly what I was seeking. Their ability to interpret my needs and transform them into concrete proposals was nothing short of amazing.

Once we had established a clear understanding of my objective, the pathway forward became significantly clearer. With the adult's guidance, I was not only able to define my goal more precisely but also embark on a collaborative journey toward achieving it. This process taught me invaluable lessons about the importance of clear communication and the power of experienced insight in overcoming obstacles and completing tasks. It underscored the fact that sometimes, the wisdom and perspective of others can illuminate solutions that we, in our limited understanding or experience, cannot see ourselves.

Embarking on a challenging endeavor often requires embodying dual perspectives: that of the uninhibited child, eager and unafraid to tackle tasks beyond their apparent abilities, and that of the pragmatic adult, who approaches the same task with a methodical step-by-step strategy. This combination of fearless ambition and deliberate execution forms a powerful approach to overcoming obstacles and achieving objectives.

Throughout my life, I've frequently found myself diving headfirst into situations or projects that seemed well beyond my grasp, embodying the spirit of a child taking on the world without hesitation. Yet it's through the application of what I call the "inch by inch" method—akin to the careful, calculated approach of an adult—that I've been able to navigate these challenges. Despite the ambitious nature of my undertakings, I've invariably arrived at a satisfying conclusion, often surprising myself with the outcomes achieved.

This enduring propensity to bite off more than I can chew yet somehow manage to chew it all underscores a mystical element to personal growth and achievement. It suggests that maintaining a childlike mindset, characterized by curiosity and boldness, even into one's elderly years, can be a wellspring of resilience and creativity. The adage "Inch by inch, life's a cinch" becomes a lived truth, reflecting the idea that any task, no matter how daunting at first glance, can be made manageable and ultimately conquered through patience, perseverance, and a step-by-step approach.

In essence, the synthesis of childlike audacity and adultlike pragmatism forms a comprehensive strategy for facing life's challenges. It is a reminder that the secret to accomplishing vast and complex tasks lies in breaking them down into smaller, more manageable pieces and tackling them one at a time. This approach not only facilitates success but also preserves the inner spark of youthfulness, a vital source of energy and inspiration that propels us forward regardless of age.

A Winning Strategy: The Best Solution Wins

In my role as an entrepreneur, I am frequently tasked with devising solutions to various challenges. Admittedly, I do not always achieve success on my own and often find myself reaching out for external assistance to overcome my personal limitations. So I adhere to a straightforward philosophy: the best solution wins. This principle dictates that the origin or creator of a solution is inconsequential; if it is effective, it merits implementation. This approach ensures that the focus remains on problem-solving rather than on the ego or prestige associated with the source of the solution. However, this philosophy also introduces a critical query: how do I ascertain whether a solution truly represents the best answer?

Determining this involves a rigorous evaluation process, considering factors such as feasibility, cost-efficiency, innovation, and impact. By applying these criteria, I can sift through the available options to identify the most effective and practical solutions, thereby adhering to my commitment to excellence and results-driven decision-making in my entrepreneurial endeavors. If those qualifying techniques fail at times, I may have to revert to a faithful and trusted method: flipping a coin.

The challenge often lies in the reality that there could be multiple excellent solutions, possibly two, three, or more, complicating the decision-making process even further. However, there's no rule that forbids pursuing several solutions simultaneously or evaluating them in a sequential manner to measure their outcomes and effectiveness. It's crucial to maintain an open-minded approach at all times and not shy away from the possibility of failure or the need to start afresh.

This is precisely how human beings evolve—by learning from their mistakes. Therefore, it's essential to be surrounded by individuals who embrace errors and are unafraid to venture into new territories without harboring regrets. People who consistently opt for the safe route unsettle me, as their contributions might stem from a desire to avoid disturbances rather than offer genuine insight, essentially embodying the "yes man" mentality. Authentic solutions, however, emanate from deep conviction and are invariably worth exploring.

I've discovered that the most effective strategy for eliciting outstanding ideas from individuals involves granting them time and space rather than demanding immediate answers in the presence of their peers. Performance anxiety can inhibit creativity, especially among those who are introverted or susceptible to peer pressure. Above all, when someone generates a brilliant solution, it's vital to acknowledge and celebrate their contribution publicly. This not only boosts morale but also encourages a culture of innovation and open-mindedness where every member feels valued and motivated to share their unique perspectives. Celebrating successes in this manner fosters a supportive environment conducive to collaborative growth and the continuous exchange of groundbreaking ideas.

Don't View Yourself through the Eyes of Your Enemies

Human beings are uniquely self-conscious creatures, deeply concerned with their external perception by the world. From the moment we wake up, we find ourselves peering into mirrors, contemplating our appearance and pondering how we will be received by the outside world. This routine continues until we retreat back into sleep, a state where external opinions and appearances momentarily lose their grip. This pervasive self-awareness may stem from our inherent social nature; the desire to interact and connect with others is fundamental as solitude is not a permanent state many wish to endure.

Because of our innate desire for social interaction, we place significant importance on public opinion, often going to great lengths to modify our appearance and behavior based on external feedback.

This external input can open up various paths, aiding us in deciding our ultimate direction. The challenge lies in discerning the sources of these opinions and advice. Sound, credible advice can streamline our journey toward our goals, facilitating forward movement. Conversely, misguided advice can lead us astray, impeding our progress. The critical question then becomes: whom do we trust for guidance while staying wary of those who might lead us astray? To navigate this, one requires a method to evaluate the credibility of the advice received. A practical approach I have adopted is to closely observe how individuals treat those around them; this behavior is often indicative of how they will eventually treat you. This observation helps differentiate valuable advice from misleading guidance, enabling more informed decisions about whom to trust and whose opinions to discount.

Acknowledging the reality that it's impossible to satisfy everyone all the time is crucial. Compromises are inevitable, and certain decisions or actions might offend some individuals. Contrarily, aligning too closely with others' expectations and consistently conforming to societal norms can erode personal individuality, rendering life unfulfilling. My counsel is to maintain your independence and strength, allowing your inner voice to guide your decisions in every situation. Trusting in oneself and valuing personal judgment over external opinions helps preserve individuality while navigating the complexities of social interactions and expectations.

Be authentic and embrace your true self rather than conforming to external expectations. In moments of uncertainty about how to act, rely on your core values and intrinsic qualities. It's crucial to slow down, pause, and carefully consider all your options. This approach allows you to be more intuitive about what feels right and recognize what doesn't resonate with you, often evident through your hesitations. Following directives on how to behave from others can lead you astray, making you a mere puppet manipulated by external forces, which obscures your true identity.

Surrounding yourself with people who have good intentions is valuable, but it's equally important to discern their true motives, as well as those of your adversaries. The age-old adage "Keep your friends close and your enemies closer" holds merit, but above all, trust your instincts when it comes to judging friends and foes. Your intuition is a powerful guide and often steers you correctly. This self-trust empowers you to navigate complex social dynamics effectively, ensuring that you remain true to yourself in all circumstances.

Transforming Ideas into Reality in Three Steps

My inquisitive nature often leads me to ponder the motivations behind my actions and the processes through which these actions take shape. With an analytical mindset, my observations extend beyond personal introspection to encompass a universal methodology employed by humanity to forge and actualize life's milestones. I've identified a distinct three-step pattern that seems to underscore this creative process, facilitating the progression from thought to reality.

The journey's *first step* begins with the inception of an *idea*, a mental spark that illuminates the realm of possibilities. This initial step is pivotal as it sets the foundation for what is to come, encapsulating the essence of our aspirations or solutions to problems. Following this cognitive inception, the *second step* involves imbuing the idea with *emotion*, allowing it to resonate on a deeper, more personal level. This emotional investment breathes life into the concept, transforming it from a mere thought into something we feel passionately about, thus amplifying our commitment and drive to see it through. The *third and final step* in this trilogy of creation involves the *physical* realm where the idea, now charged with purpose and emotion, requires a tangible plan to bring it into existence. This phase is characterized by the drafting of a blueprint—a detailed plan that outlines the necessary steps and resources, translating ethereal thoughts and feelings into concrete actions and outcomes. It's at this juncture that the idea is not just envisioned but actively constructed, manifesting into reality through deliberate effort and execution.

Building a house serves as a good example of this three-step creative process in action, illustrating how ideas transition from mere thoughts to tangible realities. Initially, the process begins with the idea where we engage in detailed contemplation regarding various aspects of the house. This phase involves thinking about the design, which encapsulates aesthetic preferences and architectural style; the location, which determines the setting and environment the house will inhabit; the size, which reflects the space requirements and capacity to accommodate family or personal activities; the cost, a practical consideration that influences the feasibility of the project; and the functionality, which ensures that the house meets the specific needs and lifestyle of its occupants.

Following this cerebral stage, we transition into the emotional phase. Here, we start to emotionally invest in the idea, imagining the house's existence and envisioning ourselves living within its walls. This imaginative exercise allows us to explore how it feels to inhabit the space, how each room caters to our daily routines, and how the house as a whole contributes to our sense of home and well-being. If this emotional reflection resonates positively, confirming that the envisioned house aligns with our desires and expectations, we are then propelled into the subsequent stages of planning and execution.

The planning stage is methodical and detailed, requiring the drawing up of blueprints and the careful orchestration of each step that will bring the house to fruition. This includes selecting materials, hiring contractors, obtaining permits, and scheduling construction phases. The culmination of this meticulous planning is the actual construction phase where ideas and emotions are finally transformed into physical form. The construction phase is a dynamic period of activity where the foundation is laid, structures are erected, and the house gradually takes shape, evolving from an abstract concept into a physical embodiment of our initial thoughts and feelings.

This journey from conceptualization through to implementation epitomizes the profound process by which we bring our ideas to life. In building a house, we see a clear demonstration of how detailed planning, coupled with emotional connection and practical execution, can realize dreams and create spaces that embody our aspirations, needs, and desires.

This three-step pattern—encompassing the mental conception of an idea, its emotional enrichment, and the physical crafting of a blueprint—delineates the intricate process by which we bring our ideas to life. Each phase is crucial, serving as a building block in the journey from abstract thought to tangible reality, demonstrating the remarkable capacity as humans possess to shape our world through the power of creativity and action.

Diet, Alcohol, Drugs, and Gambling

I have intentionally grouped the four elements of diet, alcohol, drugs, and gambling together, recognizing them as critical factors that possess a profound influence on an individual's life trajectory. These components, often intertwined, can dramatically shape and, in certain instances, fundamentally alter the course of a person's existence. My decision to consider them collectively stems from an acute awareness of their interconnectedness and the potent impact they wield on personal health, relationships, and overall well-being.

Through firsthand observations across various contexts, I have been privy to the diverse effects these elements can manifest. Diet, for instance, goes beyond mere nutritional intake; it is a cornerstone of health and can significantly affect physical vitality, mental clarity, and emotional stability. The quality and composition of our diet can either fortify our body against diseases or render us susceptible to a myriad of health issues.

Alcohol and drugs, meanwhile, present a spectrum of potential outcomes. Used within societal and medical norms, alcohol can play a role in social bonding and cultural rituals. However, its misuse can lead to addiction, health deterioration, and social disruption. Similarly, drugs, whether prescribed for medical reasons or used recreationally, have the capacity to heal or harm. The line between therapeutic use and dependency is often thin and blurred, making it a delicate balance to maintain.

Gambling, often overlooked in discussions of health and well-being, is another potent force capable of dramatic life alterations. It can evolve from a harmless leisure activity to a compulsive behavior with far-reaching consequences, including financial ruin, relationship breakdown, and mental health issues.

In many circumstances, I have witnessed the intertwining effects of diet, alcohol, drugs, and gambling on individuals and their communities. These observations underscore the importance of understanding and addressing these elements not in isolation but as interconnected factors that contribute to the complex tapestry of human life. Recognizing their potential for both positive and negative outcomes is crucial in guiding individuals toward making choices that enhance rather than compromise their quality of life.

Diet and nutrition hold a pivotal role in shaping human health and well-being. Essentially, the food and water we consume act as the fundamental fuel for our bodies, critically influencing our overall health. This relationship is evident when examining the outcomes at both ends of the nutritional spectrum. On one end, a complete lack of nutritional intake inevitably leads to the body's demise, highlighting the indispensable nature of nutrition. On the other hand, extreme, excessive consumption of nutrients can induce complications in bodily functions, such as obesity and various diseases, which can significantly shorten one's lifespan. This delicate balance underscores the intrinsic link between our physical health and mental well-being; a deteriorating physical state cannot sustain a sound mind, leading both to suffer in tandem.

Over the years, it has become increasingly clear that food and water serve not just as sustenance but as potent forms of medicine for our bodies. One of the most remarkable capabilities of the human body is its ability to heal itself, a process that is only possible with the right "medicinal" intake, comprising nutritious foods and hydration. This concept extends beyond the mere avoidance of illness, encompassing the nurturing of a state of optimal health where the body's immune, digestive, and cognitive functions are supported and enhanced. By treating food and water as our primary forms of medicine, we can unlock the body's inherent potential for self-healing, resilience, and longevity. Understanding and respecting the profound impact of our dietary choices on our physical and mental health is the first step toward cultivating a life of vitality and wellness.

Alcohol, drug abuse, and gambling exploit our vulnerabilities, acting as predators waiting to pounce on any sign of weakness.

Even the smallest crack in our defenses can become a gateway for these destructive behaviors to infiltrate our lives, potentially leading to profound and debilitating effects on our well-being. These vices, akin to treacherous paths, often begin with a seemingly harmless step, a single instance of giving in to curiosity or a fleeting desire for thrill. The notion of "just this once" or "a small try won't hurt" is a dangerous rationalization, akin to a siren's call, luring us deeper into their grasp. It's essential to recognize this voice for what it truly is: a deceptive whisper, enticing us to stray from our path of self-care and discipline. The history of countless individuals who have succumbed to these temptations serves as a stark reminder. Their journeys, marred by hardship and regret, highlight the grim reality that the end destination of these paths is seldom, if ever, beneficial. To safeguard our future and preserve our health, it is crucial to cultivate resilience against these temptations, embracing prevention as the most effective form of resistance. By steadfastly choosing to not engage with these harmful substances and activities from the outset, we protect our inner peace and foster a life of genuine fulfillment and well-being, free from the shadows of addiction and loss.

Growing up in a household overshadowed by the specter of addiction, I was inadvertently enrolled in a lifelong masterclass on the pitfalls of substance dependence. My father's battle with alcoholism, my brother's dalliances with drugs, and my mother's unwavering devotion to the horse track served as cautionary tales that etched deep into my psyche. Over the years, I bore witness to how each of them succumbed to their vices, spiraling toward an inevitable clash with the harsh realities of life. It became abundantly clear that we, as humans, are ill-equipped to juggle the burdens of addiction, which not only undermines our well-being but also steers us toward self-destruction and the endangerment of those around us.

The truth is stark—no one aspires to be shackled by a hangover, whether it's from alcohol, the aftermath of drug use, or the financial ruin that follows reckless gambling. These are not merely inconveniences but profound losses that resonate on a personal and familial level. Despite my own flirtations with alcohol during certain periods of my life, I quickly recognized that no good ever emerged from such indulgences. Thus, I made a conscious decision to eliminate it from my life entirely, a choice that, alongside quitting smoking, stands as one of the most transformative and self-affirming decisions I have ever made.

Adopting a principle of natural living, I now steer clear of anything that doesn't positively contribute to my well-being or align with my values. This guiding philosophy not only encompasses substances but extends to all facets of my life, advocating for a harmonious existence that prioritizes health, integrity, and personal growth. Through this lens, I've learned to appreciate the profound impact of making choices that foster a positive, nourishing environment for both me and those I hold dear. In doing so, I honor the lessons learned from my family's struggles, choosing a path of resilience and self-care over one marred by the shadows of addiction.

The Dirty Truth about the COVID-19 Pandemic

The COVID-19 pandemic that erupted in 2019 triggered profound social and economic upheaval across the globe, resulting in the deepest global recession witnessed since the Great Depression. Supply chain disruptions coupled with panic buying led to significant shortages, including those of essential food items and proper medical care. The pandemic also caused a dramatic, albeit temporary, reduction in pollution because of decreased human activity. In response to the health crisis, educational institutions and public spaces in numerous jurisdictions were either partially or completely shut down while countless events throughout 2020 and 2021 were either cancelled or deferred. The shift to teleworking from home became a new norm for many employees as the pandemic progressed. Additionally, the crisis was exacerbated by widespread governmental misinformation that proliferated across social media and traditional media outlets, further intensifying political tensions. It also sparked a global debate over the balance between public health mandates and individual freedoms. In essence, governments from the local to the federal level overreached their jurisdictional abilities, causing unnecessary chaos throughout the country.

Five years have passed since the COVID-19 pandemic reshaped our world, leaving enduring impacts that will be felt for generations. Today, questions linger about the origins of the virus and the rationale behind the measures that were implemented worldwide. The search for definitive answers about the cause of the virus and the effectiveness of the responses continues with no answers. There is a prevailing sentiment to "put COVID in the past" and move forward without thorough reflection on what exactly happened.

Despite the passage of time, many continue to support the actions taken during the pandemic although doubts remain about their efficacy and appropriateness. For instance, the use of surgical or cloth face masks, which was widely adopted as a preventive measure, still sparks debate over its actual impact on the transmission of the virus. Similarly, social distancing guidelines, such as maintaining six feet of separation, and restrictions on gathering sizes were seen as necessary but also as measures that created physical and emotional barriers among people.

Moreover, the rapid development and deployment of vaccines, which were a cornerstone of the public health response, have been a point of contention. Described by some as experimental because of the accelerated timelines and initially limited long-term safety data, these vaccines were met with skepticism by portions of the population. Questions about their short-term and long-term effects were significant concerns that contributed to hesitancy and fueled ongoing debates about public health freedoms versus community safety obligations. To date, there is still no proof that the vaccines were ever effective or beneficial in any way. What we do know is that the vaccines had multiple adverse side effects.

The quest for the full truth about COVID-19 and the mandates that were imposed during the pandemic may remain elusive, much like other historical mysteries that continue to perplex us. Notably, the circumstances surrounding the assassination of President John F. Kennedy bear a similar hallmark of secrecy and controversy. Despite the passage of decades, key documents related to the assassination remain highly classified, accessible only in a version controlled and released by governmental authorities. This has led to widespread speculation and ongoing debates among historians and scholars, a pattern that seems likely to follow the narrative of the COVID-19 pandemic. The parallels between these two events highlight a recurring theme in the governmental handling of public crises and significant historical incidents: the opacity of official accounts and the public's thirst for transparency. As with the JFK assassination, the complete and unvarnished details of the decisions, data, and discussions that shaped the global response to COVID-19 may never be fully disclosed. This lack of clarity fosters ongoing debate and speculation, leaving scholars, journalists, and citizens pondering what might have been withheld or misrepresented.

Moreover, the legacy of such pivotal events often leads to a persistent quest for accountability and truth. Just as researchers and conspiracy theorists continue to sift through the JFK case, health experts, policymakers, and the general public will likely scrutinize the COVID-19 pandemic response for many years to come. These examinations aim not only to uncover any obscured facts but also to ensure that future responses to global crises are more transparent and effective, learning from past oversights and errors. The dialogue about COVID-19, much like the JFK assassination, serves as a crucial reminder of the need for open government and the power of public inquiry in shaping historical understanding.

Over the course of five years since the COVID-19 pandemic began, I have closely witnessed its impact and observed the varied responses of the general public. Here is what I have concluded from these experiences:

1. Origin of the virus: it is widely accepted that the virus originated in China based on multiple data analyses and investigations into its initial outbreak and spread.
2. Death count predictions: early projections about the total number of deaths were alarming, but the actual fatalities did not reach the predicted figures.
3. Social distancing: the recommendation to maintain a distance of six feet was initially based on no scientific under-

standing. The number 6 was generated from pure fiction and was, in my opinion, pure nonsense.
4. Size of gatherings: guidelines that limited gatherings to fewer than ten people were intended to reduce transmission risks. This, too, was nonsense. It had no scientific fact to support the number 10. In fact, we later found out that herd immunity was the best defense against the virus, making large gatherings beneficial.
5. Vaccine efficacy: the vaccines developed for COVID-19 did not show to significantly reduce the risk of the disease, hospitalization, or death. Many breakthrough infections did occurred with people that received the vaccine.
6. Vaccine side effects: there have been reports of side effects such as blood clotting, myocarditis, and an abnormally high unexplained death incidents among some young athletes.
7. Shutdown measures: the decision to close schools, places of worship, and parts of the economy had a significant social and economic impacts. Because of these massive closure mandates, it will take many generations to recover back to a normal society.

Initially, I approached the COVID-19 pandemic with a healthy dose of skepticism. As a scientist with relevant expertise, my instinct was to dive deeply into the research, analyzing the virus's virulence and genetic characteristics. However, I quickly discovered that robust data were hard to come by, with most information stemming from selected governmental sources. Private analyses, on the other hand, often faced discredit. Given this context, I urged my family and the staff at my laboratory to approach the situation with rational skepticism and not be swayed by the overwhelming public reaction. We decided against wearing facial masks, believing the potential risks outweighed the purported benefits. Similarly, we did not practice social distancing or avoid large groups as I was concerned this could lead to unnecessary isolation and potential mental health issues like depression.

When it came to the vaccination, we opted for a cautious approach, observing its effects on the general population before making a personal decision. We imposed no vaccine mandates in my laboratory; the staff was free to choose their own medicine. The feedback we observed was unsettling; acquaintances who received the vaccine contracted COVID-19 multiple times and experienced significant side effects that were frequently discussed in media reports. On the other hand, acquaintances who opted out of the vaccine typically contracted a mild case of the virus and became immune to future infections.

In conclusion, our response was to not succumb to the surrounding frenzy. We chose a path guided by our understanding and observations, grateful to have maintained our course through those challenging times. Our examination of COVID-19 protocols yielded intriguing results, affirming our initial skepticism. We surveyed a group comprised of fifty individuals—family members and laboratory staff. Among them, ten had been vaccinated, either voluntarily or because of educational and employer mandates. Within this vaccinated group, five individuals experienced side effects: two reported reactions at the injection site, one developed ovarian cysts, another suffered a stroke, and one person tragically died from myocarditis. Notably, all vaccinated individuals contracted COVID-19 multiple times. Conversely, the forty unvaccinated individuals reported no such side effects. Moreover, when this group did contract the virus, the infections were mild and occurred only once. I recognized the elephant in the room. Unfortunately, many others did not.

The sense of panic among the general public was deeply disheartening. A widespread substitution of common sense for fear seemed to pervade the atmosphere, leading to an environment where everyone assumed the role of law enforcement. Citizens diligently followed government directives without question. This blind adherence fostered a culture where turning in and ridiculing neighbors became not only accepted but also expected behavior among many. This shift in societal norms underlined a distressing trend toward compliance and surveillance, overshadowing individual judgment and community trust.

Fear is a potent emotion, one that can be exploited by those in power. During the COVID-19 pandemic, government leaders across the globe utilized fear to their advantage, compelling the general populace to adhere strictly to their mandates. Often, this meant that individuals followed these directives unquestioningly, without forming personal opinions or expressing dissent. The pandemic revealed how fear could be used as a tool to control large populations effectively, managing societal behavior without resort to overt physical coercion. As we reflect on these events, it becomes crucial to recognize the lessons learned from this period. The hope is that future generations will remember the implications of wielding fear as a means of control and ensure such tactics are not repeated. In this context, one can only turn to prayer, hoping earnestly that humanity will not face such manipulation again.

The Events That Could Have Taken My Life

Throughout my life, I have often pondered with a sense of wonder and disbelief at my own survival. How is it that I have navigated through the vast expanse of time without falling victim to a catastrophic event capable of extinguishing my existence? This question looms large in my mind as I reflect on the myriad dangers that lurk around every corner—be it the sudden, unexpected calamity of accidents like my grandfather's drowning at sea, the stealthy encroachment of disease similar to my father's cancer, or the sheer misfortune of finding oneself in the wrong place at the wrong time like the family that went before my uncle Rene on the airplane ride. It's as though I've danced on the edge of a knife, miraculously maintaining my balance amid a world fraught with peril. This contemplation leads me to ponder the complex interplay of luck, destiny, and perhaps some unseen protective force that has shielded me from the myriad threats that could have easily derailed my journey. It raises profound questions about the nature of existence, the randomness of fate, and the delicate thread upon which life hangs. How have I managed to evade the clutches of fate's more grim designs, and what does this say about the path I am meant to walk in this world? Such reflections not only deepen my appreciation for the fragility of life but also instill a profound sense of gratitude and a renewed commitment to live each moment with purpose and mindfulness.

In my youthful prime, around the age of twenty-six, I found my calling not in the solitude of a recording studio but on the vibrant and unpredictable stage of a popular wedding band based in the heart of Central Massachusetts. Our ensemble, known for its lively performances and eclectic mix of music, became a staple at family-oriented gatherings, ranging from the joyous celebrations of weddings and Jack and Jills to the nostalgic reunions of classmates and the festive commemorations of birthdays. These weekend gigs provided not only a platform for our musical expressions but also a unique window into the tapestry of human connections and celebrations. By the way, I made some impressive pocket changes with my musical performances.

During the intermissions, as the echoes of our last song faded into the night, we would retreat to our chosen sanctuary away from the bustling energy of the event. This brief respite was our chance to recharge and to share a moment of tranquility before diving back on stage into the electric atmosphere of the next set. It was in these moments of quiet camaraderie, often gathered around a secluded table, that the real magic happened. As we relaxed, the air would fill with the warm buzz of conversation—tales of personal adventures, the latest rumors circulating through our small musical community, and reflections on the night's performance.

Among us was Joe, the saxophonist whose presence brought a sense of history and depth to our group. Despite being in his late seventies, Joe's spirit was as vibrant as his saxophone solos. He was a bridge to a bygone era, having served as a soldier on the Italian fronts during World War II. His stories, rich with the details of a youth spent in the throes of conflict, were a stark contrast to the celebratory nature of our gatherings. Through Joe's recollections, we were transported to the rugged landscapes of Italy where he and countless others faced the unimaginable realities of war. His narratives were not just tales of survival and bravery; they were reminders of the resilience of the human spirit, the complexities of history, and the personal sacrifices that shape our world.

These interludes, spent in Joe's company, listening to his first-hand accounts of a world torn by war, added layers of meaning to our own musical journey. They reminded us that behind every note we played, there was a story, a life, a memory that resonated far beyond the confines of our performances. As a guitar player and a far background singer in that band, I didn't just play music; I became part of a collective memory, a shared history that intertwined the joy of celebration with the solemnity of reflection. It was a profound lesson in the power of storytelling, the importance of history, and the unbreakable bond of shared experiences.

I remember vividly a story Joe shared with us one evening, a narrative so gripping and laden with the weight of history that it sent shivers down our spines. His recounting began on a day when his company was tasked with a critical mission during World War II: to fortify a position along a hillside front, digging into trenches to form a bulwark against the advancing German forces. The gravity of their task was palpable, each soldier acutely aware of the imminent confrontation that awaited them.

However, fate intervened in Joe's journey in the most unexpected manner. Shortly after their arrival and preparations on the hill, a messenger sought out Joe with orders that seemed almost surreal against the backdrop of war. He was to leave his company immediately and report to the officers' recreation hall at the main base, located some twenty miles away, to join the Army base band for a special celebration party. This directive was as startling as it was incongruous; amid the preparations for battle, Joe was to play music. He was assured that this assignment was temporary and that he would rejoin his company by the next morning after the performance.

Complying with the orders, Joe packed his gear and was transported back to the base where he performed that night, far removed from the front lines. The morning after, filled with a sense of urgency to return to his comrades, Joe presented himself at the camp operations post, ready to be sent back to the hillside trenches. However, he was met with a devastating revelation from the commanding officer;

there was no longer a need for him to return. The German forces had launched a relentless assault on the hill during the night, overpowering the American position with such ferocity that not a single soldier from his company had survived.

The news struck Joe with an unimaginable force, casting him into a profound state of shock and grief. He was the sole survivor, spared by a twist of fate so bizarre that it seemed to defy all logic. Reflecting on this and other moments of miraculous survival, Joe confided in us his deep-seated bewilderment. He spoke of advancing in battle, witnessing soldiers fall on all sides, yet somehow, he remained unscathed. The randomness of his survival, against all odds and in the most dire of circumstances, left him grappling with questions of fate, destiny, and the incomprehensible reasons why he was spared when so many others were not.

After sharing this harrowing tale, Joe's gaze met mine with an intensity that conveyed the weight of his experiences. "I still don't understand the logic why I survived the war," he confessed, his voice a mixture of gratitude and perplexity. His story, a testament to the arbitrary nature of survival in the chaos of war, lingered with us long after the music had faded. It was a powerful reminder of the fragility of life, the capriciousness of fate, and the indelible impact of wartime experiences on those who live to tell their tales. Joe's narrative was not just a recounting of personal survival; it was a window into the soul of a man who had witnessed the extremes of human conflict and emerged with a profound sense of wonder at the sheer randomness of existence.

As Joe concluded his narrative, a palpable sense of reverence enveloped me. I found myself utterly captivated, gazing at this remarkable man who had navigated through the unimaginable hazards and perils that life, in its most extreme form, had hurled at him. The table fell into a profound silence, a testament to the weight of his words and the magnitude of his experiences. None of us gathered there could genuinely wish to walk the path Joe had traversed, a journey marked by such close encounters with death and loss. Yet his story, stark and raw in its honesty, prompted a collective introspection among us.

We each found ourselves reflecting, not just on the harrowing tale we had just heard but also on our own lives and the moments where fate had seemingly intervened on our behalf. It became clear that, in varying degrees and circumstances, each of us had, at some point, danced on the edge of the abyss, narrowly avoiding the grip of the reaper. These were our own personal brushes with mortality, moments that, while perhaps not as dramatic or fraught with historical significance as Joe's, nonetheless marked pivotal points in our existence.

This reflection brought with it a profound realization of the interconnectedness of our human experiences, the shared vulnerability that binds us in our journey through life. Joe's story, while uniquely his, served as a mirror reflecting back our own stories of survival, luck, and the often inexplicable turns of fate that allow us to continue forward. It underscored the resilience that lies within each of us, the strength we draw upon in moments of crisis, and the indomitable spirit that enables us to persevere against the odds.

In listening to Joe, we were reminded of the preciousness of life, the thin line that separates existence from oblivion, and the incredible tales of survival that are woven into the fabric of humanity. His experiences, though forged in the crucible of war, resonated with universal themes of survival, resilience, and the quest for meaning amid chaos. As we sat there, reflecting on our own near misses with fate, it became an unspoken acknowledgment of the fragile yet tenacious grip we all hold on life, a bond that connected us not just as bandmates but as fellow travelers on the unpredictable journey of life.

Reflecting on the journey of my life, I realize there have been numerous instances where I narrowly skirted the finality of death. It's as though fate itself intervened, allowing me to evade the grim reaper's embrace time and again and granting me the stories to share. The first of these harrowing encounters occurred when I was just seven years old, a memory that has etched itself indelibly into my consciousness.

On that fateful day, I was walking my dog, Butch—a robust and loyal German shepherd—through the leafy tranquil paths of our

COULD HAVE BEEN; SHOULD HAVE BEEN; HERE I AM

small town's park. The world seemed vast, filled with the innocent wonders of youth, until a sudden turn of events shattered that tranquility. Butch, spotting a large collie across a bustling intersection, tore from my grasp in a frenzied dash that ended in a snarling tangle of fur and teeth. My heart raced as I watched, my young mind consumed with worry for Butch.

Young Butch

Driven by a mix of fear and desperation, I made a rash decision. Ignoring the dangers, I darted into the intersection, slipping between two parked cars with my gaze locked on the chaotic scene beyond. Midway through, a flicker of movement caught my peripheral vision—a large, looming shape barreling toward me. Turning, I was met with the wide-eyed stare of a driver, his face a mask of shock and horror. His expression, frozen in time, is a vision that, even sixty-three years later, remains as vivid as if it had occurred just yesterday.

The sensation of the vehicle's bumper colliding with my right side was both immediate and forceful, propelling me into an involuntary flight a few feet above the car. As the vehicle came to an abrupt halt, I found myself descending sharply, my body making contact with the hood before rolling off the front and onto the pavement below. There, I lay motionless, enveloped in a cocoon of shock and disbelief. Throughout this harrowing ordeal, from the initial impact to my unnerving bounce off the car's hood, our gazes remained locked—an unspoken exchange of terror and desperation. I could see the horror mirrored in the driver's eyes, a reflection of my own fear, as if our souls had momentarily intertwined in this dance with fate.

As I lay there, the ground cold and unforgiving beneath me, time seemed to distort, stretching the seconds into eternities. In that suspended moment, a thought whispered through the chaos of my mind, tinged with an eerie calmness that belied the severity of the situation, *Is this how it ends for me?* The world around me appeared to fade into a blur, the sounds of the bustling intersection receding into a distant hum. It was a profound, introspective moment, one that forced me to confront my own mortality in the face of imminent danger. This fleeting thought, born of a split second's fear, would later serve as a haunting reminder of life's fragility and the unpredictable nature of our existence.

This moment, a mere heartbeat in the span of a lifetime, was my introduction to the razor-thin line between life and death. It was the first of many lessons on the fragility of existence, each one teaching me to cherish every breath, every fleeting moment. These experiences, though fraught with danger, have imbued my life with a depth of appreciation for the precious gift of each new day.

Two years following the harrowing brush with mortality in the automobile accident, at the tender age of nine, I found myself face-to-face with death's icy grip once more. It was a bitterly cold winter day, one that had dressed the landscape in a thick blanket of snow, transforming the world into a silent frosted wonderland. My friend Jerry and I, wrapped in the fearless invincibility of youth, ventured across the seemingly solid surface of a frozen pond, our laughter piercing the cold air. Without any precursor to the imminent danger, the ice beneath me betrayed my trust in a sudden, terrifying moment. A hole appeared as if conjured by some malevolent force, and I was instantly swallowed by the frigid waters below. The shock of the cold was a physical blow, rendering my limbs numb and my breath ragged. I was swept away from the safety of the hole by an unseen current running beneath the ice, my heavy winter clothes and boots becoming my anchors to a watery grave.

Panic set in as I grasped the gravity of my situation. Fully clothed and weighed down, I was hopelessly unable to swim back to the opening through which I had fallen. The chilling waters enveloped me, and a sense of fatalism clouded my thoughts. The haunting question surfaced again, *Is this how it ends for me?* My grandfather had met his end in the frigid waters of the Canadian Atlantic ocean. Was I destined to follow in his footsteps? Escape seemed impossible. Yet in what felt like the final act of a desperate tragedy, a sudden glimmer of hope pierced the darkness. A long stick touched my shoulder, an offering from above. Summoning every ounce of strength, I grabbed it, and Jerry, driven by urgency, hauled me from the abyss.

The stick, seemingly placed by providence itself, became the instrument of my salvation. Jerry, quick to act and driven by a sheer will to save, had utilized what was at hand to rescue me from a fate that seemed all but sealed. In that moment, I was given yet another chance at life, a testament to the unpredictability of our existence and the slender threads by which it hangs. This incident, a stark reminder of my vulnerability, also underscored the profound bonds of friendship and the miraculous interventions that sometimes guide our destinies.

Once more, I found myself facing what I believed could be the final moments of my journey, this time as a result of a motorcycle accident. It was approximately five on a clear afternoon, and I was navigating my way back home atop my Harley motorcycle, returning from an appointment. The roads were unusually serene that day, with the traffic being sparse on the nondivided two-lane street I was traversing. In the distance, my eyes caught sight of a vehicle positioned in the opposite lane at an intersection, signaling its intent to execute a left turn across my path to access an adjacent street. As I drew nearer to this crossroad, I noted that the vehicle had been stationary for a considerable duration, seemingly hesitating despite several clear chances to safely complete its turn long before I would reach the intersection, which notably lacked any form of traffic signals. A nagging sense of unease began to settle over me as I approached, prompting me to decelerate from forty miles per hour to a cautious ten miles per hour, my senses heightened and my eyes fixed on the potential hazard.

Regrettably, my instincts proved accurate. Just as I edged into the heart of the intersection, the vehicle abruptly commenced its turn, cutting sharply across my lane with no warning. This sudden move left me with no viable options to evade the impending collision. We collided head-on, the impact a jarring proof to the split-second decisions that define our fates on the road. The moment my motorcycle's front wheel collided with her bumper, the bike halted abruptly, the forward momentum instantly transforming into a force that elevated the rear end, effectively catapulting me into the air above the front of the vehicle. Suspended momentarily, I found myself confronting a chillingly familiar thought for the third time: *Is this how I meet my end?*

Drawing upon the skills honed during my adolescence as a trained gymnast, my body instinctively executed a front tuck flip above the vehicle. This maneuver, practiced countless times in a gymnasium's safe confines, now served as my unexpected savior on asphalt. I landed deftly on my feet, facing the rear of the vehicle, my left shoulder coming into gentle contact with the driver's side window. The collision's drama reached a brief pause as the driver, responding to the unspoken urgency of the moment, rolled down her window. I turned my head toward her, noting with a mix of disbelief and irritation that she still clutched a cell phone in her hand. With a calmness that belied the adrenaline coursing through me, I mustered a polite request, "If it's not too much trouble, could you perhaps call an ambulance for me?"

Miraculously, despite the harrowing tumble and the total destruction of my motorcycle, my body emerged unscathed, without a single scratch to commemorate the ordeal. It seemed Joe and I were in the same boat this time. A silent prayer of thanks slipped from my lips, gratitude for my gymnastic training and the fortunate lack of any serious injuries flooding my heart. As the adrenaline began to ebb, a thought flickered through my mind, colored with a wry sense of humor, *Thank God I wasn't playing baseball—this would have been my third and final strike.* Reflecting on the incident, I couldn't help but laugh at the absurdity and the sheer luck of it all, thankful once more for escaping what could have been a catastrophic outcome.

Suicide

Suicide is the act of intentionally and voluntarily taking one's own life. It ranks among the top 10 leading causes of death in the United States, with statistics indicating that one person dies by suicide every eleven minutes. The factors leading to suicide are often complex and multifaceted, making it difficult to pinpoint exact causes. However, insights from individuals who have survived suicide attempts or experienced suicidal thoughts can provide valuable perspectives on the motivations behind such decisions. Driven by a desire to raise awareness about the often-hidden signs of suicidal tendencies, I am compelled to share a personal experience from my time working in my own laboratory many years ago. While the events in this story are entirely true, I have changed the names of those involved except for my own to preserve their privacy. Through this narrative, I hope to shed light on the subtle indicators of mental distress that might be present in those around us, potentially going unnoticed.

I remember the day vividly; it was in the early fall, and the morning was marked by a crisp, sunny ambiance that made everything seem more vivid. Around 10:00 a.m., as was customary, the lunch wagon pulled up to the front door of my laboratory, its arrival always a welcome break for my staff. The wagon was stocked with a variety of food and drinks, catering to the diverse tastes of the team.

As usual, there was nothing out of the ordinary that morning. Staff members lined up to pick their favorites, then dispersed into small groups, retreating into various offices to savor their selections. These little gatherings were also a time for sharing the local gossip of the day, a casual ritual that seemed to foster a sense of camaraderie among everyone.

However, about thirty minutes after the lunch wagon's arrival, all hell broke out. What began as a routine and pleasant break quickly escalated into chaos. The sudden shift from calm to turmoil was startling, transforming the atmosphere from one of leisurely social interaction to one of urgent confusion. A staff member burst into my office, breathless and visibly shaken, and told me that Carl had collapsed in the hallway just a few doors down from my office. Without a moment's hesitation, I rushed to the scene and found Carl lying on his back on the floor, face up. As I approached, I saw that he was unconscious, his body violently shaking uncontrollably in a frightening display of shivering. His eyes had rolled back, revealing only the whites, adding to the alarming sight before me. To make matters even more dire, he began to vomit while lying there, which heightened the urgency of the situation.

This was a terrifying scenario to encounter, especially with no prior indication that anything was amiss. The suddenness of Carl's condition created a sense of panic and helplessness among those present. We were all thrust into a crisis mode, scrambling to understand what was happening and how best to assist him. The severity and unexpectedness of the incident left us all deeply concerned for his health and safety.

We acted swiftly, rolling Carl onto his side to prevent him from choking, while I shouted for someone to call an ambulance. A staff member quickly confirmed that help was already on the way. Although Carl was still breathing, his pulse was worryingly faint, and he seemed to be slipping further into unconsciousness with each passing second. The tension in the air was palpable as we anxiously awaited the arrival of emergency services.

In just the nick of time, the sound of sirens signaled the arrival of the fire department and paramedics. The first responders swiftly assessed the situation and took charge, preparing Carl for immediate transport to a nearby trauma center. Their efficiency and professionalism brought a small measure of relief in the midst of the crisis.

As the paramedics wheeled Carl out of the building, I began rapidly firing questions at everyone involved. I needed to piece together what had happened before Carl's collapse to provide a clear picture for the medical team. Understanding the sequence of events was crucial, not only for Carl's immediate care but also for preventing similar incidents in the future. My inquiries focused on everything from Carl's recent health and behavior to any signs that might have indicated he was at risk, hoping to gather as much information as possible to aid his treatment.

Staff member Tommy piped up, providing some key details about the moments leading up to the incident. He explained that he and Carl had both gotten their food from the lunch wagon and then proceeded to his office to take a break. Tommy noted something peculiar that Carl mentioned during their meal. "Carl said his sandwich tasted funny," Tommy exclaimed, adding that just seconds later, Carl had wandered into the hallway and then collapsed.

Tommy continued, highlighting a significant detail about their interaction. "Carl never sits with anybody during break. He usually keeps to himself in his office," he said. This unusual change in behavior struck Tommy as odd; he couldn't fathom why Carl had chosen to join him that day.

Concerned about the potential causes of Carl's sudden collapse, I asked Tommy about the whereabouts of the sandwich and drink Carl had consumed. "They're still on my desk," he replied. This information was crucial as it could help determine if there was something in the food or drink that might have contributed to Carl's condition. The urgency to preserve and examine these items grew, understanding that they might hold the key to what had affected Carl so severely.

Frank, my laboratory manager, stood next to me as I spoke with Tommy, absorbing the critical details of the incident. As I listened, I couldn't help but speculate about potential causes for Carl's sudden and violent collapse. My mind raced to one of the more alarming possibilities: cyanide poisoning. The symptoms seemed to align—rapid onset and severe reaction.

Turning to Frank, I quickly instructed him to test for cyanide. "Check both the sandwich and the drink that Carl had," I told him. Understanding the gravity of the situation, Frank immediately took action. He carefully collected the partially consumed items and hurried into the lab.

Our laboratory was well-equipped for such emergencies, as testing for cyanide compounds in drinking and wastewater was a routine procedure for us. This capability was typically used for environmental testing, but now it was crucial for a potentially lifesaving diagnosis. Frank's efficiency and our lab's readiness underscored the importance of being prepared for any eventuality, even those as rare and unexpected as a potential poisoning at a casual lunch break.

Within minutes, Frank returned with preliminary results on the two items we had submitted for testing. The sandwich showed no traces of cyanide, but the drink Carl had partially consumed contained a significant level of cyanide, measuring at sixty-four parts per million. Without a moment's delay, I contacted the trauma center, urgently requesting to speak with the doctor attending to Carl as I had critical information regarding his condition. Upon reaching the doctor, I was informed that Carl was in grave condition, with the medical team struggling to pinpoint the cause of his symptoms. I quickly relayed that we had detected cyanide in Carl's drink at a concentration of sixty-four parts per million. The doctor responded promptly, confirming that he would administer the cyanide antidote to Carl immediately and requested my presence at the hospital.

Both Frank and I reached the hospital within an hour and were quickly escorted to Carl's bedside. He lay there, a focal point amid a flurry of medical staff and an array of life-supporting equipment. The attending doctor greeted us with good news; the cyanide antidote had been administered, and Carl was showing favorable signs of recovery.

As we stood by his side, Carl began to regain consciousness. It was during these hopeful moments that Carl's parents arrived, rushing to his bedside with a mix of anxiety and relief. As Carl's eyes fluttered open, his first groggy words resonated through the room, "Am I still alive?" A collective sigh of relief washed over us all as we witnessed his steady progress toward recovery.

The doctor then turned to Frank and me, his expression a mix of gratitude and respect. He acknowledged that our swift actions and the capabilities we possessed at our laboratory were crucial. "Because of your quick response and expertise, you've saved Carl's life," he said. "Job well done." This affirmation not only highlighted the critical role of our intervention but also underscored the importance of timely and precise response in medical emergencies.

Over a period of three days beginning on September 29, 1982, a series of tragic events unfolded as seven individuals, including a twelve-year-old girl, succumbed to the effects of cyanide-laced Tylenol in the Chicago area. This devastating incident prompted an immediate nationwide recall of the product and led to significant changes in the pharmaceutical industry, most notably the introduction of tamperproof packaging for over-the-counter medications. In the years that followed, persistent concerns lingered about the potential for similar acts of tampering. Questions arose about whether such a criminal act could occur again and, if so, where it might happen next. The case involving Carl seemed to suggest a possible resurgence of such crimes, possibly the work of a copycat criminal. Unbeknownst to us, we were on the brink of another startling development in this ongoing saga.

The day following Carl's harrowing experience, the situation at our laboratory escalated when the FBI arrived unannounced. They were there to conduct a thorough investigation into the incident, requesting interviews with everyone involved and asking for the remnants of Carl's cyanide-contaminated drink. Recognizing the gravity of the situation, we immediately contacted our attorney and informed him of the FBI's presence. We insisted that no further action should be taken until he arrived to represent us and provide legal guidance on how to proceed. Understanding the need for legal counsel, the FBI agents expressed no objections to our request and patiently waited for our attorney to arrive, ensuring that the investigation would proceed in a legally sound manner.

Upon his arrival, our attorney quickly met with the FBI agents to establish the ground rules for our cooperation. He advised us to fully cooperate with the investigators but made it clear that he needed to be present during each interview to ensure proper documentation and legal compliance. He also negotiated the conditions for handing over the suspected cyanide-laced drink; it was agreed that we would divide the sample, retaining a portion to preserve the integrity of the original evidence. The FBI agents consented to this arrangement, understanding the necessity of maintaining a chain of custody and safeguarding evidence.

The investigation then extended over the next several days, involving multiple visits from the agency. During this period, our laboratory became a focal point for rigorous scrutiny, with each session meticulously recorded and each piece of evidence carefully examined to piece together the circumstances surrounding the incident. This thorough investigative process underscored the seriousness with which the case was being treated, reflecting both the gravity of the situation and the urgency to prevent any future occurrences.

When the FBI's investigation finally concluded, the agents called us together for a detailed briefing on their findings. Understandably, we were all eager to learn the outcome and the implications it held. The agents began by confirming that the drink indeed contained potassium cyanide at the concentrations we had initially identified. This grim confirmation was followed by additional findings from their investigation.

The agents revealed that they had conducted extensive testing on the batches produced at the factory where Carl's drink originated. Importantly, none of the other drinks from the recalled batches tested positive for cyanide. This pivotal discovery led them to conclude that Carl's drink was the only one contaminated with the toxin.

The most shocking revelation came next. After examining all the evidence, the FBI concluded that the poisoning was an attempted suicide by Carl himself. We all stood there, stunned and disbelieving, struggling to reconcile this conclusion with the Carl we knew. The thought that he might have orchestrated this desperate act and misled everyone involved was both shocking and deeply troubling. We were left grappling with a mixture of emotions, from concern for Carl's well-being to confusion over the motives that could have driven him to such an extreme decision.

It was difficult for us to comprehend; Carl had always been an outstanding person and employee. However, the evidence presented by the FBI was overwhelmingly convincing, leading us to believe he was responsible for placing cyanide in his own drink. Following the conclusion of the investigation, Carl approached me to tender his resignation, giving two weeks' notice. I accepted it reluctantly. Since then, I have neither heard from nor seen him. Rumors suggest he relocated to another state to escape the tarnished reputation that followed him locally. Wherever he is now, I sincerely hope he finds peace and serenity.

Skydiving

On my fifty-fifth birthday, a dear female friend decided to mark the occasion by taking me out to dinner. As the evening progressed and a few spirited drinks were shared, I impulsively suggested we go skydiving—a notion that seemed brilliant at the moment but I was really joking. To my surprise, she enthusiastically responded, "That's great. I've always wanted to do that!"

Internally panicking, I thought, *What have I gotten myself into this time?* Yet I managed to muster enough courage to propose that we make the jump that very Saturday, only two days away. Again she agreed without hesitation—now I knew I was in real trouble.

As Saturday approached, I secretly hoped for a stormy forecast that would force us to cancel. However, fate seemed to have other plans. The day dawned clear and sunny, utterly perfect for skydiving. Resigned to my adventurous fate, I prepared to step out of my comfort zone, wondering how a casual dinner led to leaping from a plane.

I vividly remember an unsettling incident that occurred about twenty years ago when I was invited to witness my friend's brother's first parachute jump at Pepperell Airport—the very place I would now consider for my own first jump. As we neared the airport entrance, a shocking scene unfolded before us. A skydiver plummeted rapidly, making a distressing descent and landing harshly in the middle of a bustling street. I turned to my friend, wincing, and muttered, "Ouch! Was that supposed to happen?"

We were both stunned by the sight, especially with the knowledge that we were about to watch her brother take his inaugural leap. We proceeded into the airport, opting to keep the unnerving incident to ourselves. Fortunately, her brother's jump went smoothly, but the event left a deep imprint on me, a stern reminder underlined in my mind: never try skydiving under any circumstances. *Yet, ironically, here I am, booked to make my own jump this Saturday.* Clearly, the lesson didn't quite stick.

Saturday finally arrived, and there we were at the airport's parachute school training center, ready to be schooled in the ups and downs of skydiving. As we began our preparations, the words of my father echoed repeatedly in my mind, a mix of wisdom and wry caution: "Son, always remember what goes up must come down—that's the law of physics." His advice, though simple, seemed to carry a heavier weight as I faced the reality of jumping from a perfectly good aircraft. I couldn't help but smirk at the thought. *Thanks for the advice, Dad.* It was a playful internal nod to his practical yet somewhat obvious wisdom, which I promised myself to recall as I hurtled toward the earth. This mix of apprehension and excitement made the training more intense, as every instruction and safety check reminded me of the imminent leap that bridged theoretical knowledge with palpable experience.

The next phase of our skydiving journey was the ascent to 10,500 feet, facilitated by a twin propjet that carried twenty eager souls, including me. We hovered over the airport, our anticipation building as we awaited our turn to plunge into the unknown. The dual sensations of fear and excitement surged through me, intertwining as the aircraft's hum and the occasional chatter filled the cabin. As our turn approached, we stood and shuffled toward the jump door. For this initial dive, we were all tethered in tandem to experienced instructors, an arrangement that promised a semblance of security amid the daunting leap.

My friend, geared up and attached to her instructor, was directly in front of me. I couldn't help but laugh nervously as they jumped out the door, a mixture of disbelief and adrenaline coursing through me. My laughter was abruptly cut off by my own instructor's calm voice, "All ready? We're next." His nonchalance did little to settle my nerves. In a mere instant, as if pulled by an unseen force, we crossed the threshold of the aircraft. Suddenly, we were in free fall, the ground rushing up to meet us and the air roaring past in a deafening *whoosh* that drowned out all other sounds. The sky became a vast expanse around us, thrilling and terrifying in equal measure. As I looked up and watched the aircraft rapidly shrink in size, a chilling thought crossed my mind, *This must be what it feels like to fall from an aircraft that has broken apart, ejecting all its passengers into the open sky.*

There we were, all twenty novices, hurtling through a free fall that spanned about fifty seconds. The sudden deployment of the parachute jerked us from our rapid descent, transitioning us into a completely different experience. Initially, the sensation of being suspended by harnesses digging into my armpits and crotch was uncomfortable, bordering on painful. However, this discomfort soon gave way to awe as the sheer beauty of drifting gently toward the earth unfolded before us. Floating softly with the world sprawling beneath, it instilled a profound sense of peace within me, a calming balm that soothed the initial adrenaline rush. This serene descent offered a perspective and a tranquility that simulation could never replicate.

Our landing was smooth and uneventful, gently settling us back onto solid ground. The entire journey from the nerve-racking leap to the peaceful float down was an incredible and unique experience, deeply etching itself in my memory. Despite the exhilaration and the beauty of the experience, would I dare to do it again? Not in this lifetime. The thrill was immense but so was the relief of having my feet firmly on the ground again.

Stories I Keep to Myself

I must be forthright. My life has not always adhered to a perfectly moral path. This isn't to say that I engaged in malevolent actions, but I recognize that some of my past behaviors might be viewed as morally ambiguous or questionable. Throughout life, we all encounter moments we're not proud of, yet it's crucial to confront and accept these instances. This process of acknowledgment doesn't serve as a justification for our actions, but rather, it provides insight into why we might have strayed from a virtuous path. Understanding our missteps is vital—it helps us learn from them and can guide us to make better choices in the future, ensuring we do not repeat the same errors.

The question arises: why do we choose to partake in actions we know are wrong for us? Take for instance, a personal memory that remains vividly etched in my mind about stealing from another person. I was about twelve years old, visiting my best friend's house, when I spotted a small pocket radio tucked away on his bookshelf, concealed between a few books. At that moment, my friend was not in the room, so I picked up the radio and examined it. To my astonishment, it was the very radio that had gone missing from my possession several months earlier.

Faced with a moral quandary, I was torn between confronting him about the discovery and preserving our friendship by avoiding an awkward confrontation. After a moment of deliberation, I decided to replace the radio exactly where I found it and chose not to mention it to him. Why did I make that choice? He was a valued friend, and I reasoned that if he needed the radio more than I did, then it was best to let him keep it. This decision, while difficult, highlighted the complex interplay of ethics, friendship, and personal loss. It's an example of how we sometimes sacrifice our own sense of justice to maintain the bonds we cherish, reflecting the complicated nature of human relationships and moral decisions.

Years later, during my early college years, I found employment as a gas station attendant at a Mobil station owned by two brothers, Billy and Mike. Although the pay was only minimum wage, it was sufficient to support my modest lifestyle at the time. The brothers treated me exceptionally well, almost like a family member, generously offering perks such as using their shop to repair my own car at no charge. They were well aware of the challenges young people faced and believed that even a little help could make a significant difference. I deeply appreciated their kindness and generosity.

However, despite their good treatment, I made a regrettable decision one day: I stole from them. This act of betrayal was not driven by necessity but by an impulse I didn't fully understand myself. Reflecting on this lapse, I am reminded of the complexities of human behavior—how one can feel gratitude and respect toward others yet still commit actions that contradict those feelings. This incident became a pivotal moment in my life, forcing me to confront the contradictions in my character and the impact of my decisions on the relationships I valued.

Billy and Mike stumbled upon an unexpected trove of old unused quart oil cans—somewhere between 100 and 150 of them—left over from their father's recently retired garage business. They tasked me with retrieving these cans from storage and arranging them in the front lobby of their gas station to be sold at a discount. Eager to help, I followed their instructions and soon found myself selling about ten cans a day on average.

After about a week and having sold approximately fifty cans, I realized that Billy and Mike had not kept a precise tally of the cans I retrieved from storage; I had never given them an exact inventory. Facing no scrutiny, a dangerous temptation crept over me, and I began to pocket the proceeds from every other can I sold. This deceptive practice continued for about two weeks.

However, my illicit gains came to a sudden halt one day when Billy and Mike showed up unexpectedly during the end of my shift. They conducted a thorough recount of the oil cans and meticulously checked the cash register. It was clear they suspected something was amiss. They knew exactly how many cans had been present before my shift and were quick to notice the discrepancy in numbers that hadn't been registered in sales.

Confronted with the shortfall, I feigned confusion and suggested that it might have been an error in processing the transactions. They looked at me, a blend of disappointment and caution in their eyes, and admonished, "Eric, please be more careful." Ashamed, I hung my head, muttered an apology, and assured them I would be more vigilant about registering sales in the future.

That moment was deeply humiliating. The unspoken understanding hung heavily in the air; they knew I had stolen, and I knew they were aware. The incident was a profound learning experience for me. Billy and Mike's restrained response—not outright accusing me but warning me to amend my ways—showed their inherent kindness and perhaps their hope that I would correct my path. Perhaps it was karma from the time my friend stole my pocket radio and I let it slide. This experience taught me the value of honesty and integrity, especially when dealing with those who had extended nothing but trust and kindness toward me. I resolved then never to steal again, a promise to myself that I have kept ever since.

As I navigated the journey of my life, there were numerous instances where I strayed from the path of integrity. Much of this behavior stemmed from a deep-seated curiosity about what boundaries I could push and what I could potentially get away with. While these episodes are integral parts of my personal history, I choose to keep the specific stories private for the time being. However, these experiences are etched in my memory, serving as stark reminders of the person I once was and the lessons I've learned along the way. Reflecting on these moments has been crucial in shaping my understanding of personal responsibility and ethical conduct. They remind me of the importance of continuously striving to better oneself and adhering to a moral compass even when faced with temptations to veer off course.

A Time to Surrender

I vividly remember the days that preceded my mother's passing, a period marked by a profound transformation that left an indelible impression on my heart. Initially, she was a vibrant individual, her spirit overflowing with life and hope. She took immense joy in tending to her most cherished possessions, each item a testament to memories and moments we shared. Yet as the days passed, I watched, heartbroken, as she gradually regressed into an infantile state, becoming increasingly dependent on those around her for care. This regression was not just physical but also emotional as she began distancing herself from everything that once held great importance in her life. It was as if she was preparing for her final journey, detaching from the worldly ties that bound her. This shift was not sudden but rather a gradual fade, reflecting a deep internal process that was both poignant and profoundly moving. Her transition from the caretaker of her treasured keepsakes to someone who needed care herself illustrated a cycle of life that was both tender and bittersweet.

Witnessing the heartbreaking decline of my loved one spoke to me with profound clarity. It became evident that she had lost her will to live. No matter the extent of medical interventions we attempted, her resolution remained unwavering; for her, there was no possibility of turning back. She communicated to us, with a serene yet determined demeanor, that her new path was laid out directly before her, leaving her with no alternatives but to pursue this lone path. This decision marked the final leg of her journey in life, and she embraced all that awaited her with a sense of acceptance. Her demeanor, a blend of resignation and peace, underscored the depth of her resolve. It was a solemn reminder of the human spirit's capacity to confront its mortality with dignity and grace.

The day she passed away, I stood before her for one final time, assuring her that everything she had asked of me had been taken care of. She lay in her bed, offering a faint, serene smile that encapsulated a lifetime of resilience and grace. There was a palpable sense of calm enveloping the room, a tranquility that seemed to soften the harsh reality of our farewell. This moment marked the last instance of human contact between us—a mother and her child—sealing a bond that had been forged and nurtured over years of love, challenges, and shared experiences. There, lying in the bed, was the woman who had brought me into this world, and now, in her final moments, she was imparting one last lesson to her son: how to gracefully exit this world. This profound lesson wasn't conveyed through words but through her demeanor, her acceptance, and her peaceful surrender to the inevitable. It was a powerful reminder of the cycle of life, teaching me about dignity in departure, and the strength it takes to let go with grace.

The passing of both my mother and father marks a profound turning point in my life, leaving me to navigate the world's complexities as the sole beacon for my own path forward. In moments of uncertainty, the absence of their wisdom and guidance weighs heavily on me. They were my first port of call, offering sage advice and insight that helped illuminate the way. Now with their departure, I find myself in uncharted waters, forced to rely solely on my intuition and the lessons they imparted, piecing together wisdom with each step I take. While siblings can offer camaraderie and support, their perspectives are shaped by a shared generational lens, lacking the depth of experience and nuanced understanding that our parents, with their broader historical and life context, naturally provided. Aunts and uncles, though valuable in their counsel, simply cannot replicate the unique and irreplaceable guidance of a parent. If fortunate, their advice serves as a comforting echo of what once was, yet it's a reminder of the void that can never truly be filled.

Reflecting daily on my parents, I sense their presence weaving through the fabric of my everyday life, as if the essence of who they were—and the love they bestowed—lingers palpably in the air around me. This feeling, this intangible yet real connection, suggests that although they have passed, the energy they carried in life persists, resonating within me and the universe at large. In quiet moments, I find myself pondering how they might approach a challenge or what wisdom they would impart in a given situation. It's as though the genetic legacy we share has gained a louder voice in their absence, guiding me and my siblings from beyond, molding our instincts and choices. Their exact whereabouts remain a mystery, a question mark that perhaps adds to the profundity of their continued influence on my heart and soul. I carry this knowledge, this sense of their enduring presence, as a source of strength and guidance, a proof to the indelible impact they've had on my being and the path I tread.

Now as I continue on the later stages of my life, I find myself reflecting on my role as a parent to a son and daughter. This role has unfolded quite differently than the familial dynamic I experienced with my own parents before my siblings, and I ventured out on my own. The landscape of my children's upbringing was irrevocably altered when I underwent a divorce, their tender ages of four and seven marking the beginning of a fragmented family life. Our family unit was bifurcated, with my children splitting their time between two households until a decisive moment when, at the ages of six and nine, they came to live with me permanently, their mother fading from our lives completely because of medical reasons. Despite the bond my children and I shared, our connection lacked the bedrock of a stable two-parent foundation. As they grew into adolescence, the absence of a maternal figure and the fragmented family structure seemed to push them toward seeking guidance primarily from peers, sidelining my influence and eventually leading to my estrangement from their lives, rendering me a forgotten figure on the periphery of their existence.

This estrangement was compounded by a tragic turn of events when their mother fell ill and passed away in their thirties, a painful chapter that, to my understanding, they had to face without the opportunity for final farewells. This shared absence of closure mirrors my own disconnection from them, casting a long shadow over the complex tapestry of our family narrative. It is a haunting reality, marked by a multitude of unanswered questions and unresolved emotions that I have had to learn to navigate and accept as part of my existence.

In the face of these challenges, I hold onto a hopeful consideration that the essence of their mother and me continues to reside within them. Perhaps, in some intangible yet significant way, this genetic legacy offers a form of connection and guidance, an invisible thread that binds us despite the physical and emotional distances. It is my hope that this bond, however obscured by the trials of life, remains a source of strength and direction for them as they carve out their paths in the world. This thought, though small consolation in the wake of our estranged relationships, offers a sliver of solace that, in moments of need, the best of us may still reach them, guiding and supporting in ways unseen.

Understanding One's Death

Is there an optimal moment to prepare for the inevitable journey's end? From the moment of our first breath, survival instinctively becomes our foremost concern. This primal urge to live, no matter the circumstances, dominates our infancy, guiding us as we navigate the early stages of life. As we transition from childhood into the complexities of adulthood, this instinct remains unaltered—survival at any cost continues to be our underlying priority. Yet as we enter our twilight years, a shift occurs. The emphasis on mere survival begins to wane, giving way to a profound realization. We start to perceive the contours of our life's journey with a clarity that was previously obscured by the hustle of daily survival. It becomes apparent that the roller coaster of life is inching toward its final descent.

In this reflective phase, we find ourselves glancing more frequently in the rearview mirror of our existence, contemplating the path we've traversed with a mixture of nostalgia and introspection. The roads that once stretched before us, seemingly vast and boundless, now appear shorter and narrow, sloping gently downward toward an unseen terminus. It is during these golden years that we confront the reality of life's impermanence, leading us to ponder deeply about our purpose and the legacy we wish to leave behind. This juncture prompts a series of introspective questions. Is this the culmination of our journey, and if so, what is expected of us now? How do we reconcile with the concept of finitude and the legacies we aspire to bequeath? It is a period marked not only by reflection but also by the search for meaning beyond survival, as we strive to embrace the full spectrum of our existence, from its dawn to its twilight.

Recently, I've been drawn to revisiting the landscapes of my past: apartments and houses that once provided me shelter, workplaces that shaped my professional journey, and schools where foundational memories and learnings were forged. These locations serve as a rich tapestry of my history, offering me a wellspring of inspiration and the comforting reassurance that, in the end, everything has unfolded as it should. I consider myself lucky to have these landmarks within easy reach, a privilege not everyone enjoys. Although many of these places have withstood the test of time and remain standing, change is a constant companion. Some of the structures are showing signs of neglect, succumbing to the ravages of time, and stand on the brink of disappearing forever. Witnessing this transformation evokes a bittersweet sentiment, a reminder of the impermanence of life and the relentless march of progress.

For some individuals, the journey back to their roots is hindered by geographical distances or logistical constraints. Whether it's due to being born in a distant locale, perhaps hundreds of miles away, or in another country across the seas, the ability to revisit one's place of origin can be challenging, if not, at times, insurmountable. My father's story illustrates this sentiment poignantly. Born in the bustling borough of the Bronx, New York, he spent his formative years immersed in the vibrancy of his neighborhood, surrounded by a close-knit circle of friends and family. His childhood and adolescence were marked by the typical joys and trials of growing up in such a lively environment, attending local schools and forming bonds that he hoped would last a lifetime.

As he transitioned into adulthood, my father made the move to Massachusetts, a place he would eventually call his final home. Despite this new chapter, he often expressed a deep yearning to return to his old stomping grounds in the Bronx, to reconnect with long-lost friends, and to recapture the essence of his youth. This longing was akin to an unfulfilled dream, much like an envisaged boat trip down the scenic Connecticut River that never came to fruition. Unfortunately, his penchant for procrastination often led to regrets, a sentiment that was all too common in his later years. He would share with me, with a hint of melancholy, how he felt like a visitor in his own town, highlighting a profound sense of displacement and longing for a past that seemed increasingly out of reach.

In stark contrast, my mother's experience was rooted in a deep sense of belonging and continuity. Born, raised, and having spent her entire life in the same town, she was enveloped by the familiar faces of family and friends. This ever-present support network imbued her with a profound sense of home, a feeling that she cherished deeply. It's ironic then that at her funeral, the interior of her casket door, the inscription was "Going Home"—a reminder of her unwavering faith. A deeply religious woman, my mother often spoke of the dual concept of home: the physical place where she lived, surrounded by loved ones, and the spiritual home awaiting her in God's kingdom. This duality of home, grounded in her faith, offered her comfort and a sense of eternal belonging, starkly contrasting my father's perpetual search for a connection to his past.

Did my parents understand what the end was all about? I believed that my mother did and my father was taken by surprise. During my mother's later years, she, in small increments, prepared herself to depart this world. She worked most of her life as a secretary that was very rewarding for her but when she turned sixty-five a few years after my father's passing, she retired. This left her plenty of time to complete the things she always wanted and needed to do by disbursing her personal wisdom and belongings among her family. For her, she had plenty of time for goodbyes with no regrets until her passing at the age of eighty-one.

My father was confronted with the harsh reality of his mortality in a manner that allowed little room for the leisurely contemplation of life's final chapter. Diagnosed with terminal cancer at the age of sixty, he was suddenly faced with a drastically abbreviated timeline, having just a year to come to terms with and prepare for his imminent departure at the age of sixty-one. This abrupt revelation was a source of profound distress for our entire family. To him, the diagnosis felt like an irrevocable decree, marking the beginning of an inexorable countdown to an unavoidable conclusion. The question lingered in the air: did he fully grasp the magnitude of what needed to be accomplished in this condensed time frame to achieve a sense of fulfillment in his life?

Contrastingly, my mother's journey toward her life's end was marked by a readiness and acceptance that my father sadly lacked. Whereas she seemed to approach her final days with a sense of peace and preparation, my father was, in the simplest of terms, disillusioned. It was painfully clear that he had not managed to realize his aspirations of a leisurely retirement filled with golf, literature, and the joys of unhurried days. The divergence in their experiences taught me a profound lesson about the inevitability of the end and the importance of living one's life in a manner that allows for peace and fulfillment when that time approaches.

Both my parents, through their distinct paths to life's conclusion, imparted to me a crucial understanding about the essence of readiness and the value of cherishing each moment. Their experiences underscore the importance of not only pursuing one's dreams with vigor but also preparing oneself emotionally and spiritually for life's ultimate certainty. This lesson, learned through the lens of their contrasting departures, will undoubtedly shape my own approach to life, ensuring that I live fully and prepare wisely for the end, whenever it may come.

Standing at the threshold of what many consider the twilight years, I find myself peering into the future with a clarity and resolve that has been honed by the experiences and lessons of those who came before me. At seventy years old, I am grateful to acknowledge the gift of a long life characterized by robust health and a tapestry of rich experiences that have colored my existence. Yet with the wisdom that comes with age, I recognize the immutable truth that time marches on, its inexorable advance reminding me that each moment is precious.

Physically and mentally, I find myself in an enviable position, often feeling as spry and sharp as individuals decades my junior. This vitality fuels my optimism and drive, yet it also serves as a reminder that the clock, relentless in its ticking, continues to wind down. It is with this awareness that I approach the planning of my remaining years, which I hope will extend into a vibrant and fulfilling three decades.

In the quiet moments of reflection, informed by the stories of my parents and their divergent paths to life's inevitable conclusion, I have pondered deeply on how I wish to curate the chapters that remain. My plans, while solid in their foundation, are imbued with a flexibility that acknowledges the unpredictable nature of life. I aspire to strike a balance between achieving long-held dreams and embracing the spontaneous opportunities that life may yet present.

Key to my approach is a commitment to living intentionally, ensuring that my actions and choices reflect the values and passions that have guided me thus far. Whether it's dedicating time to hobbies that have always ignited my spirit, engaging more deeply with my community, or embracing opportunities to travel and explore the world's vast wonders, I aim to fill my days with activities that bring joy and fulfillment. Moreover, I am acutely aware of the importance of leaving a legacy that extends beyond material wealth. My focus also lies in imparting wisdom, fostering relationships, and contributing positively to the lives of those around me. Through these endeavors, I hope to not only enrich my own life but also touch the lives of others in meaningful ways.

In embracing the journey ahead with open eyes and a full heart, I am buoyed by a sense of purpose and anticipation. My plans, though subject to life's whims, provide a road map for a future that I approach with excitement and a deep appreciation for the beauty of life's impermanence.

Preparing for our final chapter is a deeply personal endeavor, yet it embodies universal principles that resonate across the myriad of human experiences. My advice, drawn from personal reflection and the wisdom of those who have navigated this path before, centers on the imperative of conducting a comprehensive assessment of one's life. This introspective process is as unique as each individual, influenced by our diverse lifestyles, health conditions, and financial circumstances. Just as no two snowflakes are identical in their intricate designs, no two life assessments will mirror each other perfectly. However, beneath these differences lies common ground—a universal need to address and resolve unfinished business.

This preparation begins with a holistic review of our lives, encompassing not only our financial affairs but also our personal relationships, emotional well-being, and the legacies we wish to leave behind. Tying up loose ends means different things to different people; it could involve settling debts, ensuring our wills and estate plans are up-to-date, or even reaching out to mend fences with estranged friends or family members. It's about creating peace, both externally in our affairs and internally within ourselves.

Beyond the practical aspects, preparing for our final chapter also means reflecting on our values, desires, and the mark we wish to leave on the world. It's an opportunity to think deeply about what matters most to us and how we want to be remembered. This could involve drafting a living will that outlines our wishes for end-of-life care, planning meaningful ways to bequeath our possessions, or considering charitable acts that align with our values. Moreover, this journey toward closure is not just about tying up our own loose ends; it's also about facilitating conversations with loved ones about their wishes and hopes for the future. It's a process that encourages openness, fosters deeper connections, and helps all involved to embrace the full spectrum of life, including its final stages.

In essence, preparing for our final chapter is a multifaceted process that challenges us to look at our lives from a comprehensive perspective. It's about making peace with the past, living fully in the present, and setting the stage for a departure that aligns with our deepest values and aspirations. By embracing this approach, we not only enrich our own lives but also offer guidance and comfort to those we leave behind, ensuring that our legacy is one of love, resolution, and fulfillment.

Embarking on a journey to leave behind a tangible legacy, I've chosen to fulfill a desire that my father once harbored: the creation of a written document for future generations to cherish. This decision was fueled by a longing for connection to my ancestry, a sentiment born from the realization that so much of my family's history has slipped away, unrecorded and untold. The stories of my grandparents and their forebears, their thoughts, feelings, and aspirations, remain largely unknown, obscured by the passage of time. Like many, my family's past is scantily documented, particularly from the 1900s and earlier, leaving us to rely on fragmented folklore or mere speculation to piece together our ancestral narrative.

In bygone eras, the scarcity of cameras and virtually nonexistent recording media have left us with precious few images and no auditory legacy of our predecessors. This dearth of tangible memories is a great loss, the magnitude of which is felt more acutely as generations pass. The absence of detailed accounts and personal reflections means that many potentially enriching and instructive experiences from our past are irretrievably lost to time. I often ponder the invaluable lessons and insights that could have been gleaned from such records had they existed.

Contrastingly, the advent of modern technology has revolutionized our capacity to document and preserve our lives for posterity. The ease with which we can now capture photographs, videos, voice recordings, and store vast amounts of data ensures that current and future generations will have unprecedented access to their family history. This technological boon offers a way to bridge the gap between past and future, allowing personal stories and achievements to be shared and preserved.

In the twilight of my father's life, he expressed a wish to leave behind his own mark, requesting a tape recorder to document his final thoughts and reflections. I honored this request, hopeful that this endeavor would allow him to convey the wisdom and insights accumulated over a lifetime. Concurrently, he turned to art, a passion that had lain dormant for much of his life because of the demands of daily responsibilities. Despite his latent talent as an artist, the opportunity to fully explore this gift had always eluded him.

After his passing, I discovered that the recordings he intended to leave were blank, a sad reminder of intentions unfulfilled and words left unspoken. However, I found solace in one completed painting—a depiction of flowers—that now adorns the wall of my office. This solitary piece serves as a bittersweet testament to his artistic ability and a visual reminder of what might have been had he pursued his creative passions.

Inspired by my father's last wishes and the stark contrast between the lost histories of our ancestors and the abundant possibilities of today's digital age, I am compelled to document my own journey. Through writing, I aim to capture the essence of my experiences, thoughts, and hopes for the future, ensuring that my descendants will have a wellspring of knowledge and connection to draw upon. In doing so, I honor both the unfulfilled dreams of my father and the silent stories of my ancestors, bridging the gap between past, present, and future with every word penned.

By Leo Koslowski

Reflections on My Fiftieth Class Reunion: A 2022 Retrospective

The year 2022 descended upon me with the full force of a freight train loaded to capacity, barreling down the tracks directly from 1972. It was an unstoppable force of time that, upon halting, starkly reminded me that fifty years—a half century—had elapsed since my high school graduation and the momentous occasion of my fiftieth class reunion. There, in a spacious dining room, around 120 of us were seated, exchanging tentative glances and hesitant smiles as we embarked on the task of weaving together the threads of our past and present, endeavoring to understand the imprint of time on our lives and the mysteries behind the loss of sixty-eight of our classmates to the realms beyond our understanding.

This reunion was unlike any other I had attended. There was an indescribable aura that enveloped us all, making it a unique, almost sacred gathering. We were not just celebrating a milestone but also confronting the reality of our shared journey through time. For many of us, this reunion marked a significant life threshold; we were mostly around the age of sixty-eight, having just surpassed the traditional age of retirement. This was a pivotal moment, a tribute to reaching what many consider a pinnacle of life—a point signifying not only survival but success in health and finances, the promise of a new chapter where life can be embraced with the innocence and freedom of youth. Retirement, for many, symbolized a return to a carefree existence, a time when every day holds no obligations and every moment is an opportunity for leisure and exploration, akin to a perpetual play day in our final tranquil haven. This reunion served as a reflective pause, a bridge connecting the dreams of our youth with the realities of our golden years, a chance to celebrate our achievements, reminisce about days gone by, and ponder the infinite possibilities that lie ahead.

At the far corner of the room, my eyes settled on a familiar figure from my earliest school memories: Philip. I vividly recall him as the young boy who, on our very first day of grade one, found it impossible to hold back his tears as he watched his mother walk out of the classroom. Time, the ever-persistent sculptor, had molded him into a different person now. There he sat, exuding a quiet sense of contentment, alongside his wife. They seemed to bask in the great atmosphere, a serene bubble amid the lively reunion, surrounded by friends whose journeys had intersected with his not just in that first-grade room but in various chapters of life across the years.

Adjacent to us, another integral thread in the fabric of our shared history, was Dave and his delightful wife, Collin. They were a pair known not just for their endearing personalities but also for their commendable service to others, a testament to the kind of spirits they were. The evening unfurled like a spellbinding narrative, filled with magical moments that were further embellished by sincere smiles and warm embraces. It was an unspoken agreement, a collective acknowledgment that despite the inevitable conclusion of our gathering within a few hours, the connections rekindled in those fleeting moments were timeless.

We had all started as a large family—originally four hundred strong. Now with sixty-eight cherished souls less, the countdown continued, each departure a reminder of the transient nature of our meetings. Yet in that reflection, there was no room for despair. The spirit and love that permeated the room that evening felt eternal, offering a comforting assurance. It whispered of a reunion, a hope that beyond the confines of time and space, all four hundred of us would once again converge, united as one extended family in a gathering devoid of final goodbyes.

Unlocking the Secrets to a Fulfilling Life

I often assert that the essence of a fulfilling life is to "live within your means, spiritually, mentally, physically, socially, and financially." Reflecting on my life's journey, I ponder whether the paths I chose or forsook were predestined by external forces, determined by biological genetics before birth, or entirely the result of my own decisions. Numerous theories attempt to explain life's trajectory, and while many hold merit, I've come to believe it's likely a blend of many factors.

I posit that no one exists in isolation, devoid of influence from our surroundings. Picture yourself in an expanse of absolute void; without distinguishable paths, movement becomes meaningless, anchoring us to a singular point, possibly akin to our pre-birth state. This concept raises profound questions: where were we before existence, and is that where we return postmortem? These queries intrigue me as they transcend our conscious understanding, challenging us to consider realities beyond definitive comprehension.

While some anticipate that death unveils these mysteries, perhaps introducing us to a higher entity or returning us to our origin, others adopt a more pragmatic view, suggesting that life simply ceases. Despite the diverse beliefs and theories, the truth remains elusive, a puzzle wrapped in the enigma of existence and the universe's vast mysteries.

Humans stand unique among earth's creatures, possessing an acute consciousness of our own existence. We understand the cycle of birth, life, and the inevitability of death, a realization apparently absent in other species. This awareness manifests in our actions, as humans are known to prepare for their demise, passing on belongings and knowledge to subsequent generations, aiming for their betterment and survival, a practice not observed in animals like cats, dogs, or even primates. This behavior raises the question: what drives humans to act this way? I believe it is influenced by a significant force, offering us multiple life choices with the autonomy to decide our paths.

From the instant we are born, a pivotal choice is presented—to breathe. This initial decision sets the stage for a series of choices and paths, leading ultimately to life's end. One crucial realization I've encountered is the universal "law of asking." According to this principle, expressing a desire for something positions you to eventually receive it. This process involves envisioning oneself at the center of a personal universe, surrounded by endless possibilities awaiting selection. By articulating a desire, you invite the possibility of its fulfillment into your life though it demands patience and discernment, as all possibilities, including undesirable outcomes, are within reach.

The law of asking resonates because it presupposes that all desires are attainable for everyone in the universe, influenced by the individual's unique requests. This explains the diversity of human conditions and possessions; like snowflakes, no two people harbor identical aspirations. Hence, it poses a philosophical inquiry: do we encounter our desires by chance, or do we carve a path toward them? Given our individual uniqueness, it seems that our specific desires and the paths to achieving them are as distinct as we are, reflecting the complex interplay between individual agency and the vast expanse of universal potential.

CHAPTER 7

Time to End

And in the end, the love you take, is equal to the love you make.

—Lennon-McCartney

Everything Must Come to an End Someday

The ancient adage rings with an unvarnished truth, "If you are fortunate enough to be born, then, regrettably, you are also destined to die." These words, though not the most uplifting, encapsulate an undeniable reality. From the moment we draw our first breath, we are bound to experience, repeatedly throughout our lives, the phenomenon of endings. These terminations can manifest in myriad forms, ranging from the simple transition of day into night, to the culmination of a long journey, to the more profound and life-altering finality of losing a loved one or a cherished pet. Regardless of their nature, these endings serve as a constant reminder of life's impermanence. Yet amid this ceaseless cycle of beginnings and conclusions, two entities stand as exceptions to the rule: time and the universe.

Time, it appears, might have commenced at a point we can conceptualize as "zero," akin to the initiation of a numerical sequence, but it relentlessly marches forward, unfettered by any notion of cessation. Similarly, the universe, in my perception, defies the constraints of start and finish, existing instead as a boundless expanse, stretching into the vastness of infinity. This eternal continuum, where neither time nor the universe succumbs to an end point, underscores the unique nature of their existence, contrasting starkly with the ephemeral nature of everything else within our tangible reality.

If time and the universe, in their vast expansiveness, defy the notion of an end, and we find ourselves existing within these boundless realms, then the pervasive experience of endings in our lives presents a profound paradox. This conundrum leads me to surmise that what we perceive may not fully represent the essence of reality but rather merely its facade. To delve deeper into this mystery, let's consider the dual constituents of the universe: matter and energy.

Matter is the easier of the two to comprehend, being any substance with mass that occupies space and is often perceptible through our senses. Everyday examples include the physical bodies of living organisms, the structures we inhabit, the vehicles that transport us, the clothes we wear, and numerous other objects that constitute our tangible world. Astonishingly, despite the diversity and complexity of these forms, they share a fundamental building block: the atom. This minute unit, the cornerstone of all matter, weaves the fabric of the physical universe, from the grandest galaxies to the air we breathe.

The atom, that essential cornerstone of matter, has enthralled me for as long as I can remember. It serves as a symbol of the universe's enduring and tireless essence. In theory, every atom in existence today has been around since the beginning of time and is fated to continue into the boundless expanse of eternity. Furthermore, the atom represents the nearest thing we have to a perpetual motion machine, with electrons in constant motion around their nuclei in an everlastingly captivating dance.

Despite our advancements in science, the atom's intrinsic behavior remains shrouded in mystery. We can observe its activities, measure its properties, and even harness its energy, yet the fundamental reasons for its unending vigor and the rules governing its interactions are still subjects of inquiry and awe. It is a humbling thought that every atom composing the very fabric of our being has traversed the expanse of time from the universe's inception.

What is truly remarkable, and perhaps even a bit mystical, is the way in which a specific assemblage of these ancient atoms comes together at a precise moment to form a unique entity—each one of us. This gathering is not a mere chance but a complex result of the laws of nature and the history of the universe. Just as these atoms have come together to create life, so, too, will they one day disband and merge into new forms, be it other living beings, objects, or the stars themselves.

This cyclical journey of atoms, from their formation in the hearts of dying stars to becoming part of living organisms and eventually returning to the cosmos, mirrors the endless cycle of the universe itself. It serves as a reminder of our interconnectedness with the cosmos and the perpetual cycle of renewal and transformation that defines existence. In this grand cosmic cycle, we are but temporary custodians of the atoms that compose us, participating in the eternal ballet of the universe.

On the other hand, energy is often taken to be a mysterious and all-pervading force that propels and animates the universe toward its manifold display, from the sparkling light of stars to the soothing heat of our sun, from the unseen forces at work in every galaxy to those upholding the fabric of space.

What is interesting about these forces of energy is that they are immaterial, not consisting of matter, yet wield the awesome power to reshape landscapes and move mountains if need be. Immaterial forces, such as radiation, light, and gravity, are eminent examples of such forces—forces that exist without material form but play essential roles in our universe. Basically, the energy is changing and perpetual, having power to change from one form to the other, but, however, its existence is eternal, never in any way dimming or ceasing to be. The position of these, what its position in the universe seems to put into sharp focus, is the dynamic interaction between the visible and invisible that underlines its crucial part in the perennial story of existence.

This dichotomy between matter and energy and their interplay suggests that while the components of our reality may undergo transformations or endings, they are part of a larger continuous cycle within the infinite expanse of time and space. Therefore, the endings we experience are not absolute ceases but transitions from one state to another within this grand continuum.

The idea that our perception of everything must come to an end holds truth, especially when considering the transformation of atoms and the shifting forms of energy. This constant state of flux implies that all things, including events, undergo a process of ending and morphing into new events. Yet despite the relentless pace of these transformations, the overarching change in the universe remains neutral—marked by a balance where nothing is genuinely added or subtracted. It's a concept that aligns with the principles of conservation, suggesting a universe that exists as an infinite continuum.

In summary, the adage that everything must come to an end holds true only within the finite boundaries of our personal timelines, not in the context of the universe, which transcends the very notion of time. This perspective challenges us to rethink the concept of endings as absolute terminations, encouraging us to view them instead as markers of transition within a broader, timeless continuum. In the grand cosmic scheme, where the universe operates without a clock, what we perceive as an end is merely a point of transformation, a segue into new beginnings and possibilities. Thus, while our human experiences are punctuated by beginnings and endings, the universe itself unfolds in an unending sequence of changes, untouched by the constraints of time that shape our understanding of existence.

Final Wishes: Crafting Your Will and Planning Your Legacy

Creating a will and making final arrangements might seem morbid at first glance, but in truth, these actions are essential aspects of life planning. Reflect for a moment on the satisfaction and sense of completion that comes from finishing a significant project. Whether it's preparing a Thanksgiving feast for a large family, building a house that becomes a cherished home, publishing a book that shares your insights with the world, or the proud moment of receiving a diploma—these milestones represent the culmination of hard work and vision. In the same vein, a will and final arrangements are comparable projects, albeit on a grander scale. A will is more than just a legal document; it's a final testament that ensures your wishes are respected and carried out when you're no longer here to oversee them yourself. Meanwhile, final arrangements provide a structured plan for your last moments, allowing you to shape the narrative of your life's closing chapter. Together, they offer peace of mind, not just for you but also for those you leave behind, ensuring that your legacy is honored in the way you envision.

Unfortunately, not everyone has the opportunity to draft a will or make final arrangements. Life is unpredictable, and unforeseen circumstances such as accidents, sudden medical issues, or the call of duty in times of conflict can lead to an unexpected departure from this world. In the absence of these crucial documents, families are often thrust into a state of turmoil and distress. The burden of decision-making, now resting heavily on the shoulders of grieving loved ones, can become a source of contention and conflict among family members. This division, born out of the chaos of unresolved wishes and the complexities of estate distribution, can leave deep rifts within the family fabric. I have personally witnessed the devastating impact this can have, observing families torn apart by disputes that seem insurmountable. The absence of a will or final arrangements not only complicates the practical aspects of dealing with a person's departure but also can inflict long-lasting emotional wounds on those left to navigate these choppy waters without guidance. It underscores the critical importance of proactive planning, not just as a means of asset distribution but as a vital act of care for those we love, aiming to spare them additional heartache in their time of loss.

Embarking on the process of drafting a will and making final arrangements is a task that can be initiated at any point in an individual's life, reflecting the understanding that life's circumstances are ever evolving. The beauty of these documents lies in their flexibility; they can be modified and adapted as life unfolds, ensuring they always mirror current wishes and circumstances. However, it's crucial to remember that this malleability is only applicable during one's lifetime. Upon passing, these documents become immutable, their directives as binding as if set in stone, unless a probate court intervenes because of disputes or grievances presented by family members.

Importantly, not every detail of one's final wishes needs to be meticulously outlined by the individual themselves. Much can be entrusted to designated family members—be it a spouse, children, or even legal representatives—who can be assigned specific roles and responsibilities. The aim is to alleviate the burden, not add to it, by allowing trusted individuals to manage affairs in accordance with the decedent's wishes. Moreover, these documents do not require complex legal jargon to be effective. Often, simple, clear instructions and objectives are far more valuable than an exhaustive list of demands, providing a straightforward path for those left behind to follow.

From my personal experience, I opted for a straightforward approach when drafting my own will and arrangements. My primary goal was to ensure a seamless transition of responsibilities to my wife, granting her the authority to make decisions in my stead, with the exception of a few specific final wishes concerning the equitable distribution of assets among our children. Beyond these explicit directives, I chose not to dwell on the minutiae of the arrangements, trusting in the judgment and discretion of my loved ones to handle the rest. This decision underscores a profound trust and the recognition that, ultimately, the specifics of these arrangements hold less significance for me personally, allowing those I care about the freedom to act according to what they believe is best. Hopefully after my passing, the families will unite in good will and not divide in despair.

On Top of the Hill, What's Next?

The phrase "over the hill" often conjures up a variety of meanings, depending largely on who you ask. In my experience, the obstacles I've faced rarely resembled mere hills; they felt more akin to towering mountains. Reflecting on my journey through the span of seventy years, I acknowledge it wasn't a walk in the park, yet it was undeniably thrilling. If the saying "On top of the hill" symbolizes reaching the zenith of one's life, then I'm inclined to concur. My path from infancy, through the formative educational years, into the quest for a career, the joy of expanding my family, to the trials of health challenges, and eventually settling into a lifestyle that's both manageable and sustainable paints a vivid picture of what it means to reach that apex. But the question remains: is this pinnacle the ultimate achievement, or is there more beyond the horizon?

The laws of physics remind us that what ascends must eventually descend, yet the precise moment when one reaches that plateau—the peak before the descent—remains a profound mystery. How do we recognize that turning point, and once there, how long can we bask in the glory of our achievements before we embark on the downward journey toward life's conclusion? This metaphorical "hill" in life's landscape serves as a reminder of the transient nature of our existence, prompting us to ponder the true essence of our personal summits and valleys.

At the age of seventy, I firmly believe that I have yet to encounter the zenith of my life's journey. The horizon continues to expand before me, revealing uncharted frontiers and weaving new pathways of opportunity that beckon with the promise of adventure and discovery. Such revelations prompt a profound contemplation: should I declare that what I've achieved is sufficient, drawing the curtains on further pursuits, or do I recognize that the decision to cease exploring might not solely rest in my hands? This pivotal question underscores the eternal dance between contentment and aspiration, pushing me to ponder the extent of my agency in charting the course ahead. It's a reflection not just on age but on the nature of human ambition and the endless quest for meaning that defines our existence.

Throughout my career, I've delved into various professions, embracing the worlds of electronics, aviation, music, chemistry, biology, and business. Yet despite the breadth of my experiences, I continue to encounter new opportunities that knock on my door, inviting me to explore further. Interestingly, these so-called "new" opportunities aren't entirely unfamiliar territories. Rather, they are nuanced variations of disciplines I've previously mastered, allowing me to blend my past experiences with fresh challenges.

Take for example, my venture into the realm of vintage electronics. I've established a workshop dedicated to testing and repairing electronic devices, with a particular focus on tube circuit citizen band (CB) radios from the 1960s and 1970s. These radios, once heralded as the epitome of luxury and innovation in the United States, represented the pinnacle of consumer electronics during their heyday. Despite their superior quality, the high production costs made them accessible to only a select few, positioning them as the "Cadillac" of radios. Over time, competition from overseas manufacturers, who offered similar products with new transistor technology at lower prices, led to the decline of these domestic companies. Today, the remaining radios are rare finds, often in a state of disrepair.

Electronics workshop

What's fascinating is the niche market that exists for these vintage radios. Enthusiasts and collectors are willing to pay premium prices for units that are restored to their former glory. Leveraging my background in vacuum tube electronics, I've developed a method to rejuvenate these historical pieces, turning them from forgotten relics into desirable collectibles. This endeavor, while occupying the margins of my time, has evolved into a rewarding hobby-business hybrid. It allows me to exercise my electronics skills in a way that's both satisfying and profitable.

This journey into the revival of vintage electronics is just one example of how my varied career path has equipped me with the unique ability to identify and seize upon these blending opportunities. It's a testament to the value of diverse experiences and the endless possibilities that arise when we're open to combining our past expertise with new ventures.

This phenomenon of discovering new opportunities within familiar territories extended beyond electronics into other areas I've passionately explored, such as aviation, music, chemistry, biology, and business. The journey into aviation not only allowed me to earn a pilot's license but also led to the acquisition of two small private airplanes. This venture blossomed into a dual-purpose endeavor; it provided me with the sheer joy of personal air travel while also serving as a profitable rental service. Similarly, my foray into music, particularly my experiences playing in a rock band, inspired me to construct a recording studio. This space became a crucible for creativity, not just for my own musical expressions but also for fellow artists seeking a quality production environment.

In the realm of chemistry and biology, my interests merged seamlessly with my entrepreneurial spirit, culminating in the establishment of a research and testing laboratory. This facility became a nexus for innovation, offering valuable services that leveraged my scientific expertise for practical applications. Moreover, the insights and knowledge gained from my diverse career path have recently guided me into the world of authorship. With a plethora of experiences to draw upon, I've embarked on a journey to write and publish, aiming to share my unique perspective and insights with a global audience.

This continuous emergence of new vocations and pursuits underscores a fundamental truth about my journey; so long as I continue to breathe and engage with the world, opportunities will invariably seek me out. It is a proof to the idea that a diverse set of skills and experiences can pave the way for unexpected ventures, each building upon the last in a symbiotic progression. My story is a living example of how varied interests, when pursued with passion, can converge to create a multifaceted and fulfilling life path.

A Message to My Unborn Son

I felt that there is yet a thorn in the shoe, and each and every step I walk reminds me of my unborn son. I was eighteen years of age, a senior in high school, when a careless, unforgettable event happened in my life. There was a young girl that I was dating, eighteen also. We were at that age where experiment seems to be the best order of the day, especially on sex. Just that she got pregnant was very unfortunate for the both of us. This wasn't a time for this to be happening, both of us still in school, raising a baby with no incomes to do it. I do not remember, and perhaps, I don't want to remember all the details as we tried to choose how to do an abortion; but in general, a way out of this bad situation was very fast and easy.

Young minds, however, and under the cover of secrecy, this could be the only solution. Without letting our parents know or guiding us through this, we took the matter in our hands. I borrowed the money from my sister's friend, and she traveled to New York City where, at the time, the procedure was legal.

Whichever times I try to rationalize my decisions in the case, I seem to never find a justification for them. The right words escaped me—none gave solace, let alone be the much-needed redemption for a choice that weighed heavy on my conscience. It is a decision ringing through with both regret and sorrow, leaving a hole that no explanation or apology can fill. It was at this moment of great introspection when I pondered that maybe the road to healing does not lie in justifying the unjustifiable but in seeking forgiveness from that higher power and the soul that our choice touched—our unborn son. It is hence a serious understanding that some behaviors supersede what man can fully comprehend and forgive. One needs to look beyond and above the earth with its explanations, hoping for divine mercy and receiving.

In the depths of my reflection, I now understand that a day will come when I must confront the repercussions of my actions. That would have been the weight of my sins upon my soul, so heavy, and I would have taken one wish: to be able to turn back time right before that fateful decision of mine and change its course, to be spared from all that pain and regret. Alas, I realize such a possibility hangs somewhere out there in the area of realness, just a vision to salve the ache of remorse. In this light then, I can see my road ahead quite clearly, though not without its difficulties. I commit to tirelessly seeking forgiveness, not just from those I have wronged but also from myself. This is, in the end, a way of redemption—long and uncertain but with hope that one has to travel, directed by the light of atonement and the desire to heal the splits of the past. To my unborn son, I am deeply sorry for what I have done. Please forgive me.

You Will Soon Become a Memory

As I navigate the journey of my life, a profound realization dawns upon me; the fabric of our world is intricately woven with the threads of past memories. Reflecting on this, it becomes evident that the extensive knowledge amassed over countless years is meticulously chronicled, serving as a beacon for future generations. This cyclical process, which I fondly term the "leapfrog effect," encapsulates the essence of human progress. Each generation meticulously curates the wisdom of its predecessors, amalgamating it with contemporary insights. This fusion of past and present knowledge sets the stage for subsequent generations, fostering a continuous cycle of growth and innovation. This forward momentum is not just a proof to our resilience but also a mechanism through which we strive to enhance our collective existence. Through this perpetual interplay of learning and evolving, humanity embarks on an endless quest for improvement, each step forward a tribute to the legacies that precede us, ensuring that our journey through time is both transformative and enriching.

The concept of harnessing the echoes of bygone memories to fuel our journey forward can aptly be described as progress. This term encapsulates not just the advancement of knowledge and technology but also the emotional and spiritual inheritance passed down through generations. My ancestors, in their wisdom, generously bequeathed to me a rich tapestry of knowledge, which I cherish as a vivid memory of their lives and legacies. These memories serve as a cornerstone of my identity, providing me with both a biological blueprint—my physical characteristics—and a sociological grounding—the community and cultural milieu I identify with.

Beyond the tangible, these inherited memories offer a profound connection to my forebears, anchoring me to my roots while propelling me forward. They imbue me with a sense of belonging, linking me to a lineage that has navigated the vicissitudes of life with resilience and fortitude. This ancestral knowledge and the memories it conjures are not just a reflection of the past; they are a beacon that illuminates my path, guiding my steps in the maze of life. They equip me with the wisdom to face contemporary challenges, allowing me to adapt and innovate. In this way, the memories of my ancestors are not merely recollections of who they were but are instrumental in shaping who I am and aspire to be. Through them, I am empowered to contribute to the tapestry of human progress, ensuring that the legacy of learning and growth continues for generations to come. Soon, I will be a memory too.

My Final Thoughts

As I approach the twilight years of my life, a profound sense of finality envelopes me, casting its long shadow over every facet of my existence. It feels as though I have entered a countdown, a psychological realm where each moment is imbued with both preciousness and brevity. Time seems to accelerate inexplicably—a day now passes in what feels like an hour, a week in a day, a month seems to last only a week, and a year rushes by too swiftly to grasp all the details fully.

Contrary to what one might expect, time does not slow as we grow older. It seems akin to a snowball rolling downhill, gaining speed as it grows larger. Perhaps it is the accumulation of life experiences that propels the acceleration of time. This intense awareness of life's impermanence has sparked a transformation within me, profoundly altering my outlook and behavior in ways I could never have anticipated. Every action and thought is now filtered through this new lens of urgency and clarity, compelling me to live with purpose and cherish the fleeting moments.

While the demands of survival—health, family, and financial stability—remain paramount, a subtle shift in perspective has begun to take root. It's as if a new strand of thought is weaving itself into the fabric of my being. Increasingly, I find myself drawn to the tapestry of my past, exploring its intricate threads with a newfound intensity. Perhaps this shift signifies a need for reconciliation, a microscopic examination of the choices and actions that have defined my journey thus far. In revisiting the milestones and moments that have shaped me, I seek a sense of closure, a chance to "set things straight" before the final curtain falls.

As the sands of time continue to slip through my fingers, I am compelled to confront my legacy, to ensure that the chapters I leave behind are written with intention and integrity. Though the future may hold uncertainty, I find solace in the opportunity to make peace with the past and embrace the moments that remain.

COULD HAVE BEEN; SHOULD HAVE BEEN; HERE I AM

Take care, my beloved friends and fellow travelers on life's journey. May the vast, benevolent universe guided by God's grace pave your way home safely. Always remember, there is a deeper purpose woven into the grand tapestry of life, and each of you is a living testament to this profound truth. Carry this knowledge in your hearts as you journey forward, knowing that every step you take is part of a greater plan designed to bring out the best in you and generations to follow.

ABOUT THE AUTHOR

Eric Koslowski was born and raised in a quaint town nestled in the heart of Central Massachusetts. From a young age, his insatiable curiosity often led to minor mischief, which occasionally vexed his parents.

However, as he matured, Eric managed to channel this restless energy into more constructive pursuits, ultimately shaping a fulfilling and productive life for himself. A staunch advocate of the philosophy that life's outcomes are largely determined by the paths one chooses to follow, Eric has always aligned his choices with his inner callings.

His academic and professional background is deeply rooted in the sciences, particularly chemistry and biology. He also possesses diverse skills that span across electronics and music, which further showcase his multifaceted interests and talents.

Eric is the author of *Wellwaterology*, a comprehensive book that delves into the intricacies of private well water systems, offering problem-solving techniques and maintenance advice. Today, he continues to reside near his childhood home with his wife, Lori. Here, in his well-equipped laboratory, Eric dedicates his time to developing innovative products designed to enhance the quality of people's lives, ensuring his lifelong passion for science and technology brings practical benefits to others.

Printed in the USA
CPSIA information can be obtained
at www.ICGtesting.com
CBHW030518091124
17088CB00028B/139